Elementary English Teaching

A Source Book for Teacher Educators

A.K. Sinha
Former Professor
Delhi University, Delhi

SHIPRA

Rs. 950

ISBN: 978-81-7541-847-9

First Published in India in 2016

Elementary English Teaching: A Source Book for Teacher Educators

Published by:

SHIPRA PUBLICATIONS
LG 18-19, Pankaj Central Market,
I.P. Ext., Patparganj, Delhi 110092, India
Ph.: 011- 2223 5152, 2223 6152
Email: info@shiprapublication.com
www.shiprapublication.com

Preface

Deficiency in English language teaching in India has given rise to numerous English language coaching schools throughout India which focus on spoken English. They promise inter-active learning and technology support for correct pronunciation. As the National Education Framework prepared by NCERT (2005) admits, while recommending the teaching of English from class I of primary schools, the level of introduction (of English) is a matter of political response to people's aspiration rather than an academic or feasibility issue. This book has been written to meet the demand of teachers who intend to teach spoken and written English in primary schools.

In the past, even in schools where English was taught from class I, the focus was on reading and writing. The skills of listening and speaking were confined to listening to the material in the text book and answering orally questions on what was taught. Now the priorities have changed. In the elementary classes, the emphasis is on spoken English and the focus is on acquiring listening and speaking skills which can be useful in everyday life. English will no longer be taught with a view to being used as a library language but for everyday communication where other Indian languages do not prove helpful or where English is the only language of communication.

The book is divided into six parts. The first part explains why English has been introduced from class I and what the impact of this decision is on primary education system in India. Chapter II comprises the needs analysis of Indian public with reference to English whereas chapter III discusses the objectives of language skills development. Chapter IV discusses the main characteristics of the English language and points out how and why it has become the lingua franca of international forums. Chapter V suggests how an appropriate environment can be created for teaching English from class I. Chapter VI points out what is expected of an English language teacher at the elementary level in the changed environment.

In part II, chapter VII discusses how to develop the skills of listening and speaking among small children in India. It offers a detailed analysis of various aspects of the pronunciation of English so that the teacher can develop himself/

herself successfully. It also discusses the ways and means of improving students' listening and speaking abilities.

Part III comprises two chapters. Chapter VIII discusses various ways of improving students' reading ability as well as their speed. Chapter IX suggests how to learn the writing system of English and how to correlate its pronunciation with its spelling. It gives some tips on the spelling of English words. It shows how children can be taught to write their own composition under controlled situation and how it could lead to writing free composition.

Part IV talks about the basics of lesson planning and material development in English. Chapter XI discusses several approaches to language teaching—behaviourist and developmental—and their implications on language teaching methods. Chapter XII discusses various methods—grammar-translation methods, various versions of monolingual direct method and the bilingual method which the current academic proposal seems to favour. It also discusses, in chapter XIII, how to develop material aids for language teaching.

Part V chapter XIV discusses various ways of evaluating learners' achievement. It emphasizes the role of continuous and comprehensive evaluation.

Part VI is practicum. It contains four lesson plans, one each on listening, speaking, reading and writing. It also contains five lessons on 'word games' of five different types 'chain spelling' (*antakshari*), anagrams, antonyms, definitions and scrambling.

The proposal to introduce English from class I is ambitious but absolutely necessary. The book discusses the critical period hypothesis which states that a child can be exposed to more than one language before he/she attains puberty and it does not adversely affect the development of his/her mother tongue. The hypothesis also points out that the initial learning in acquiring correct speech habit (pronunciation) will have a lifelong effect on the language learner. However, much depends on the quality of the teacher. The Knowledge Commission suggested that talented young teachers should be assigned the job. If such teachers find the book useful, the author will be amply rewarded.

The author acknowledges his indebtedness to Dulay, Burt and Krashen (1982), Howatt (1984) and Cook (2008) for their comprehensive approaches to the subject. He is obliged to Dr. Bikram Jora for preparing the type script and to Mrs. Usha Kiran Sinha for her cooperation and support. He appreciates the help of his grandsons Aayush and Apoorv in procuring the books taught in elementary classes and sharing their own experience as students in an English medium school. They made him aware of what is actually taught in the English class these days. He is very much obliged to Mr. D. Kumar, Shipra Publications, for commissioning the job and for his continuous critical interest in the work and helpful comments for its improvement.

Contents

UNIT I: ENGLISH LANGUAGE IN PRIMARY SCHOOL CURRICULUM

1

Knowledge of Language

Language, says the *Oxford Dictionary of English* (2005) "is the method of human communication, either spoken or written, consisting of the use of words in a structured and conventional way". There are other methods of communication, mainly non-verbal (i.e. the use of gesture and body movement) which human being share with other living beings but language is unique to them. Other animals have signalling system of various kinds which they use for various purposes, but only man is endowed with the ability to communicate verbally. Serious attempts have been made to teach animals to speak but they have uniformly failed. Parrots can imitate a few human expressions but they cannot use any of their own. As Bertand Russell observed once: "No matter how eloquently a dog may bark but he cannot tell you that his parents were poor but honest."

Language: Unique to Human Beings

In their natural habitat primates (e.g. monkeys, gorillas, chimpanzees) communicate with one another in systems that include visual, auditory and tactile[1] signals. Many of the signals are associated with the animals' immediate environment and carry meaning. For instance, they convey a sense of danger, aggressiveness, love, anger and other emotions. However, their natural sounds are highly stereotyped and convey limited messages. They are their immediate response to a situation. They have no way of expressing their past experience or future programme.

Guided by natural system of communication, scientists have tried to explore whether they can learn a human language. In 1930s Dr. and Mrs. Kellogg raised Gua, an infant chimpanzee, with their infant son and gave them equal exposure to human language. Gua picked up some isolated words but could not produce or understand any sentence. In another experiment, Dr and Mrs Hayes brought up Viki, another chimpanzee. After years training she could utter words like *papa* and *mama* with great difficulty but that was the end of her language production.

1. Concerned with the sense of touch.

Experiments with the Children of Primates

Psychologists Allen and Beatrix Gardner tried to teach Washoe, another chimpanzee, the American Sign Language. They put her among deaf and dumb children who acquired the sign language on their own from the community of hearing-challenged people whereas Washoe was taught how to produce them. At the end of four years, these children could use the sign language freely and fluently whereas Washoe could produce signs for eighty five words and fragments of sentences such as "more fruit", "you drink" and "hug hurry". Another psychologist couple, Premacks, raised Sarah, a chimpanzee and tried to teach her an artificial language. She learnt to associate certain symbols which she displayed only when she got a cue from trainers. Dr. Patterson taught Koko, a gorilla, to associate signs with objects and concepts and to combine them into short sentences. However, Koko could do only what she was taught and could not come up with new combinations on her own. Besides, her combinations had a lot of redundancy. It may be noted that these primates did not lack stimulus[1] but inspite of that, their achievement were frustrating if we compare them with what a human child acquires without any external stimulus.

Innateness[2] Hypothesis

The failure of these experiments and research reports on child language acquisition leads us to Noam Chomsky's claim that human children have innate ability to acquire language and this ability is unique to human beings. Though chimpanzees like Sarah and Lara could manipulate some symbols and Washoe and Nim Chimpsky could use some signs of American Sign Language, their acts were essentially imitative. They could not come up with an expression of their own spontaneously nor did they display any syntactic awareness even after four or five years of rigorous training. It may be pointed out that a human child becomes a fluent speaker of his/her mothertongue by that time. The hypothesis claims that a child is born endowed with the principles of Universal Grammar[3] which enable him/her to come up with the rules of a language specific grammar in course of his/her linguistic development. Though the child makes mistakes in the process and overgeneralizes some rules, he/she discards them in the course of his/her language acquisition.

Language Development of a Child

The psycholinguistic research on language acquisition by speakers of various languages points out that language acquisition process is universal and involves

---

1. Stimulus is a thing or event that evokes a specific functional reaction in an organ.
2. inborn, natural
3. The capacity that human beings have with regard to the acquisition of language; the inborn ability to the principles of language, applicable to any language.

similar stages of development. Children start with babbling. At the end of one year, they utter one word expressions. After a few months they speak two or three words together. These words have definite patterns, express syntactic characteristics and carry meaning. During this telegraphic stage of language learning, they do not use function words or morphemes, but they use correct word order which suggest that they have some sense of structure. Gradually they produce sentences that are closer to adult's language. Eventually the child starts using complex structures which display complex grammatical systems.

The Mother Tongue

The first language the child acquires is his/her mothertongue[1]. It is based on the language which his/her parents, family members and neighbours use. However, it is not the imitation and reproduction of their utterances. In fact the child is likely to use a sentence which he/she has never heard before but is a possible sentence of the language he/she speaks. It may be pointed out that the mothertongue of a child is not necessarily the language his/her mother speaks. Suppose a Telugu-speaking mother gives birth to a child who is adopted by a Hindi-speaking couple and the child is taken to a place where he/she never comes across Telugu. The child will pick up the language spoken by his/her foster parents and that language will be his/her mothertongue.

The Second Language

Suppose the parents of the child move to an area where most of the people he/she comes in contact with speak Punjabi. Such a child is likely to pick up Punjabi as well. In that case Punjabi will be considered to be his/her second language even though he/she learns it simultaneously with his/her mothertongue. It may be pointed out that the child will go through the same process of language development which he/she went through (or is going through) while acquiring his/her first language.

Some pedagogues hold the view that the child should not be exposed to a second language till his/her knowledge of the first language is firmly established. However, this view can be easily refuted if we look at a child growing up in a bilingual society. He/she picks up the second language on his/her own much before he/she is introduced to that language at school. In fact, if it is not a national language or the state language, he/she may never be formally introduced to it at school. The author knows two young sisters whose father is the speaker of Malayalam and mother is the speaker of Kannada and they speak English very often at home. The sisters picked up all the three languages. Besides, they picked up Telugu and Urdu, the languages spoken in Hyderabad where they grew up. They became multilingual because of the unique environment in which they lived. They never applied the rule of one language while speaking another,

1. The first language, the language that a child learns to speak first.

though they would sometimes mix lexical items. However, as soon as they did so, they realised that they had used a 'mixed code' and would try to find (or ask for) its equivalent in the language they used.

Characteristics of a Language

A bilingual[1] or multilingual[2] child knows which language he/she is using or listening to at a particular time, though he/she may not be familiar with the technical aspects of the language he/she is differentiating between. He/she knows that these languages have sound systems of their own which may resemble, as in the case of Hindi and English. He/she knows that their vocabularies differ and so do the rules of their grammars, for examples, the rules that add morphological[3] endings to words for functional purposes or the rules which direct the arrangement of words in sentences. In other words, two languages may differ with reference to—

(a) The sounds and their arrangement in words,
(b) The words with or without functional morphological features (e.g. plural markers) attached to them,
(c) Arrangement of words in phrases and sentences, which involve not only word order, but rules of agreement between various constituents of the sentence.

The system of a language can be discussed in terms of its (a) phonology, (b) lexicon,[4] (c) morphology, (d) syntax, and (e) semantics[5]. Of course every utterance carries meanings which is the sum total of the meaning of its constituents. Each constituent carries a substantive meaning (which is listed in a dictionary of that language) and the functional meaning which is the outcome of the attachment of grammatical markers to specific words and, also, arrangement of words in the utterance. For example, the words '*he*', '*is*', '*a*' *doctor* ' have their meanings but when combined in a sentence *he is a doctor* is a statement and *is he a doctor* is a question. The Hindi sentence '*wo ghar par hæ*', 'he is at home' and *wo ghar par hæ*? 'is he at home' are different in meaning though they have the same words and the same word order. They are different because they have different intonations,[6] when spoken and different punctuation marks, when written.

Knowledge of a Language

Knowing a language means knowing its main features which are as follows:

---

1. A person who knows two languages.
2. A person who knows more than two (many) languages.
3. Involving morphology, i.e. the forms of words, particularly with inflictional ending.
4. List of words in a language.
5. meaning.
6. The rise and fall of the voice when speaking.

(i) Its sound system,
(ii) Its words and their meanings,
(iii) Its morphological markers and their functional value,
(iv) its phrases (i.e. how words are grouped together in chunks)
(v) its sentences (i.e. how chunks of words are put together to form a sentence)
(vi) its paragraphs (how logically related sentences are put together in a paragraph which has a theme) and,
(vii) its texts (how paragraph are put together to form a unified text which may be an essay, a short story, a novel or a series of dialogues that constitute a play).

Knowing the sound system of a language means knowing which arrangement of sounds carry meaning (i.e. make sense) and which arrangements are not possible (and are nonsense). Knowing the words means having the ability to associate each word with a meaning. For instance, one who knows English knows what the word *student* means; its means "someone who is studying in order to gain knowledge or enter a particular profession". If one knows Hindi as well, one knows that such a person is called a *chhatra* or *vidyarthi.* The person who knows the words *student* and *chhatra* can easily conclude that the word and its meaning are arbitrarily associated; otherwise why should the same entity be called *student* in English and *chhatra* in Hindi? The fact that a student is called *chhatra* in Bengali, Assamese, Marathi, Gujarati, and Punjabi as well simply points out that all these languages are offsprings of the same Indo-Aryan language, Sanskrit.

Definition of Language

We have already pointed out the definition of language, as given in the *Oxford Dictionary of English.* It covers the follow ing points:

(i) Language is a method of human communication.
(ii) It is either spoken or written.
(iii) It consists of words.
(iv) Its words are structurally well arranged.
(v) These structures are conventional, i.e. they are based on or are in accordance with what is generally believed or done.

Knowing a language means being able to produce a new sentence which may not have been spoken before. It also means to understand sentences which have been never heard before. This is what Noam Chomsky calls the creative aspect of language use. According to him, the human faculty of language "seems to be a true 'species property' varying little among humans and without significant analogue elsewhere". It is based on elementary property that seems to be biologically isolated "property of discrete infinity".

According to Chomsky (2000:10), every language has a system of computational operation[1] which involves three kinds of elements:

- The properties of sound and meaning, called 'features'
- The items that are assembled from these properties called 'lexical items' and
- The complex expressions constructed from these 'atomic units'.

Legibility conditions impose a three way division among the features assembled into lexical items:

- Semantic features, interpreted at the semantic interface[2],
- Phonetic features, interpreted at the phonetic interface,
- Features that are not interpreted at either level.

Many linguists define language in terms of its use. For instance, Edward Sapir (1921) viewed language as "a purely human and non-instinctive method of communicating ideas, emotions and desires by means of a system of voluntarily produced symbols" (p. 8). He believed that human beings were "very much at the mercy of the particular language which had become the medium for their society". Benjamin Whorf, a follower of Sapir, asserted that language is "not merely a reproducing instrument for voicing ideas but rather is itself the shaper of ideas". Whorf's theories about the relationship between culture and language had many supporters during the pre-Chomskyan days. His claims that language compels its speakers to think in certain ways was challenged by many linguists but his view that language and culture interpenetrate each other was widely appreciated. Chomsky calls such a characterization of language E-language[3] where 'E' stands for externalised'. He characterises it as 'I' language[4] where 'I' stands for 'internalised'. Whereas the former is based on the speaker's performance, the latter depends on native speaker's competence.

Human language is not only creative and innovative but also unique in several ways. For instance, it can be used as a 'metalanguage' to discuss the rules of any language. It is a cultural asset. Cultural developments were not possible until language, the tool of significant expression, took its shape. Language cannot be separated from the totality of human behaviour. In each speech community, its language mirrors human life- the personalities of its speakers, their attitudes and beliefs and their styles of thought and expression. In short, language categorizes the totality of human experience and makes it understandable.

---

1. Smallest units.
2. A point where two systems meet and interact.
3. Language in use.
4. Language that is within a person, potential language.

2

The Importance of Teaching English at the Primary Level in India

Academic Need

Education has been a primary concern in India since Independence. In 2009, Indian Parliament passed the right of children to free and compulsory Education (RTE) Act which was enforced with effect from April1, 2010. It secures the right of children to free and compulsory education till they complete elementary education in a neighbouring school. The District Primary Education Programme is meant to operationalize the strategies to achieve universal primary education through district specific planning and target setting. Besides, there are other programmes such as Sarva Shiksha Abhiyan, the Kasturba Gandhi Shiksha Yojna and the Midday Meal Schemes to attract children to primary education. The RTE Act 2009 lays down norms and standards for improving primary education.

The secondary education system in India serves as a link between the elementary and higher education. It plays a pivotal role in shaping and directing the future of a child. The National Council of Educational Research and Training (NCERT) helps the Central Board of Secondary Education (CBSE) in shaping the curriculum of central schools and other schools affiliated to the CBSE. It does primary research on various aspects of school education and publishes important textbooks, manuals and monographs to guide them in implementing the academic policy of the government.

In 2005, the Government of India formed the *National Knowledge Commission* to meet the knowledge challenge of the twenty first century and to increase India's competitive advantage in the field of knowledge. The commission submitted its report in 2007, in which it observed:

> *"An understanding and command of the English language is a most important determinant of access to higher education, employment possibilities and social opportunities. School leavers who are not*

> *adequately trained in English as a language are always at a handicap in the world of higher education... and those who do not know English well enough find it exceedingly difficult to compete for a place in our premier educational institutions. This disadvantage is accentuated further in the world of work, not only in professional occupations but also in white collar occupations overall."*
>
> *[Report; 32]*

In short, the *Report* highlights the following points:

(i) In India, a student needs a good knowledge of English to have higher education.
(ii) It is a must for admission to good academic institutions.
(iii) It helps in getting good jobs.
(iv) It is an aid to one's social mobility.

Undoubtedly, the *Report of the Knowledge Commission* reflects the reality in so far as the language situation in India is concerned. Every year we read the news about some students of Indian Institute of Technology and other premier colleges killing themselves out of frustration because they could not cope with the burden of carrying on their academic activities in English even though they had managed to get good marks at the higher secondary examination. Even those who join such colleges or institutes where classroom discussions are carried on in Hindi or regional languages feel disappointed because most of the standard textbooks are in English. They find them difficult to comprehend. They find it hard to compete with the products of English-medium schools. For them, English is not a language of the exclusive upper class but a language they need to have for their own upward social mobility.

Job-Oriented Needs

The product of such schools where the teaching of English is casual find themselves severely handicapped when they enter the job market and face interviews. They rush to privately-run English language teaching shops. They undergo training, attend mock interviews and communication skills classes but they are of no avail. When they face interviews, they are hardly able to express their thought clearly and coherently. They are unable to express even simple concepts explicitly because of their poor language.

They need good English not only for getting jobs in multinational companies, corporate houses, centres for business process outsourcing (BPOs), Information Technology enterprises, Indian construction companies working abroad and hospitals, schools and colleges in the developing countries but also for better paid jobs in malls, retail chains, airlines, hotels, restaurants, fancy show rooms, banks and various financial institutions in India. Even taxi drivers and tourist guides need working knowledge of English to deal with customers from abroad. Globalization has opened so many doors but at every point of entrance there is a chance of getting rejected if a candidate lacks fluency in written and spoken English. In short, there is a large scale demand for job-oriented learning of English.

Needed for Interstate Communication

People's mobility has increased inside the country. Young men and women are ready to move to any corner of India if they get suitable jobs. However, they realise that once they are out of the region where their mother tongue is the language of social interaction, they need the working knowledge of two languages, Hindi and English, Hindi for the market place and English for social interaction with educated public. As these languages act as link languages almost all over India, one ought to have a working knowledge of both of them.

English was introduced in India by the British colonial rulers for their own convenience. They ran their administration with the help of English-educated Indians. Now that they are gone, the role of English should have been marginalised, but it is not the case. Now we need English to keep ourselves in touch with one another when we come across people who do not know our language and there is no dirth of such occasions in our lives whether we move out of our region or not. Most educated Indians are bilinguals, some even multilinguals, out of social and economic necessity. English is one of the components of our bilingualism. As there is a shift in the pattern of communication and the focus has been increasingly on English as a second language, a new orientation is needed for its teaching.

Introducing the Teaching of English from Class I

It is because of these trends and such demands that the policy of introducing English as a compulsory subject from class I has been adopted. It may be pointed out that the situation had already changed by 2005.

- Nine Indian states had already introduced English as a compulsory subject from class I. Out of these, six were in the North East India and three were union territories.
- Twelve states had English as a compulsory subject latest by class V.
- In *National Curriculum Framework (2005)*, prepared by the National Council of Educational Research and Training (NCERT), the experts had recommended that English be taught from the beginning of elementary education.
- They had observed that it was not an academic issue but "a matter of political response to people's aspiration."

- The *Knowledge Commission* recommended that English be introduced as a subject right from class I along with the regional language and the mother tongue.
- It found it essential to do so "to create meaningful learning experience for the child."
- The new policy is intended to make the teaching of English accessible from the initial stage of education to meet the demand of the public.
- It is in accordance with the perceptions of Indian public.

Importance of Teaching English

Figures 2.1 and 2.2 point out why English language teaching is important in India.

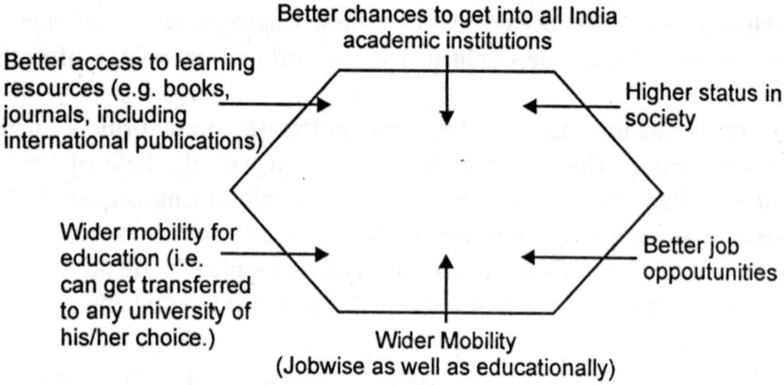

Fig. 2.1: External Influences on the Learning of English in India

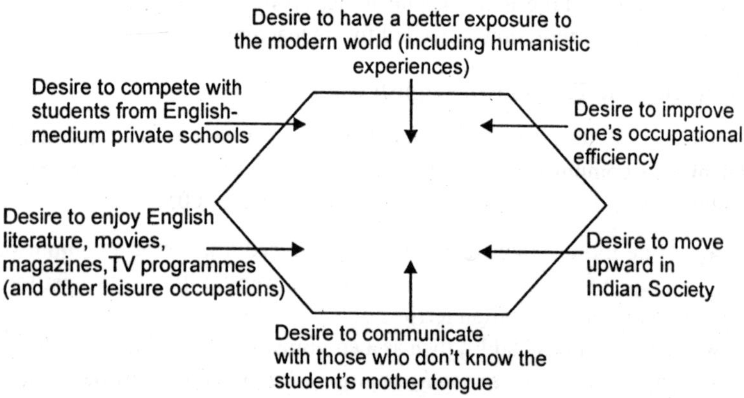

Fig. 2.2: Internal Factors that Affect the Learning of English in India

Implications of the Recommendation

The importance given to teaching of English right from class 1 has its implications. It is not going to be just one of the subjects to be taught but a tool (medium) for the teaching of atleast one of the content subjects from class 3. It raises at least two points:

(i) Are not we moving towards bilingual education?
(ii) Is it desirable to expose students to a second language so early in life when the learning of the mothertongue is yet to be consolidated?

A Move towards Bilingual Education

The Knowledge Commission observed that the introduction of the teaching of English from class I should not be treated as "a shared-alone, add-on subject"; it should be an integral part of school curriculum. In order to do so, it recommended that it should be integrated with "the learning of the content subjects". The Commission thought that it could be done after two years of the teaching of English, i.e. from class III. As to which subjects could be taught through the medium of English has been left to individual schools. They could decide the issue keeping in view the content subject teacher's proficiency in English and the availability of suitable teaching material. The commission felt that such a step would help in reducing the gap between English-medium private and missionary schools and the government-run public schools. Such a programme of bilingual language teaching has been successfully implemented in Canada and has been in practice in many countries which were the colonies of the British earlier.

The French Immersion Programme[1] in Canada

The programme was initiated in Ontario, Canada, for English-speaking children to have education through the medium of French in some selected subjects. The teachers were encouraged to use approaches similar to those being used by their English language counterparts. The immersion programmes was of various types. Some students were introduced to French as a medium at an early stage of schooling. Out of them, some were exposed to the medium completely and some, partially. Some students were exposed to the French medium at a later stage, either completely or partially. Johnson and Swain (1997) have evaluated their achievement and found the efforts successful in terms of their objectives. They found that the students with positive attitude towards the language were more successful than others.

Transposing this model to India will not be hazardous because of the positive attitude of the parents and students towards English. However, it may be diffIcult to find suitable teachers of content subjects who are proficient

1. The method of teaching a language by using that language exclusively.
2. Using only one language.
3. Using two languages as media of education

to teach specific subjects through the medium of English. As the emphasis is on exposing students to the language with a view to enabling them to use it fluently and not on explaining the rules of grammar, teachers should be fluent in English. He/she should have positive attitude towards students and encourage them to express their thought in English. In short, the immersion programme could be successfully implemented to create meaningful learning experiences which is what the Knowledge Commission wanted.

Monolingual[1] vs. Bilingual[2] Education

Many linguists, psychologists and educationalists hold the view that every child should have his/her elementary education through the medium of his/her mother tongue. Such people are likely to oppose the recommendation of the Knowledge Commission. They would be dead against any scheme that resembles the immersion programme because they believe that only the mother tongue as the medium of early education promotes creativity and helps concept formation in the child. However, in a country like India where children are usually at home with two or more languages or dialects right from the beginning, bilingual education is not a burden. Schools where Indian languages are media of education have provision to teach English as a second/foreign language but they cannot be claimed to be bilingual because English is taught only as a subject there. In some schools social science and humanities are taught in Hindi and physical science in English, such school may be called bilingual.

Experiment at Central Institute of Indian Languages

The Central Institute of Indian Languages (CIIL) has proposed and experimented with some bilingual schools in which students start reading and writing in their mothertongues and are exposed to a mainstream language in its spoken form; they learn to read and write it later. It is hightime to evaluate the success of such bilingual schools and profit from their experience. The bilingual elementary schools in India do not have the same compulsions which have led the members countries of the European Union to go in for the Immersion Programme. There those who are exposed to bilingual education are mostly minority immigrants in a dominant monolingual society, as in France or Germany (Johnson and Lapkin, 1982).

Bilingualism in India

In India, bilingualism and multilingualism is an overwhelming phenomenon

1. Using only one language.
2. Using two languages as media of education

to which the scheme intends to add one more language, English. However, unlike in the colonial era, it is not imposed on the unwilling or uncommitted public. It has been made available because of people's demand or willingness to have it. It is not a utopian dream. It is a realistic vision which emerges out of the strong desire of the Indian community to share the English language. Undoubtedly, students will feel empowered if they get a working knowledge of English at school. It will fulfil the desire of their parents as well.

The Critical Period Hypothesis

Before we conclude, we would like to respond to those psychologists and pedagogues who are against bilingual education on theoretical ground. Their main argument is that it is against the interest of the child to expose him/her to a second language at an early stage of life. They should be aware of a recently developed theory called the *Critical Period Hypothesis* based on psychological research. It states that there is a limited developmental period in a person's life during which it is possible to acquire a language, be it L_1 or L_2, to normal native-like levels. Once this window of opportunity is closed, the ability to learn language declines. Psychologists cite the example of Genie in the USA who was kept in complete isolation by her mother for thirteen years. By the time she was brought in contact with human civilization, she had attained puberty and her language acquisition ability had declined. As Curtiss (1977) reports, she could not acquire language as a normal child inspite of the best efforts of psycholinguists.

Neurological Evidence

Lenneberg (1967) was the first neurolinguist to offer a neurological explanation for the time-locked decrease in one's ability to fully acquire a language. He attributed this decrease to a progressive loss in the hemispheric equipotentiality (i.e. the ability of either cerebral hemisphere subserve language) resulting in the lateralization of language to the left hemisphere. He also indicated that this lateralization is completed by puberty. This claim was first supported by Oyama (1976) with reference to Italian-English bilinguals in America. It was further substantiated by Kim (1995) who compared grown up Korean English bilingual's acquisition of some sounds (i.e. [I] and [i]) with that of young native Americans. The data collected from these studies provide evidence for the critical period effect. The earlier a person is exposed to the second language, the better is his/her native language like acquisition.

The proponents of the "earlier-is-better" assert that there is a critical period for the acquisition of an L_2 sound system and other language components. Though no rigorous research has yet been conducted to arrive at a firm conclusion, one can conjecture on the basis of research done so far that, in general Arab students fail to acquire English sounds correctly because they are exposed to the teaching of English late there, very often after the learners have crossed the critical period.

In view of the evidence discussed above, we consider it desirable that the teaching of English be introduced from class I in India. Psycholinguistic research on bi-/multilingual acquisition points out that the acquisition of a second or third language at a very early age does not interfere with the acquisition and consolidation of the first language. On the other hand, as Weber-Fox and Neville (2003) point out, judgement accuracy for syntactic structures in bilinguals differ in relation to the timing of second language acquisition. It is therefore, prudent to introduce English as a second language in elementary classes as early as possible.

To sum up

- there is a public demand to introduce the teaching of English from class I in India.
- It has been decided to fulfill this demand.
- It may be implemented on the model of Immersion Programme in Cananda.
- It is not against the interest of children. The psychological research favours the early introduction.
- The critical period hypothesis supports it. So does neurolinguistic evidence.
- Bilingualism is a widespread phenomenon in India. Many children grow up as bilinguals.

3

The Place of English in Primary School Curriculum

As we have already seen, the Knowledge Commission has recommended that the teaching of English as a language should be introduced from class I at the primary level along with the teaching of the pupil's mothertongue or the regional language. It has also been recommended that this phase of language learning should focus on using both languages to create meaningful learning experience for the child. It wants some content subjects (e.g. social studies) to be taught through the medium of English from class III onwards. In other words, it wants it to become one of the tool languages from class III. This suggestion creates a unique problem. The child has to be not only able to communicate simple facts about himself/herself and his/her environments in English, but also to comprehend concepts of and information about some selected content subjects in English. The ability to comprehend and reproduce what he/she has learnt in English is a necessary qualification he/she must have during the first two years of acquisition of English.

Bilingual Medium of Instruction

The bilingual system of education has to be introduced in such a way that the child does not become indifferent to his/her mother tongue, as most children going to as English-medium public school in India do. At the same time he/she should feel confident in English. The teacher should, therefore, show enthusiasm for and interest in the English language from the beginning. His/her attitude will create interest in students. His/her spontaneity will determine the success of their performance. If he/she creates a proper environment in the class, there will be active participation by students and the quality of teaching/learning will improve. As the centre of learning is the interaction between teacher and his/her students, the main objective of the curriculum should be to develop in them that ability to interact. It is only through this ability that the knowledge of the content subjects can be acquired well in English.

In order to enable students to communicate in English, the teacher will have to adopt monolingual approach while teaching English. He/she can begin with the help of clearly understood hand signals. He/she can introduce himself/herself and ask a student his/her name which he/she should be able to answer in simple and fluent English. The student should learn how to greet the teacher and fellow students. He/she should be able to identify and name objects around him/her in the classroom, in the playground and at home. He/she could participate in choral speaking, enunciating the English sounds.

Learning the Four Skills

Initially efforts should be made to let the student develop an auditory sensitivity to the sounds and structures of English. When the student responds to a question, he/she should be allowed to finish even if his/her sounds or words are not correct. Other students should be asked the same question before the teacher corrects the errors.

After the student has gained skills in listening and speaking, he/she should be helped in developing reading skills. After he/she has learnt to recognize the letters of the alphabet, he/she should be encouraged to recognize his/her name in the written or printed form. He/she should be taught how to read the names of objects around him/her and how to talk about them in simple sentences. Reading reinforces his/her newly acquired ability to speak. The student should be asked to read only that material which he/she can understand and speak about. When he/she is able to read it, he/she should learn to write it. The four skill areas-listening, speaking, reading and writing- should be acquired in sequence with regard to the development of the knowledge of relevant contents. At a point when multiple content items are being developed, a student may not have gained equal confidence in all of them. Reinforcement programmes may be introduced at this stage, keeping their specific skill requirements in view. Special attention should be paid to pronunciation. If correct pronunciation is taught at the initial stage, it helps the student throughout his/her life. It helps him/her speak clearly and be easily understood. He/she will not have to unlearn the wrong pronunciation.

Steps in Language Learning

When a new item (i.e. a sound, a word or a sentence structure) is introduced, the student is led through the following basic steps:

(a) **Perception[1] and comprehension[2]:** The student must be able to recognize and understand the new utterances. The teacher should provide

1. The ability to see, hear or become aware of something through the senses.
2. The ability to understand something.

usual cues, paraphrases and repetitions to ensure comprehension.

(b) **Repetition:** when the student is asked to repeat an item, the teacher should pay attention to his/her pronunciation, intonation, stress and rhythm. Necessary correction should be made after the student completes his/her response.

(c) **Practice:** Situations should be created for the student to repeat the item in a variety of ways. Mechanical repetition makes the experience monotonous and should be avoided.

(d) **Application:** The student should be encouraged to use new material in conversation and classroom activities. His/her creative urge should be stimulated. Once the student becomes successfully interested in reading and writing, he/she should practise dictation. It reinforces the newly learned language pattern and is an effective way to practise spelling. The simplest dictation may involve only the writing of a word, a phrase or a sentence, while a complex task may involve the writing of one or more paragraphs.

Skill Development Activities

Students should be given basic sentence patterns to satisfy their immediate needs, such as,

May I have a glass of water?
May I go to the bathroom?
May I shut the window?

They should be supplied with vocabulary to talk about the objects in the classroom, such as

It is a piece of chalk/a blackboard/a chair.
I want a pen/an eraser/a piece of paper.

They should be given names of various geometric shapes (such as round, circle, square, rectangle, triangle, etc). They should be taught to use words with the same or opposite meaning in structures, such as

He is happy/cheerful/joyous.
He runs fast/slow.
It goes up/comes down.

At a later stage, students may be encouraged to play word games. For instance, one student utters the word *mango*; another student has to speak another word starting with the last letter of the word, 'o', e.g. *orange* and a third with its last letter 'e', e.g. *egg* and so on.

Another game that may be played is scrambling.[1] Students may be asked to put scrambled letters of a word in a correct sequence. They may be shown a sequence of pictures or photographs and asked to describe the event systematically. They may be encouraged to write down what they speak.

Students may be asked to name things they play with or work with and then use the words in their own sentences. They may write down their sentences.

Special attention should be paid to increase the comprehension skills of students. The teacher may tell them stories or narrate an event and then ask questions to find out whether they have followed what was told. They may be given simple stories to read silently and asked question about them. They may be given a factual narrative and asked to list the facts they have come across. They may be told to read action stories. They may play character roles from them. They may be told a long story and asked to narrate it in brief. In short, they may be exposed to various functions of the new language.

All these learning activities may be in addition to the reading of prescribed text books and doing the exercises given under each lesson. An imaginative teacher may be able to integrate the steps mentioned above with the given lessons. The Knowledge Commission suggests that multiple textbooks in English should be made available to suit the diversity of language environment in the country. However, certain guidelines should be prepared to develop pedagogically sound English textbooks for every level. The body of experts which prepares textbooks should keep the broad goals of English language teaching in view, i.e. it should provide a meaningful learning experience to the child.

Objectives—Converse and Express

The overall objectives of teaching English at the primary level are two:

(i) To enable students to converse in English.
(ii) To equip them with minimum reading ability to comprehend content subjects taught in English and to express them orally or in writing.

In order to enable students to converse in English, the following steps need to be taken:

- They should be given opportunities to improve their pronunciation so that they can distinguish between sounds that often confuse them (e.g. distinguish between
  (i) /dʒ/,/z/and/ʒ/
  (ii) /s/and/ʃ/
  (iii) /v/and/w/
  (iv) /t/and/θ/

1. The action of alternating the letters of a word.

(v) /d/and/ð/
(vi) /pʰ/and/f/
(vii) /æ/,/e/and/əɪ/
(viii) /ɔ/and/əu/

- Steps should be taken to enable them to hear the difference in isolation and in words and sentences.
- They should be enabled to hear stress on words and note the intonation pattern in sentences.
- Listening practice should be followed by speaking practice, keeping the confusing items in view.
- Attempts should be made to increase their speech fluency while reciting nursery rhymes or practising to speak dialogues.
- To practise choral speaking and group recitation to improve their enunciation[1] and voice.
- To practise conversation in a natural and relaxed atmosphere.
- To use language laboratory facilitate, wherever feasible.

In order to improve their listening comprehension, students should listen to children stories and enhance their auditory perception. The teacher should see to it that students concentrate on listening and do not get distracted.

- The teacher should ask questions to find out how well the students have understood and how much they can recall.
- If they fail to recall some events or dialogues, they may be exposed to them again to find out whether their listening comprehension has improved because of revisiting the lesson.

Various Modes of Reading

In order to meet the second objective, i.e. to improve the reading comprehension of students, the teacher should demonstrate the difference between

(a) *Skimming* (i.e. reading a text quickly just to understand the main idea),
(b) *Scanning* (i.e. while reading one may have specific points in mind and be looking for them quickly in the text) and,
(c) *Reading for detail* (i.e. reading a text very carefully for specific information).

He/she may do so by reading different texts. The teachers ask his/her students to follow him/her in the act. The teacher may mention the strategy

1. The act of speaking clearly.

he/she is going to adopt while reading a text and then point out what he/she may get after finishing the task of reading. Separate suitable passages may be selected for the specific task and the teacher may state in advance his/her objective of reading the text.

Reading for Listening Comprehension

- Reading for listening comprehension should be used to teach better speaking skill if attention is paid to how different sounds are articulated when they occur in words and how function words are reduced when they occur in sentences. While playing the tape for listening comprehension, the teacher may do so. The significance of stress and intonation should be pointed out. Students should be told to follow these strategies when they speak.
- Reading lessons should highlight the techniques used by writers so that students adopt similar techniques when they write their composition.

In short, improvement in listening skills should lead to the learners' improvement in speaking skills. Likewise better reading skills should inspire them to adopt better writing skills. Though the curriculum aims at the acquisition of better oral skills, it implies that they should lead the learner to the acquisition of better expression skills in their speech and writing.

Importance of Fulfilling the Objectives

The objectives discussed above aim at attaining proficiency in all four skills of learning English as second language. It is because English is going to play a significant role in the learner's life as a tool to learn other subjects in course of their higher education. Knowledge is expanding at a tremendous speed and new knowledge is available more easily and faster in English than in any other language, Indian or foreign. That is why English has been playing a prominent role in higher education, in every aspect of learning, be it science, technology or arts.

With speakers of various Indian languages coming closer because of their mobility to get engaged in various jobs, the role of English as a link language has increated for inter-state communication in India. In cosmopolitan cities, English-medium schools are needed for educating children of various language families. For that reason we need a large number of teachers who can teach various subjects through the medium of English.

Globalization has made it possible for technically trained professionals and skilled factory workers to move to any part of the world where such jobs are available but they are eligible for them only if they have at least the working knowledge of spoken English. Those experts who prefer to stick to a job available in India need to learn from books and journals in English. They can participate in seminars which conduct their business in English. They can share their own experience with experts around the world through English-medium journals.

All Skills Equally Essential

The role of English is of increasing importance in all walks of enlightened life. The young mind should prepare himself/herself from the beginning by studying English. Gone are the days when English in India served only administrative and academic purposes. Now we need people who have expertise not only in reading comprehension but also in listening, speaking and writing in English. Since they have an interwoven fabric, no single skill can be acquired in isolation. The interrelationship among them is manifested in every walk of life of an educated Indian. Any programme of teaching English must acknowledge it.

4

Nature and Characteristics of the English Language

Spread of English

English spread in the British islands during sixth to fifteenth centuries. During the sixteenth century, almost the whole of the British Isles came under the rule of one authority and English became their mothertongue. Soon after that, the British expedition to the new world started. It resulted into their settlements in America. By the eighteenth century the British settlement spread all over northern America. It led to the majority of inhabitants of the new world speak English as their mothertongue. It is claimed that the English language was a major factor in keeping the USA united in spite of its cultural diversity because of immigration from various European countries. The situation was slightly different in Canada which had a sizable number of French-speaking inhabitants. Though English became the national language of Canada, French also flourished and was declared its co-official language in the mid-twentieth century.

The Caribbean islands had British settlement during this period with English as their dominant language. Their interaction with the Black population led to the growth of Pidgin English which is now recognized as creole English.

The British explorers reached Australia towards the end of the eighteenth century and by mid-nineteenth century the country had a large settlement of English-speaking people. Soon after their arrival in Australia, some British immigrated to New Zealand. In 1820, the British settlement began in South Africa, which was then dominated by the speakers of Afrikaan; English became a significant language there. During the Apartheid, the local Black population perceived Afrikaan as a language of authority and repression and English as a language of protest and self-determination. They opted for English because they considered it a language of upward social mobility.

The UK, USA, Canada, New Zealand and Australia: these are the countries which have the English-speaking people in majority. The people of Sierra Leone, Zambia, and Cameroon in Africa speak English-based creole (Krio). Botswana, Malawi, Namibia, Uganda and Zimbabwe have English as the official language and Kenya and Tanzania have it as an important language of communication. So have the Philippines, Guam, Samoa, Singapore, Malaysia, Hongkong and Papua New Guiena. English has become a prominent language in India, Sri Lanka, Pakistan and Bangladesh as well.

Inner and Outer Circles of Speakers of English

Kachru (1985, 2001) has presented the spread of English around the world in three concentric circles:

(a) *The inner circle* in which English is the primary language, as in USA, UK, Ireland, Canada, South Africa, Australia and New Zealand.
(b) *The outer circle* where English is used as an important second language, as in India, Singapore, Malaysia, Malawi, Namibia, Uganda, Zimbabwe, etc.
(c) *The expanding circle* which includes countries such as China, Japan, Korea, Vietnam, Thailand, Cambodia, Indonesia, Turkistan, Kazakhstan, Uzbekistan, Greece, Russia, and countries of the European Union. In these countries English is learnt as the most important foreign language.

These countries were not the colonies of British Empire but they have recognized the significant role that English plays as a global language and teach it as a foreign language. It is taught as foreign language in almost all Arab countries. According to Crystal (2003), nearly 329 million people of the world use English as their first language and 430 million people as their second language. According to British Council, nearly a thousand million (i.e. One billion) people learn English as a foreign language. No other language has spread around the world as extensively as English.

English in the Post-colonial Era

The spread has been very fast after the Second World War and is becoming faster now. Till the middle of the twentieth century, English was a prominent language because Britain was the leading colonial power. Now it has its influence because it is the language of international trade and commerce, of diplomacy and international exchange. The economic globalization has spread the network of multinational companies. The corporate houses with headquarters in non-English speaking countries prefer to conduct their business in English and so do international banking systems. The communication revolution has introduced internet and computer-based communication, including documents handling software. Audio-visual cultural products, such as films, television programme and popular music made in English are more popular worldwide than the products of any other language. Besides, English is the working language of international organizations and conferences, it is used for scientific and other academic publications of international repute and for widespread translation and interpretation. It is the language of tourism and air services.

Rich Vocabulary

English has a rich vocabulary because it has adopted several ways to expand it.

Coinage

The world has undergone profound socio-cultural changes and English has changed accordingly to maintain its relevance. New words have been coined to capture new natural phenomena, scientific concepts and socio-political developments. Words such as *sitcom* (=satellite communication), *intercom, interlanguage, biodiversity, biodegradable, audiophile, neurobiology, technopreneur, technospeak, armsgate, choppergate, fast food, roadmap*, etc. are of recent origin. In 1980s the word *cybernetics* became popular. Now we have a dozen of compound words such as *cybercafé, cybercrime, cyberphobia, cyberpunk, cyberapace, cyber stalking, cyber terrorism, cyberwar* and *cybernaut,* associated with it. From the word *video,* which refers to the system of recording, reproducing or broadcasting moving visual images, we have words such as *videotape, videocamera, videorecorder, videogame, videography, videopiracy, videoconference, videophil* etc. From the word *web,* which refers to a complex system of interconnected wiring network, we have words such as *webcam, webcast, weblog, webmaster, webpage, website, webspace* etc. From *blog* (i.e., add new material to or update a weblog), we have *blogging, blogger,* and *blogsphere.* Numerous new words have been coined to meet the requirements of the speakers of English. Such a flexible process of formation of words exemplifies the vitality of the English language.

Extension of Meaning of Existing Words

Sometimes an old English word is given a new meaning and is profitably used. For instance, the word *mouse*, which was traditionally used to denote a small rodent, is now used by the users of computer to refer to a hand-held device which is moved across a mat or a flat surface to move the cursor on a computer screen. Traditionally, the *server* is a person who serves; in the USA, it is used for a waiter or waitress. Now, for a computer user, it is a computer programme which manages access to a centralised resource or service in a network. Even in ordinary use, some words have undergone change in meaning or extended their meanings. For instance, the word *cool* which refers to 'moderately low temperature', is now used to refer to 'an emotionally restrained, fashionably attractive or impressive person'. To *chill* is to 'cool' but now it means 'to calm down' as well. To *dig* is 'to extract from the ground by breaking up and moving earth'. Now it means 'to understand, enjoy or appreciate' as well. Earlier *lousy* meant 'inflected with lice', now it means 'worthless'. Usually *window* refers to an opening in the wall or roof of a building or vehicle, now it also refers to 'a framed area on the display screen of a computer for viewing information.

Liberal Borrowing

The English language has kept its door wide open to admit words from other languages it comes in contact with. For instance, it has borrowed from Hindi names of objects such as *kebab, kofta, korma, khichri, pulao (pilaf), raita, curry, khaki, kurta, pyjama, pagri, topi, sari, salwar etc.* It has also borrowed words such as *karma, nirvana, shanti, samadhi, sadhana, sangh, gherao, band, hartal, yaar, jugar* etc. From Arabic, it has borrowed *burka, candy, alcohol, cotton, algebra, camphor, coffee, halal, amber, albatross, tariff, cipher, elixir, satin, assassin, bark, kafir* etc. It has borrowed words from many Asian, African and Australian languages. Of course it has a huge number of words derived from French, Latin and Greek. Most of its technical terms have Latin or Greek roots, prefixes or suffixes. Its willingness to borrow words which its speakers consider apt expressions indicates its dynamic character. It makes it a welcome language outside the English-speaking world.

Idiomatic Use[1]

The COBUILD English vocabulary lists fifty structure words (such as articles, prepositions, conjunctions, pronouns and deictic terms) and fifty most frequently used nouns, verbs and adjectives. It claims that knowing these words allows a person to recognize half of the words he/she may come across in English. It has twenty verbs such as *be, becomes, come, find, get, give, go, help, know, look, make, mean, say, see, seem, tell, take, think, use* and *want*. Most of them can be combined with a particle to form a phrasal verb. For example, from *come*, we have *come about, come across, come along, come around, come at, come back, come before, come between, come by, come down, come down to, come down with, come for, come forward, come from, come in, come in for, come into, come of, come off, come on, come on to, come out, come out of, come out in, come out with, come over, come around, come through, come under, come up, come upto, come up with, come upon,* etc. The phrasal verb has a meaning different from that of the verb alone. One has to familiarize oneself with some frequently used phrasal verbs.

1. Expressions that are natural to a native speaker.

Synonyms and Antonyms

Many English words have near synonyms. For instance, the verb *make* has form, *fashion, pattern, fabricate, assemble, manufacture, build, construct, compose* and *constitute* as its synonyms. However, there are collocation restriction on their use. We *make* a dress, *build* a house, *manufacture* some products and *construct* a road. Just as synonyms have subtle differences, so have antonyms of a word. For instance, the word *artistic* has two antonyms: *unartistic* (not artistic) and *inartistic* (showing lack of artistic talent).

Compound Formation

English has compounds of noun-noun combination (e.g. *girlfriend*), noun-adjective combination (e.g. *nerve-breaking*), preposition verb combination (*outdo*), etc. Some compound words may be put in a reverse order to get another word e.g. *turn-over, overturn; take-over, overtake*. It has *Bahuvrihi* compounds such as *bluechips, stonewall, wishbone, videofit, Indian summer*, etc. All these point out the dynamic characteristics of the language.

Varieties of English

Apart from the features discussed above, the language has developed its local varieties in countries where it is used as a first or second language. Thus we have American, Canadian, Australian, Indian, South African and other varieties of English. While the use of English as a language of wide communication continues to exert pressure towards global uniformity, the shift in its status in many countries from foreign language to second language is leading to the development of a large number of local varieties. Though the trends are contradictory, they are natural. English has two main functions these days. On the one hand, it is growing as the language of international communication,

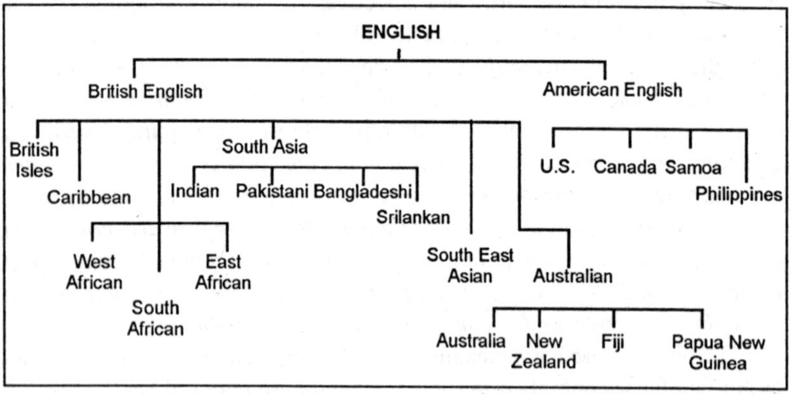

Figure 4.1: Varieties of World Englishes

on the other, it is the vehicle of national identity in many new nations which have adopted it as a language of national unity. They encourage the development of new forms and hybrid structures to establish their separate identity.

Need for a Uniform Standard

Earlier the print media played a vital role in maintaining a uniform standard, now it is being gradually displaced by the electronic media. However, the electronic media is getting a more widespread range than the print media. The BBC and CNN are attracting more viewers worldwide than the number of readers of world's leading newspapers have. Recently Al Jazeera has gained international popularity. Though it is based on the Arab soil, it broadcasts in English. Such channels are likely to act as a uniting force and maintain an acceptable standard. The growing trend towards the internationalisation of education and the increasing importance of world youth culture are likely to promote the cause of international intelligibility of the language. The grip that the standard British English had over Indian English may become loose in favour of Indian and American English but the goal of international intelligibility will not be lost.

English as a Lingua Franca[1]

English no longer belongs to its native speaker the way it did in the past; it has become the *lingua franca* of a sizeable section of world population. Consequently, while teaching English, the emphasis has shifted from approximation to the native speaker's usage, i.e. received pronunciation, to international intelligibility. The globalization of English has affected all aspects of its use, function and learning. Recently some scholars have started insisting that the English presented in the classroom should be authentic and natural and not products for instructional processes. The debate goes on whether the context of use should get priority over the context of learning. The communicative language should be able to meet the needs of its speakers but in the context of English, it should be able to meet the global needs as well which is the reason for its widespread use.

Modern Usage

Usage is concerned with the way people actually speak. It refers to those acceptable practices which make understanding possible between hearers and speakers. It is important that children acquire information about several areas

1. A shared language of communication between people whose mother tongues are different.

of usage so that they conform to the accepted practices. There are three basic points to be noted in the context:

1. Grammatical usage must meet the contemporary standard.
2. The words chosen to be used should be colloquial.
3. The structure of sentences must meet the prevailing standard.

The Changing Syntax of English

The English language has been changing gradually and some irregular plurals are giving way to regular ones. For instances, the plural of *forum* is *forums* and not *fora* anymore. More people say *corpuses* rather than *corpora*, *indexes* rather than *indices*, *syllabuses* rather than *syllabi* and *formulas* rather than *formulae*. The past tense of *quit* is either *quit* or *quitted* and that of *broadcast* is either *broadcast* or *broadcasted*. The past tense of *thrive* is *throve* or *thrived* and that of *shine* is *shone* or *shined*. The native speaker of English says "it is me" rather than "it is I"; *who do you want to meet* rather than *whom do you want to meet*. A lot of people of younger generation say *I am good* rather than *I am well*. They say *who did you vote for* rather than *for whom did you vote*. A sentence such as *the person did his job* is now used as *the person did their job*. Some people prefer saying *his* or *her* instead of only *his*. All these are instances of the changed usage and a modern teacher of English should not frown at a student if *he/she* (or *they*) uses the current usage, rather than the one prescribed in the grammar books of English.

In short, we have seen how the language of the residents of a small island has now become a world language. It is not because the native speakers of English represent a colonial power but the language has developed remarkably to meet the growing demands of people all over the world. English is dynamic enough to borrow words from other languages and to create new expressions to represent new concepts. Its grammar and usage are changing. One needs to be aware of these changes and accept what is in common use.

5

Need for Creating an Environment to Learn English

The initiative to teach the English language from class I of elementary schools is a welcome step but how will it succeed? One must create an environment for the learning of English. Most primary school children in India are taught all subjects by one teacher who has little experience of bilingual teaching and may not know enough English to teach even elementary students. To learn English for upward social mobility, properly trained teachers are to be made available in every school. They should be aware of the fact that they have the twin task of making students familiar with internationally acceptable usage of the language and the usage which fits the surroundings in which learning takes place.

New Textbooks

Language teaching experts suggest that multiple textbooks should be made available to address the diversity of English language environments in the country. The government should set up agencies to develop pedagogically sound English textbooks for every level from class I to class XII. These textbooks will act as models for the development of textbooks at the state level, with the help and collaboration of civil society organizations which may have expertise in the domain. The lessons should contain relevant cultural contents which must be familiar to students. It is not necessary to present a British or American scenario because students are unfamiliar with it and will fail to empathise with it. Instead of western folk tales which may be difficult to comprehend, one could use local folk tales, the contents of which are familiar to children. They will concentrate on how these well known stories are presented in English. The same strategy should be used when the teachers tell a story orally. If it is told in a simple and fluent language with proper accent, the class will not sound like a Hindi class.

Experience of an American Child in Hyderabad

An anecdote will make the point clear. An American professor came to Hyderabad with his family and sent his six year old daughter to a Telugu-medium school for some time. The girl picked up Telugu real fast inside and outside the classroom. She was exposed to a nursery rhyme in English but its pronunciation and rhythm were so different that she thought it was in a new language. She knew it was not in Telugu but she could not imagine that it was in English. One day she was persuaded to sing some nursery rhymes in Telugu. She did it reasonably well and then volunteered to sing something in 'Indian'. When she sang it, the parents realised that it was in English, with perfect Telugu accent. The parents were very amused to find the girl's perception that it was in a different language which she called 'Indian'. Had the teacher played the tape of that nursery rhyme, the girl would not have got confused about the identity of the language. The point is that the teaching should take place in the proper environment which, in this context, could have been provided by the use of a tape-recorder or a record player. In the absence of a proper environment, the purpose of teaching a nursery rhyme in English was defeated. The child could not get its correct pronunciation or rhythm.

Teaching Aids

If the teacher wants to create a proper environment for the child to learn English well, he/she should equip the classroom with appropriate audio-visual aids. He/she can take the help of non-technical teaching aids such as blackboards, pictures, charts, scrolls, flashcards, photographs and cartoons. He/she can use technical aids such as slides, transparencies, films, videotapes or television. Videos and television can be used to provide audio-visual background to the classroom discussion. Wherever possible, a multimedia approach can be undertaken. Flash cards can be used to present main lexical items and filmstrips or tape-recording to present the items in a context. The cassette-recording of a conversation can be used for listening practice. If the school has a language laboratory, it can be used for intensive practice through contextualised drills. It can be used to get the voice of the learner recorded so that he/she may compare his/her pronunciation to the prerecorded standard pronunciation. These days there is provision for computer-assisted language learning (CALL) and mobile assisted language learning (MALL). These are flexible language learning tools which make learning contextualised and interactive. Innovative teachers and enterprising schools should make full use of them.

Dramatization

Dramatic plays are an integral part of living for a young child. For instance, when a child looks at the picture of an animal or a bird, he/she likes to imitate the sound it creates. Such a play creates a make-believe world in which the child undergoes familiar experience and explores new ones. In his/her dramatic play, he/she likes to play the role of daddy, a mom or a teacher. He/she spends a lot of time in dramatic plays of many sorts. A lonely child plays the role of an imaginary companion, if no real one is available.

As young children are keenly interested in dramatic plays, the teacher may give this natural tendency a purposeful turn by presenting teaching items through dramatization. They may be lured to play various roles and speak their dialogues as directed. It will expose them to listening practice and encourage them to speak in a natural manner. They will forget that they are using a language which is not their mother tongue. An episode may be dramatized in such a way that children participate in it enthusiastically. Even nursery rhymes can be sung while enacting the scenes mentioned therein. As young children enjoy playing roles, they want to experience it. They do not care for the stage setting or other paraphernalia, as most of the playing will be done just for pleasure. It creates a suitable environment for proper learning. No school experience gives a child a better opportunity to be creative than does play making. As play making calls for careful thought with regard to timing and attention to sequence of events, the teacher has to preplan the whole episode carefully so as to make it purposeful.

Puppets and Marionettes[1]

To give a chance to children to carry out the dramatic interpretation of a story or a dialogue is a favourite way of creating an environment for teaching. There are other ways that can be adopted to add to the variety of experience. In elementary schools in the USA puppets of a number of kinds are used. Children who do not play the roles themselves like to play with puppets. These puppets are made with bottles that are wrapped with papers of various colours and are pushed around on a table. Children enjoy to do so and talk for them with confidence. An alternative way is to use hand puppets made of paper bags or scraps of cloth. Children enjoy manipulating them and talking for them without any inhibition. Sometimes stick puppets are also manipulated. Slightly grown up children can use marionettes which work by strings. The children who are mature enough to handle them enjoy producing plays. Pantomimes based on fairy tales or nursery stories are also popular in elementary classes in the West.

1. Puppets which work by string.

Use of Mass Media

The use of these activities are considered to be more desirable than making them watch episodes on television. They make them active participants, and not passive observers. The use of the mass media in the classroom exposes them to new ideas. However, they do not make them creative like play acting does. The latter develops vital creative interest in children. As these devices are cheaper than having electronic equipment, the teacher should prefer them and use them profitably to create the right environment.

Illustrations and Charts

The teacher should have charts illustrating how various vowel and consonants are pronounced. These charts may not be so interesting for students of class I but can prove to be useful if the teacher refers to the place and manner of articulation of a sound while demonstrating how to pronounce it. For instance, while pointing out the difference between/p^h/and/f/, the teacher can refer to the charts, as in figure 7.4. The practical demonstration, accompanied by the illustration to show how the tongue moves will help the child in understanding the point more clearly than its mere articulation and description by the teacher.

The tables of patterns of syntactic structures can be profitably used in the class. For instance, one table may illustrate the following:

Table 5.1: Substitution Table Concerning Self-Identification

My His Her	name	Is	Ramesh. Amit. Rita. Radha.
what	is	my his her	name?

Likewise, another table may refer to the objects in the classroom.

Table 5.2: Concerning Identification of Objects

This That	is	a my your his her	table. chair. blackboard. chart. pencil. box. bag
These	are		books. exercise books. pens. pencils.

Pattern Practice

Such tables can be used for pattern practice in the class. Drills and pattern practices are no longer considered to be as important as they were some decades ago when it was thought that language learning involved habit formation. Though recent research has shown that they are not as significant as they were thought to be, they do add to the process of language learning. If used imaginatively, they can stimulate creative thinking. For instances, the teacher may begin by saying,

> "My name is Rita Bhandari, what is your name?"

To this a student may respond by saying: 'My name is Ankita'.

She can then turn to the student sitting next to her and ask,

> 'What is your name?'

The next student will mention her name and pass on the question to her neighbour. That way the whole class may get involved. Each student will get a chance to identify himself/herself. The same table may be used with variation.

One student may identify her neighbour and ask about another one:

> 'Her name is Neeta; What is his name?'

Or, 'She is Neeta; Who is he?' (and so on).

In this process of introduction, one learns how to use pronouns such as, *you, he, she, it, we, they*, and *their* possessive forms: *my, her, your, its, our, their*, etc. The teacher does not use the term possessive pronoun but the concept becomes clear in the process of its use. A chart can be used to consolidate their learning.

In short, a classroom should have enough visual aids, electronic as well as non-electronic, to facilitate the process of learning. They should be used in a meaningful manner so that they attract students and make them concentrate on the points the teacher wants to highlight. It is upto him/her to use some of the techniques mentioned above to achieve the specified objectives of each lesson. He/she has to plan his/her lesson in such a way that all the teaching aids available to him/her are exploited in a natural manner. The classroom activities should appear to be spontaneous rather than contrived. Language ability grows in an environment that is suitable and stimulating. Elementary school children will use English in a situation where they really need it. It is the duty of the teacher to create such an environment.

6

Creativity and Innovation

Expectation from the English Language Teacher

> You must train your children to their studies in a playful manner and without any air of constraint with the further object of discussing more readily the natural bent of their respective characters.
>
> — *Plato*

Modern educators lay a lot of emphasis on the concept of creativity. Earlier it was thought that only genius manifested their latent through their creative activity. Now we believe that all human beings have creative potential; they have a distinct impulse to make original things. A child can learn much from the making of things but he/she can learn even more by sharing it with others and receiving appreciation for what he does. It is at this point that the teacher's role becomes crucial.

The world influences the child by exposing him/her to complex natural phenomena and social relationship. He/she selects what he/she considers feasible. The teacher helps him/her by drawing out his/her inherent power and facilitating him/her to respond to the world. Ideally the child should have the freedom and facility to choose. It could be in the fields of three distinctive activities:

(i) the activity of self expression,
(ii) the activity of observation and
(iii) the activity of appreciation.

Though the activity of self-expression cannot be taught, the teacher can play the role of a mid-wife; he/she can be a guide and inspirer. As observation is almost entirely an acquired skill, the teacher can train his/her students in direct perception of the world around them. He/she can help them in responding to other person's mode of expression and in preserving their original intensity of reaction to the sensuous qualities of expression. Though the teacher should not impose himself/herself unduely upon the child, he/she must not simply stand aside. As a child is in a constant state of transformation, the teacher's duty is to watch over this organic process. He/she should see that its tempo is not forced. As the values of the child change with the years of growth, the vigilant eyes of the teacher should see to it that the poetic vision of one age continues, with required changes, as the poetic vision of another age takes over and the sense of value does not lose its instinctive base. In short, the teacher should look at the development of the child as a progressive enlargement of his/her personality and interaction with his/her social groups: the family, the successive classes at school and the society in which he/she grows up. The function of education is to foster growth and the job of the teacher is to nurture the growing child.

The Facilitator of the Child's Growth

Educational psychologists say that the ideal of primary education is the growth of an individual child in whom all the natural functions grow harmoniously together. It is in this sense that the function of education is considered to foster growth, which includes the growth of the ability to express oneself. The Infant School (i.e. Nursery School/Kindergarten) is supposed to emphasize play activity. The teacher is supposed to offer sympathetic encouragement, rather than directly train children to acquire skills. He/she should give them full opportunity to express their ideas and experience through language, through singing and chanting, through miming and other dramatic action. The basic skills of listening, speaking, reading and writing should be acquired incidentally. They should originate in course of these activities.

Teaching through Interaction

The primary school teacher should play the role; a facilitator rather than an instructor. The language teacher, especially the teacher of English, should not forget it. Instead of forcing children to practise patterned drills, he/she should encourage them to express themselves in the language they are supposed to learn even though they are poor at it. The teacher should create an atmosphere in which the learning of English becomes a practical necessity for purposes of intergroup communication. In the group activity organised in the class, the English language should play a key role. Whether it is enacting a drama or reading a poem or telling a story, the target language should be the medium. Such a step would make students realise, indirectly but effectively, the intimate value of the language. A continuous inter-communication in English would lead to not only the refinement of language but also of learners' thought. Though the teaching of language is often promoted on practical, rather than aesthetic ground, the teacher can create an aesthetic interest in students in a subtle manner. The grammatical structures of the language must be introduced imaginatively to infuse life into them. And that is what an ideal teacher of English must aim at to make students sensitive to the language.

Experience the Needs of the Learner

Language teaching demands a high degree of joyful responsibility for the life entrusted to teachers; it must be influenced without any suggestion of dominance. Though the relation of the teacher with his/her students must be impersonal, it should not exclude emotive communication. Though the teacher need not identify himself/herself with the personal feelings and emotions of his/her students, he/she must experience the give and take of a mutual relationship both from his/her own as well as the students' points of view. The act of understanding must be a constant condition of reciprocity. It must be so on the part of the teacher, though he/she knows it well that students cannot experience the act of education from the point of view of the teacher. It is not enough for the teacher to represent the pupil to himself imaginatively; he/she must expression and appreciate the individuality of the students' disposition. He/she must try to identify himself/herself with his/her students and feel as they do.

The teacher gradually learns to distinguish and anticipate the real needs of his/her students. As he/she becomes aware of these needs, he/she understands more profoundly what they need to be real human beings. As he/she understands the civilizing effects of language, he/she becomes aware of his/her own limitation and tries to improve himself/herself by self-education. The education of students is, thus, always the self-education of the teacher. The educator absorbs the positive forces at work and rejects the forces that prevent him/her from playing his/her role creatively. He/she knows that his/her main task is to make his/her students articulate. He/she also knows that being fluent in the language is not enough, one must be clear in what one says. The teacher should, therefore, encourage both fluency in language and clarity of thought in his/her students.

Creative Teaching

The main task of a creative teacher is to create an atmosphere around him/her inside and outside the classroom in which his/her students try to make full use of their language potential and feel enthusiastic enough to express their creativity. If they find the classroom atmosphere relaxed and encouraging, they feel free to express their experience and views. The teacher prompts them to interact without interruption on his/her part. He/she adopts a flexible attitude towards them so that they interact with fluency and flexibility. His/her brain-storming technique may enable shy and withdrawn students to overcome their inhibition. They may come up with a variety of ideas. Some of them may not be relevant but he/she in careful enough not to make any adverse remarks. He/she may raise encouraging questions to find out what made them offer such observations.

Creativity gives birth to imagination which leads to the growth of new and significant ideas. It encourages one to take a chance and try novel ideas. When such ideas prove to be successful, they develop one's self-confidence and motivate one to contribute further to interaction, acting as an effective driving force.

Encouraging creativity among students is the most important objective of a creative teacher. He/she encourages them to open up. They feel that there is someone to appreciate them, recognize their talent and be sympathetic if they falter. A creative teacher knows his/her subject well and communicates his/her ideas effectively. If he/she teaches English, he/she pronounces all the sounds of English well and is wellversed in its stress patterns, intonation and rhythm. If a student mispronounces a word, he/she does not interrupt him/her to correct his/her pronunciation. Rather, he/she makes it a point to use that word correctly in his/her own speech. As young children are fond of imitating their teachers, his/her effort, though indirect, creats the desired effect. A creative teacher does not compel a student to repeat an expression for reinforcement; he/she reinforces it by repeating it himself/herself consciously in a natural course.

The English teacher must be dedicated to his/her students. He/she must have an understanding of the socio-cultural background of his/her students. Many of them may have no exposure to English outside the classroom and in spite of their enthusiasm to learn English, they may feel deprived. The job of the teacher is to give them protection and encouragement. His/her positive role in the development of Oral Skills will lead to success of his/her students.

Awareness of English Vowels

At the level of class I, the teacher should emphasize the development of listening and speaking. The skills of reading and writing could be added later on. His/her goal should be to develop in students an accurate auditory perception of sounds. The teacher should be able to keep in view the similarity and differences of sounds in the child's mothertongue and English. For instances, Hindi and most Indian languages have the following vowel sounds:

ə, a, I, i, U, u, e, æ, o, ɔ:

They have two diphthongs (i.e. sounds that are produced by the sequence of two vowel sounds): *əi* and *əu*. English has all these vowels (though the place of articulation of some of them are slightly different). Besides, it has/ei/, as in *day*,/ai/as in *time*,/œi/as in *boy*, and/au/as in *house*. The teacher could distinguish between/I/and/i/by referring to the contrast between *fit* and *feet* and *sit* and *seat*. Likewise *pull* could be contrasted with *pool,* and *foot* with *boot.* The sound/e/could be contrasted with/æ/, as in *bed* and *bad* or *beg* and *bag*. Similarly/ɔ:/could be contrasted with/au/as in *don* and *dawn.* He/she is supposed to have a list of simple words which provide such contrasts. The teacher should be prepared to provide minimal sentences to make the contrast meaningful, as in the following:

1 a. Please *sit* down.
  b. Have a *seat*.
  c. Please *sit* in the *seat*.
2. a. Where did you *get* it?
  b. Was it at the *gate*?
  c. Did you *get* it at the *gate*?
3. a. It is an ugly *hat*.
  b. I *hate* it.
  c. I *hate* this ugly *hat*.
4 a. He *caught* a *kite*.
  b. It was under the *cot*.
  c. He *caught* the *kite* under the *cot*.

(Please see the diagram 7.3 on page 48.)

Awareness of English Consonants

The teacher should be aware of the fact that English has some consonant sounds that Indian language do not have, e.g. th/θ/, as in *thin* and th/ð/, as in *that*. It has/ʒ/as in *pleasure* which is different from /dʒ/ as in *jar* and /z/as in *zero*. The teacher should be able to pronounce them correctly. Like Hindi-Urdu, English has *k, g, t, d, p, b, l, r, s,* /ʃ/. *m, n,* and /ŋ/ but /tʒ/ and /dʒ/ in English are affricates whereas *c* and *J* in Hindi-Urdu are plosives (stops). English does not have *gh, jh, dh* and *bh*. Thus *ghost* is pronounced as /gəust/, *bhakti* as/bakti/, *dhoti* as/doti/and *jhuggi* as/jugi/. As no double consonants are pronounced in English, *coffee* is pronounced as /kofi/, *dull* as /dʌl/and *upper* as/ʌpə:/. Retroflex sounds (T, Th, D, Dh) do not exist in English. Instead of dental sounds, it has alveolar ones (e.g. *t* as in *ten* and *d* in *dog*). It has *f* and *z* as Urdu has. Hindi does not have contrast between *v* and *w* as English has in *west* and *vest*. The teacher should pay special attention to English sounds which differ from those of the child's mothertongue. Though there is no meaningful contrast between *k* and /k^h/ and *t* and /t^h/, the pairs are in complementary distribution. For instance, *kin* is pronounced as /$k^h in$/ but in *skin, k* occurs without any aspiration. Similarly we have *pit*/p^hit/and/spit/, *table*/t^heibl/and/steibl/.

The teacher should be aware of how stress is assigned to English words and how the intonation pattern works in English sentences. (We will refer to them in some detail in chapter seven)

Knowledge of Syntax

The teacher is supposed to be aware of the difference between simple and complex sentence patterns. He/she should introduce students to simple sentences first. Once they learn them, he/she should encourage his/her students to produce new sentences on their patterns. He/she should use one basic sentence pattern at a time with natural intonation. Once students have learnt to use simple sentences, they should be encouraged to use compound and complex sentences in a natural context. They should be familiarised with different ways of saying the same thing. Special attention should be paid to the word order of English and to the fact that the movement of words in a sentence can shift the emphasis or change the meaning of the sentence. For instance, there is a difference in emphasis between (5a) and (5b).

5a. I like these mangoes.
5b. These mangoes I like (those I donot).

While discussing the contents of a lesson creatively, an enterprising teacher may come up with several innovative techniques. He/she may adopt a brainstorming technique to stimulate the imagination of his/her students. His/her questions and comments may help them elaborate their ideas which he/she may guide them to organise well. He/she may help them think aloud and arrive at a conclusion in a logical manner. From the beginning, he/she needs to focus at the reasoning ability of his/her students.

The teacher may encourage students to play roles and actively participate in the development of the plot of a lesson. The students play their roles by using their own imagination and come up with their own dialogues to develop the theme. When the role-playing is over, they may be invited to comment on their activity, point out their achievements and failures and decide for themselves whether they were faithful to the text.

The teacher may decide to present a lesson through open-ended questions and answers. Some of them may be relevant, some, superfluous. The teacher can guide them to weed out superfluous questions and answers.

A creative teacher comes up with innovative programme involving activities, exercises and oral interaction. He/she can innovate various types of language games, puzzles and riddles. He/she can encourage students to write short stories or compose poems, hold recitation sessions or elocution competition. His/her vigilance and acute observation can create a situation in which students become aware of the power of the English language and feel tempted to use it effectively. The value that he/she inculcates in them will stand in good stead throughout their lives.

Need for Careful Planning

All such activities need careful planning by the teacher. It needs lesson planning and material development. All primary schools may not have audio-visual aids. The teacher has to be innovative to prepare low-cost teaching aids. He/she has to improvise language games suitable to the children. As the teacher is an important part of each child's language curriculum, his/her choice of words and sentences in the class carries immense influence. He/she is the ever-present model for children. If students feel comfortable in the company of the teacher, they admire him/her and their process of learning is smooth and fast. As children react to the personality of the teacher as much as to his/her language, a lot is expected of him/her. He/she can use language to stimulate his/her students to think. He/she may help them have self confidence to express themselves without any inhibition or hesitation. The value he/she inculcates in them will stand in good stead throughout their lives. As a poet says,

> The sacred power that is thine
> To work with human souls;
> With heads and minds that speak and live,
> Oh! Could there ever be a work more noble and sublime.
>
> —"The Power of the Teacher"

Qualities of a Good Teacher

The society entrusts the teacher with the task of polishing, and shaping the mind and character of his/her students but they are not clay. They have a natural urge to grow. They all, and not only a selected few, have potential to be creative. Much depends on the ability of the teacher to create the environment for their linguistic growth. He/she must create the most delicate type of relation with the children entrusted to him/her. It may be expressed through glances, smiles, rarely perceptible movements as well as commands and well intentioned enthusiasm. Though the teaching process should be uniform, the teacher should pay the greatest attention to his/her pupils's personalities, this mental gifts and abilities and their inner world. It required the teacher to be a gifted and skilled educationist. Each teacher should try to develop his/her abilities to the highest level of teaching skills and an orientation towards students' individuality. An English teacher can make both his/her and students' life truly interesting and creative by improvisation, dramatisation and inventiveness.

Teaching is like love. It is a form of love. Just as it is impossible to love by order, one cannot communicate in accordance with a specified pattern. Each teacher can develop his/her abilities to the highest level if he/she is truly committed.

7

Listening and Speaking

To Listen vs. To Hear

To *listen* means 'to give attention to a sound'; to make a conscious effort or endeavour to hear'. One may hear without listening. For example, one may suddenly hear words spoken in an adjoining room. Likewise, we may listen without hearing. In listening the ear is intent upon the sound. The difference between listen and hear is like the difference between *look* and *see*. To *look* means to direct one's gaze is a specific direction just as to *listen* means to direct one's ears to a specific sound. The act of listening involves paying attention to something. A person learning English as a second/foreign language pays attention to the sounds he/she hears and tries to figure out what they mean. To the ears of a layman the English sounds he/she hears are meaningless; they are mere noise.

Development of Speaking and Listening Skills in the Child's Mothertongue

Language is used to serve many purposes. A child learns to use it primarily to express his/her feelings, thought or intention. A small child thinks aloud. Before he/she goes to a nursery or primary school, he/she learns to listen to the language spoken by his/her parents, relatives and neighbours. He/she learns how to respond to the person who speaks to him/her. As he/she grows up, he/she discovers how to speak his/her mothertongue to respond to the person who addresses him/her. He/she also knows how to use the language to draw attention. In everyday interaction, he/she not only listens and understands but also speaks. He asks questions and makes statements and requests. By the time he/she is ready to go to an elementary school, he/she is familiar with the communication skills of listening and speaking in his/her mothertongue. If the language of the neighbourhood is different from his/her mothertongue, he/she picks it up on his/her own to communicate with his/her peers and elders.

If parents mispronounce words in the mothertongue and use inaccurate grammatical expressions, the child may pick them up but acquires better expressions ultimately at school.

Bilingual Environment

If the child grows up in a bilingual environment and English is one of the languages spoken around, he/she picks it up before going to school. In case the spoken language he/she is exposed to is substandard and inaccurate, he/she has to 'relearn' it at school. If he/she is completely unexposed to English, the teacher has a raw learner at hand. It is in his/her power to expose the child to the correct forms of speech. Most children learn how to read and write at school. In case the learner is a raw hand, he/she learns all these four skills-listening, speaking, reading and writing–at school. Of these skills, listening and reading are receptive and speaking and writing are productive. The student knows how to be proactively involved in learning all these skills. The objective of introducing English at standard 1 in India is to familiarize students with all the four processes. However, it is better to give priority to listening and speaking.

The Beginners of Three Types

The class I student in India may belong to any of the three categories:

(i) He/she has been to a nursery school or kindergarten and knows some spoken English;
(ii) He/she comes from a bilingual family or neighbourhood and has some knowledge of spoken English.
(iii) He/she comes from the background in which he/she has never heard English being spoken, nor had he/she been to a nursery school or kindergarten.

In most of the primary schools in rural India, the child belongs to the third category. In urban areas, he/she might have been to a nursery school which lacked competent teachers of English. If parents used English at home, they might have lacked competence and exposed the child to the substandard spoken English. It is the duty of the teacher to find out the category to which the child belongs. He/she may separate unexposed students from those who have been poorly exposed. He/she may have separate strategies to deal with them.

Listening

Listening is a process of giving attention to certain incoming sounds which combine into words and sentences and convey meaning. Traditionally listening was regarded a *passive process* in which our ears receive what sounds go in them. All a listener has to do is to register the message passively. Now listening is regarded as an *active process*. A good listener is as active while listening as a speaker is while speaking.

Listening is a complex process that requires effort and attention. As a person listens, he/she recognizes the nature and pattern of sounds and attaches meaning to them. He/she reacts to the sounds on the basis of his/her experience. If the sounds deal with things or ideas outside his/her experience, he/she is unable to understand them. Sometimes he/she attaches meanings to such expressions which are quite different from what the speaker intended to convey. Usually he/she puts the sounds into perspective. He/she pays attention to pitch, stress and intonation of the speaker. They help him/her in interpreting the sequence of sounds. He/she remembers the sense of what he/she hears. When listening to an utterance in a language he/she does not know, he/she fails to attach meaning to it or interprets it on the basis of his/her understanding of such a sequence in the language he/she is familiar with.

Types of Listening

There are two types of listening; one-way listening and two-way listening. When a student listens to a teacher's lecture in the classroom, it is an act of one-way listening. When he/she listens to a programme on radio or watches a discussion or a dialogue on television, it is an act of one-way listening. However, when one character talks with another character on television, it is an act of two-way listening for the participants. A two-way listening act is a dialogue; when one person speaks, another person listens to him/her. When he/she responds, the first person listens. As they speak by turn, at every point in turn-taking, the speaker becomes the listener and listener becomes the speaker. In any interlocution, the roles of participants (interlocutors) are reserved.

In *one-way listening* the purpose of the listener is clear. He/she listens with a view to getting the sense of the lecture, so that he/she can summarize it. All acts of purposeful listening are not alike. Some listeners listen to a talk critically; they not only listen but also think about what they are listening. *Critical listening* is a systematic act in which the listener concentrates on the main points made by the speaker and ignores digressions, including anecdotes and jokes. *Appreciative listening* suggests that the listener is favourably inclined towards the speaker and may not have a critical appraisal of whatever he/she listens to. *Creative listening* takes place when the listener feels inspired by what the speaker says and tries to reconstruct the idea in one way or another.

In *two-way listening*, the listener is the next speaker and is more actively involved than in one-way listening. He/she is normally polite and courteous and goes on thinking about how to respond while he/she is listening. In one-way listening, the listener may become indifferent but in two-way listening he/she is thoroughly involved. As the span of concentration is relatively small in primary school children, it is advisable that the teacher turns his/her classes in two-way listening. He/she should approach the topic he/she wants to discuss in a conversational style and give his/her listener opportunities to ask questions or give comments. Making them victims of long lectures is neither productive nor profitable.

Purpose of Listening

In one-way listening in the classroom the purpose of listening is either to understand the *gist* of what is being spoken or to get specific information in detail.

Listening for Gist

When one is listening for gist, one ought to know what information one is listening for. Then only one will be able to concentrate on the main point and ignore what the speaker has said but is not relevant or necessary. The word *gist* refers to the substance or general meaning of a speech or text and that is what the listener should be looking for.

Listening for Specific Details

While listening for specific details, the listener is not supposed to miss any point. He/she must listen to the whole speech carefully and make a mental note of all the points. For instance, when we listen to an announcement about the arrival or departure of a train, we pay attention to the train number, the platform number and the time of arrival and departure of the train in which we are interested. We do not pay attention to the detailed announcements about other trains. In short, listening with a purpose means developing the ability to concentrate on the points of one's interest and ignoring other information that we do not need to know.

Listening Environment in the Classroom

When children come to a class, they know that they have to listen to the teacher. However, all of them are not equally alert. Some students may be preoccupied with other ideas. They may be distracted by what other students do or by other things in the environment. They may experience little conscious listening or half listening. They may be apparently absorbed but show little or no reaction. They may hear some portions of the utterance and start reacting to them mentally, disassociating themselves from what is said later on. Probably every individual responds at times in each of these ways depending on his/her interest in the subject, his/her attitudes towards the speaker and his/her own mental condition at the moment. A teacher should be able to watch his/her students' focus to find out how deeply listening is going on and when and where a student has got off the track. Often one can tell this by watching their eyes and faces. The teacher should try to turn marginal listeners into appreciative listeners. Some students may find it very difficult to acquire the practice of listening when they are spoken in a foreign or unknown language. The period during which a child can listen an utterance attentively is initially very short. It increases by practice. However, listening cannot be forced. Rather than being unduly persistent and strained, the teacher should adopt pleasant manners to converse. He/she should give an opportunity to students to speak and share their views. If the teacher speaks nicely, if his/her pronunciation is clear and rhythmical, if he/she does not speak rapidly and does not have high pitch, children can listen to him/her without any strain. The teacher must provide physical conditions conducive to good listening. An interesting way to introduce the subject provides students with a purpose for listening. The voice quality of the teacher is important because it stirs emotional reaction in students. A lilting voice with a smile and a relaxed, appealing attitude attracts children's attention more than a cold and stern voice.

Objectives of Getting Trained to Listen

The main objectives of listening exercises are

- To discriminate between sounds (e.g. between/t/and/θ/).
- To recognise specific sounds in words, (e.g./t^h/in *tanks* and/θ/in *thanks*).
- To identify stressed words (e.g. 'export (n.) vs ex'port (v).
- To recognise grouping of words (due to intonation)
- To recognise a sentence as a unit (i.e. the role of a period ⊙ or other punctuation marks signalled by pauses of various duration (e.g. , for a short pause)
- To identify modulation of the speakers's voice.
- To connect linguistic expressions to non-linguistics (kinesic) cues, such as eye movements and postures in order to convey meaning.

Objectives of Learning to Speak

Listening and speaking are two sides of the same issue: oral communication. The objectives of training in listening have been mentioned above. It is believed that a language learner will speak correctly only when he/she can listen to sounds correctly. Assuming that the learner has achieved the target set for listening properly, he/she should take up the task of speaking properly. The learner should try to achieve the following goals:

- To articulate vowel and consonants sounds correctly, first in isolation, then in words and sentences.

- To differentiate between the sounds he/she finds contrasting, for instance, between/dʒ/,/z/and/ʒ/,/t/and/θ/,/l/and/r/,/pʰ/and/f/,/w/and/v/,/e/and/əi/,/æ/and/əi/,/o/and/ɔ/,/ɔ/and/əʊ/.
- To practise these differences in minimal pairs of words and in sentences.
- To use stress and intonation correctly in sentences and to understand the difference in meaning because of a change in intonation.
- To modulate one's voice according to the need,
- To synchronise correct pronunciation of expressions with the correct gestures and postures,
- To use pauses on appropriate occasions

Besides, the speaker should

- concentrate on what he/she is saying,
- speak distinctly, keeping her/his voice neither too high nor too low,
- avoid digression and repetition.
- use apt vocabulary.

Factors Affecting Listening and Speaking

Speech sounds uttered in a pleasant voice which are loud and clear enough to be heard facilitate listening whereas harsh and coarse voice hampers it. If one speaks very rapidly and sharply, one distracts the listener or causes strain to him/her. Any manner of speech that needs extra efforts to understand affects listening adversely. The spoken language must be clear and intelligible. Clarity of speech involves accurate articulation of sounds and their clear enunciation. The pronunciation should be easily understandable. The choice of words should convey his/her intention. The usage should be acceptable. Use of uncommon words or unacceptable expressions has an adverse effect on the listener.

Listening to English Sounds

The articulation of sounds of English may present a problem to children, especially if they do not occur in their mothertongue. For instance, Indian children can pronounce/p, b, t, d, k, g, l, r, n, m, ŋ, s, /ʃ/ 'sh'correctly but may have difficulty in pronouncing th/θ, ð/and/ʒ/. Some children may face difficulty in pronouncing/f, v, w/as well. If a child cannot pronounce a sound, he/she has difficulty in listening to it accurately. For instance, some Hindi-speaking children hear/f,/as/pʰ/,/θ/as/tʰ/and/ð/as/d/. Children learn the pronunciation of sounds from the family members at home and from other people they associate with. The mispronunciation of English sounds may be due to lack of these sounds in the children's mothertongue or an attempt to match these sounds with other sounds which they consider to be identical. It may also be because the people they listen to constantly mispronounce them. Language

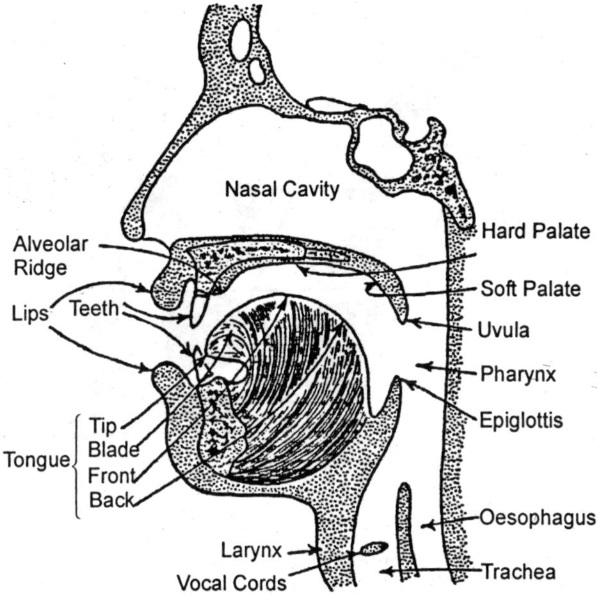

Fig. 7.1: Organs of Speech (Schematic diagram)

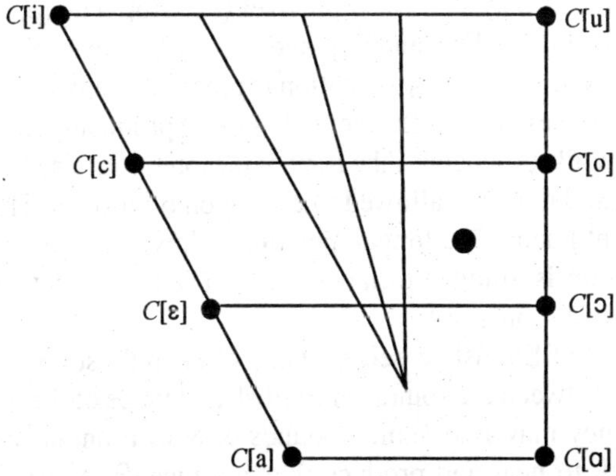

Fig. 7.2: The Primary Cardinal Vowels

development takes place through the use of the language. In so far as sounds and stress are concerned, the main problem the primary school children in India face is that most of the people they associate with do not use them correctly. The only remedy is that they are exposed to correct speech in the classroom. It means that the teacher should use proper expressions and pronounce them clearly. His/her efforts can be reinforced with the help of audio-visual aids. Videocassettes can not only produce correct sounds but show how these sounds are produced.

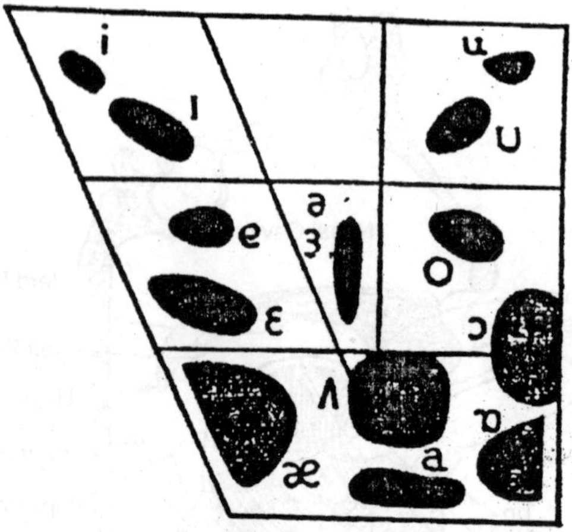

Fig. 7.3: Vowels in Indian English

Identification of Sounds

The teacher may produce a sound in a word and ask students to identify it. He/she may tell them how he/she has produced that sound. If videotapes are available, they may be played to demonstrate the production of the sound. For instance, he/she may show how plosives (i.e. Stops) i.e./p, b, t, d, k, g/are produced by closing the lips, and c/tʃ/ and j/dʒ by their partial closure. While pronouncing/f, v, θ, ð, s, z, ʃ, ʒ/, frication is produced. While producing these sounds, the air passes through the mouth but while producing/m, n, ŋ/, it passes through nose. While producing/l/the front of the tongue is raised in the direction of hard palate and the air is allowed to escape on both sides. The sound/r/is a frictionless continuant. The tongue position is lowered while speaking it so that the airstream is allowed to move freely. (See the articulation on these sounds in figure 7.4 on p. 49)

The teacher of English as second language should study the similarities and difference between the sounds of English and those of the mothertongues of children. They may find similar sounds easy to pronounce but different sounds difficult to hear and produce. For instance,/θ, ð, ʒ/do not occur in most Indian languages. They should be produced clearly in the class so that students may learn to recognize them. Only after their recognition, they may be produced correctly. On can do so by practising them.

Indian children may have no difficulty in differentiating a voiced consonant from its voiceless counterpart because they are there in their language. They have a contrast between aspirated sounds such as/k^h, t^h, p^h/ and their unaspirated counterparts/k, t, p/. They need to be told that in English these contrast do not create meaningful difference as they do in many Indian languages. However they have their own carved out areas in which they are

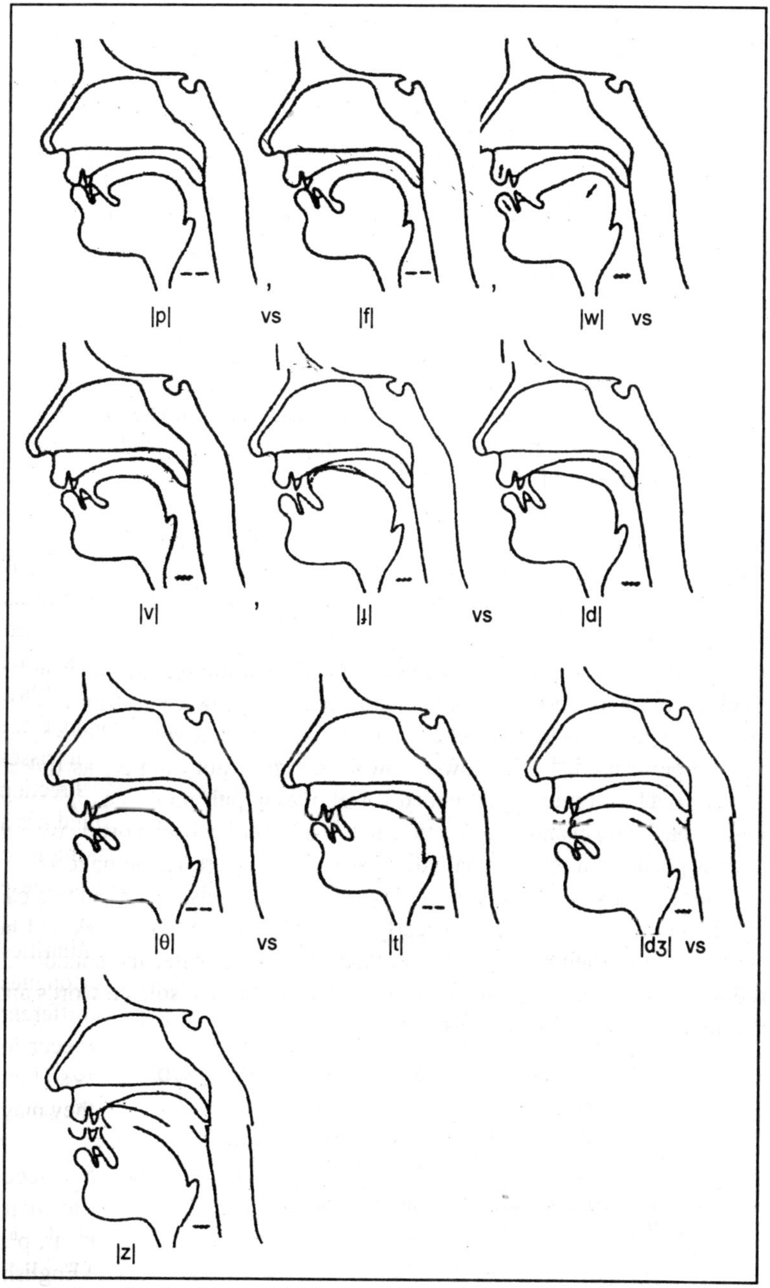

Fig. 7.4: Indicating Place and Manner of Articulating Some Consonant Sounds

used. If/k, t, p/occur in a stressed position, they are spoken as/kh, th, ph/, otherwise they remain unaspirated.

Like Indian languages, English has/ə, a, I, i, U, u, e, æ, o, ɔ/as vowels. They have double vowels (diphthongs) such as/ei, ai, əi, əu, au, iə, uə, uə/. Hindi-Urdu has only/əi, au/. The rest will have to be practised by listening to them. Besides, in English there is a difference between/ə/,/əː/and/ʌ/,/e/and/ei/and/ɔ/and/au/. The teacher will have to make students familiar to them, by using them in words. (See figures 7.3 on p. 47 on the point and manner of articulation of vowels).

Sound Contrast and Phonetic Drills for Speaking Distinctly

Vowels are the outstanding sounds in syllables because their presence indicates syllables. Unlike in the production of consonants, there is no audible friction in their production. They are voiced sounds. They are produced by an uninterrupted stream of air from the lungs.

The classification of vowels depends on whether they are pronounced in the front, back or middle of the tongue. If we look at the cardinal vowel diagram in figure 7.2 on page 47, the lower high front vowel/I/is lax, as in/sIt/ *'sit'* but a slightly lower front vowel is tense as in/siː t/ *'seat'*. The sound /e/, as in/bet/ *'bet'*, is a mid-front tense vowel whereas/æ/, as in/sæt/, is a lower front tense vowel./ə/, which is called 'schwa', is a mid-central unrounded vowel, as in/əbaut/about./a/, as in /faðəː/'father' is low central unrounded vowel whereas/o/, as in/obei/'obey' is mid back rounded vowel. The sound/ɒ/is an open rounded back lower vowel as in/pɒt/'pot' and/ɔ/, as in/kɔt/ 'caught', is a lower mid back rounded vowel./u/as in/pul/'pool' is a high tense rounded back vowel and/ʊ/as in/pʊt/, 'put' is a lower lax back vowel. We can see their position in the cardinal vowel diagram in figure 7.3 on page 48.

The teacher who knows how and where these vowels are articulated can help the child to produce them clearly. However, first, the child should be able to listen to them, if possible, on tape or cassette. After the sounds are produced several times, he/she may produce them first in isolated words and then, in minimal contrasting sets:

/i/	/I/	/e/	/æ/	/u/	/ʊ/	/ɒ/	/ɔ/
Seat	sit	set	sat	suit			sought
Feel	fill	fell		fool	full		
Peat	Pit	pet	pat		put	pot	–
Beed	bid	bed	bad	boot	–	–	
Deed	did	deal	dad	–		–	–
Neat		net	nat			not	naught

These words can then be used in sentences, such as the following:

Please *sit* in this *seat*.
They *sat* on the sofa *set*.
These shoes *fit* in my *feet*.
She *met* me in the *meat* market.
Those *men* are *mean*.
He *hid* his *head*.
She *begged* for the *big bag*.

English has some diphthongs, i.e. sounds produced by the sequence of two vowels. However they are produced so rapidly that we cannot tell where one sound begins and the other ends. They are/ei/as in *day,*/əi/as in *time,*/ɔi/ as in *boy,*/əu/as in *home,*/au/as in *cow,*/Iə/as in *dear,*/eə/as in *care,* and/uə/as in *poor.* Of these,/əi/and/au/are familiar to Hindi-Urdu speakers. The rest will have to be practised, first in isolated words and then in contrasting pairs. The following pairs may be tried:

Eat-ate; feel- fail; lead-lead; bleed-bled.
Paid-pad; sake-sack; pain-pan; cane-can.
Boat-bought; note-naught; so-saw; pose-pause.
Let-late; get-gate; bet-bait; pen-pain.

The contrasting sounds in the words given above will help the children to differentiate between them and to pronounce them correctly. The teacher may draw their attention to their contextualised use, as in the following:

I *hate* the *hat/heat*.
He picked up the *mail* after the *meal*.
This *pin* caused me *pain*.
She was *mad* at the *maid*.
He *planned* to catch the *plane*.
He bought a *cake* and a *coke*.
I *sat* at the *site*.
The *man* was in the *mine*.
It is *not* in the *note*.
His shirt got *caugh*t on the *cot*.

The children will have fun repeating these lines:

Betty Botha bought some *butter*
But, said she, the *butt*er is *bitter*
If I put it in my *batter*
It will make my *batter bitter*
But a *bit* of *better butter*
Would make my *batter better*.

The teacher may point out that there is/I/in *Betty*,/əʊ/in *Botha*,/ɔ:/in *bought*,/ʌ/in *butter*, and *but*,/æ/in *batter*,/ə:/in *bitter*, and *better* (in '*ter*'). If *but* is spoken in its contracted form, the vowel/ʌ/will be reduced to/ə/. Thus this stanza has a contrast between/ə/,/ə:/and/ʌ/, between /əʊ/ and /ɔ:/ and between /I/, /e/ and /æ/.

Consonants

English has six plosive (stop) consonant phonemes in pairs. Each pair consists of an unaspirated voiceless phoneme and unaspirated voiced phoneme./p/,/t/ and/k/as in *pin, tub* and *king* are voiceless and/b/,/d/and/g/are voiced./p/,/t/ and/k/are aspirated, except when they occur after other consonants. Thus, *pin* is spoken as/p^hin/, *tub* as/t^hub/and *king* as/k^hiŋ/. However,/p/,/t/and/k/are not aspirated when they occur in words such as *spine, station* and *scale*. English has/f, v, θ, ð, s, z, ʃ, ʒ/as fricatives. Of these,/θ, ð,/do not occur in Indian languages and students will have to make efforts to speak them. Some Hindi speakers replace/f/with/p^h/but that is a mistake./p^h/is a voiceless aspirated stop whereas/f/is a voiceless continuant; it is spoken when the lower lip touches upper teeth. The following contrast may be noted:

Pad-fad; pan-fan; pat-fat; pit-fit

We may look at the contextual clues in the following sentences:

It will *fit* in the *pit*.
He had to *leap* to get the *leaf*.
He had *fun* when he heard the *pun*.

/s/and/z/occur in many Indian languages but some dialects of Hindi do not have/z/. Their speakers use/dʒ/ for /z/. The teacher may point out that /dʒ/ in English is an affricate, a continuation of a plosive and a fricative, whereas /z/ is hundred per cent fricative. We can use the following contrasting pairs for practice:

Jig-zag; jest-zest; fudgy-fuzzy; rage-rays.
Stage-stays; page-pays; fudge-fuzz; huge-hues.

The following sentences provide contextual clues:

He said so in *jest* will *zes*t.
She *pays* for each typed *page*.
They *raised* their voice in *rage*.

Many speakers of Indian languages tend to replace/θ/as in *thing*, with /t^h/; for instance, they say/thiŋ/for/θiŋ/. Students need to be told that/th/is a voiceless, aspirated stop (plosive) which is pronounced when the tip of the tongue touches the tooth ridge whereas /Θ/ is a voiceless continuant which is pronounced when the top of the tongue touches the top teeth, as is clear if the following pairs of words are pronounced correctly.

> t^hank-thank; t^hen-then; t^hick- thick; t^hiŋ- thing
> t^hin- thin; t^hie- thigh; t^haught-thought; mat^h- math.

The following sentences may be used for practice:

> He *taught* what he *thought* proper.
> India *thanked* Russia for *tanks*.
> The *team* had a good *theme*.
> The box had a *thin* layer of *tin*.

Those who use/t^h/for/Θ/, use/d/for/ð/. They forget that/d/is a voiced stop which is pronounced when the tip of the tongue touches the tooth ridge, whereas/ð/is a voiced continuant which is pronounced when the tip of the tongue touches the top tooth. The point can be clarified by articulating these pairs of words accurately.

> Dare- their; den- then; day- they; die- thy; udder- other.

We may note the following sentences with their contextual clues:

> I do not *dare* to go *there*.
> Will *they* come that *day*?
> *Those* who *doze* in the class are lazy.
> By *then* the tiger will be in his *den*.

The children who do not differentiate between /s/ and /ʃ/ need to be told that/s/is a voiceless continuant which is pronounced when the tip of tongue touches the tooth ridge whereas /ʃ/, which is also a voiceless continuant, is spoken when the front of the tongue touches the hard palate. The following minimal pairs should be pronounced correctly:

> Said-shed; same-shame; see-she; self-shelf;
> Sell-shell; sip-ship; so-show; sign- shine.

The following sentences may be drilled to keep the distinction clear:

> She put a *sheet* on that *seat*.
> *She* went to the *sea* shore.
> It *perished* in *Paris*.
> These *classes clash* very often.

The sound/ʒ/as in *leisure* should not be confused with either/dʒ/or/z/ because /ʒ/ is a voiced fricative which is pronounced by taking the tip of the tongue very close to the alveolar ridge while the middle of the tongue is close to the palate; the tongue is grooved. The lips are pushed outward and the teeth are closed together. We have already noted that/z/is a fricative which is pronounced when the tip of the tongue touches the tooth ridge and /dʒ/ is an affricate which is articulated while moving the front of the tongue to the hard palate. We have discussed the contrast between /dʒ/ and/z/. We should now differentiate between *leisure*/leʒəː/and ledger/ledʒəː/, vision/viʒ n/and pigeon/ pidʒin/and confusion/kənfjuː ʒn/with Confucian/kənfjuʃn/.

In North Indian English/a/and/əː/are spoken as/aː/./ei/is spoken as/eː/ and/ou/as/o/.

> /a/is often spoken as/ə/. Like American, Indians do not drop the final r, as the British do. Thus, /kaː/*car* is spoken as /kar/, /bɔː/ *bore* as /bɔər/ and /betəː/ *better* as /betər/.

Consonant Clusters

Some speakers of Indian languages have some difficulty in pronouncing consonant clusters with initial *s*. For instance, Hindi speakers from the eastern region add/i/ initially while speaking sk, sp or st clusters, as in/iskul/,/ispik/,/ isteiʃn/. Those from the northern belt of the Hindi region break the cluster by adding/ə/(schwa) between the cluster, as in/səkul/,/səpik/and/səteiʃn/. If children have picked up either of these habits, they have to be persuaded to say/spiːk/,/skul/and /steiʃn/.

Many English words have double consonants as in *doll, bubble, giggle, twitter* etc. but they are spoken as single consonants, as in/dʌl/,/bʌbl/,/gigl/,/ twətəː/, etc.

Many Indian languages have voiced aspirated stops such as *bh*, *dh*, and *gh*. Even if an English word has such consonants in spelling, they are spoken without aspiration. For example, *Bhutan* is spoken as/butān/, *dhoti* as/dəuti/, *ghost* as/gəust/, *ghetto* as/getəu/and *ghastly* as/gaːstli/. If the teacher keeps these points in mind and helps students in acquiring the correct pronunciation, there is no reason why their spoken English will not be up to the mark. The points mentioned above are intended to help the teacher to guide his/her students to distinguish various vowel and consonant sounds. The figures in 7.4 will help them in understanding the difference. The goal can be achieved by listening to them correctly and reproducing them successfully.

If Indian children in the elementary classes are given a chance to learn spoken English, they need help in listening as well as speaking. Listening requires attention to sounds and registering and reacting to them at the rate at which they are heard. Children should be made aware of the fact that listening provides them only one chance for intake. Whereas in reading one may reread the text for a better comprehension, there is no such chance while one listens, for sounds come and pass away. If the listener loses track of what has been said, he/she misses the message. He/she has to have good control over himself/herself while listening.

Stress

Listening requires that sounds in a sequence be put into some sort of perspective. We have discussed above how various sounds of English are articulated but there are some variations when they are spoken in a sequence. For instance, there are three articles in English: *a, an* and *the*. In isolation they are pronounced as/ei/,/æn/and/ði:/but in a sequence they may be spoken as/ə/,/ən/and/ðə/or/ð/. (See Table no. 7.1 for a list of some accented words in English and their unaccented (unstressed) forms). Stress involves emphasis given to a particular syllable or word in speech. it is manifested by speaking the syllable with relatively greater loudness or at a higher pitch. Here pitch refers to the quality of a sound governed by the rate of vibration in producing it. It indicates the degree of highness or lowness of a tone.

Though there are no foolproof rules to determine which syllable of a word should be stressed, certain observations can be safely made.

(i) A great majority of two syllable words are accented (stressed) on the first syllable. For instance, *brékfəst* (breakfast), *mʌndi* (Monday), *névə:* (never).

(ii) In a compound word, the primary stress falls on the first element of the compound and the secondary stress on the second element, e.g. *drʌ´gstɔə:* (drugstore), *futpa:* θ (footpath).

(iii) In a compound verb, the primary accent is on the second component. For example, *ʌndə:stæ'nd* 'understand', *əuvə:'luk* 'overlook' *autspéukən* 'outspoken'.

(iv) When a suffix is added to a word, the new word is stressed on the same syllable as was on the root word, as in
Háppy- háppiness
Beáuty- beáutiful
Góod- goodness

(v) Numbers ending in *–téen* get the stress usually on the last syllable, e.g.
Thírty- thirteén

(vi) Several words which may be used either as nouns or verbs have a difference in stress to indicate the difference in their usage, e.g.

Noun	*verb*
Digest/dáidʒest/	digest/didʒést/
Insult/ínsʌlt/	insult/insʌ'lt/

[see Table no. 7.2 for more words of this type.]

Table 7.1: Accented and Unaccented Forms of Function Words in English

Word Form	*Accented Form*	*Unaccented*
a	ei	ə
am	æm	əm, m
an	æn	ən, n
and	ænd	ənd, ən, nd, n
are	a: (a:r)	ə
as	æz	əz
at	æt	ət
be	bi:	bi
been	bi:n	bin
but	bʌt	bət
can (aux)	kæn	kən, kn
could	kud	kəd, kd
do (aux)	du:	du, də, d
does (aux)	dʌz	dəz, z, s
for	fɔ:	fər, fr
from	frɒm	frəm
had (aux)	hæd	həd, hd, d
have	hæv	həv. əv, v
he	hi:	hi, i:, i
her	hə:	hə:, ə: ə
him	him	im
his	hiz	iz
is	iz	z, s
must	mʌst	məst, məs
not	nɒt	nt, n
of	ɒv	əv, v, ə
shall	ʃæl	ʃəl, ʃl
she	ʃi:	ʃɪ
should	ʃud	ʃəd, ʃd
than	ðæn	ðen, ən
that	ðæt	ðət
the	ði:	ði, ðə, ð
them	ðem	ðəm, ðm, m
there	ðeə:, ðɛər	ðe, ɜ
to	tu:	tu, tə:
us	ʌs	əs, s
was	wɒs	wəz
we	wi:	wi
were	wɜ: (r)	wər, wə
who	hu:	hʊ, h:, u

Word Form	*Accented Form*	*Unaccented*
will	wil	l
would	wud	wəd, əd, d
you	ju:	ju

A.C. Gimson, 1965, pp. 240-242.

Table 7.2: Change in Stress due to Grammaticalization

Word	Noun	Verb
accent	[ˊæksent]	[æk'sent]
	or	or
	[æksənt]	[ək'sent]
concert	['kɒnsət]	[kən'sə:t]
conduct	['kɒndkt]	[kən'dʌkt]
contract	['kɒnˌtrakt]	[kən'trakt]
convict	[ˈkɒnvikt]	[kən'vikt]
contrast	['kɒntra:st]	[kən'tra:st]
digest	['dai,dʒest]	[dai'd ʒest] or [di'dʒest]
desert	['dezət]	[di'ze: t]
discount	['diskaunt]	[dis'kaunt]
frequent	['fri:kwənt]	[fri'kwənt]
import	['impɔ:t]	[im'pɔ:t]
impress	['impres]	[im'pres]
increase	['iŋkri:s]	[in'kri:s]
insult	['insʌlt]	[in'sʌlt]
object	['ɒbdʒikt]	[əb'dʒikt]
perfect	['pə:fikt]	[pə'fekt]
permit	['pə:mit]	[pə'mit]
present	['preznt]	[pri'zent]
produce	['prɒdju:s]	[prə'dju:s]
progress	['prəʊgres]	[prə'gres]
project	[prɒdʒekt]	[prə'dʒekt]
protest	['prəʊtest]	[prə̂test]
rebel	['rebl]	[ri'bel]
record	['rekɔ:d]	[ri'kɔ:d]
refuse	['refu:s]	[ri'fu:z]
segment	['segmənt]	[seg'ment]
subject	['sʌbdʒkt]	[səbdʒekt]
survey	['sa:vei]	[sə'vei]

[from Gimson 1965: 228-29]

All words are divided into two classes.

(a) *Content Words* which have their own meanings, and
(b) *Function Words* which have little meaning other than the grammatical idea they express.

- Nouns, verbs, adjectives and adverbs are content words which are usually stressed.
- Articles, prepositions, personal pronouns, possessives, relative pronouns and conjuncts (e.g. *and, but, if, so* etc.) are unstressed. Unstressed words have reduced vowels. In order to improve one's pronunciation, one should know how to pronounce them correctly.

Intonation

Intonation involves the rise and fall of the voice. It is the combination of musical tones on which we pronounce the syllables that make up our speech. It is closely related to sentence-stress but it is not equivalent to it. Often a syllable with a sentence-stress is spoken on a higher musical note than the unstressed syllables.

- English has mainly four types of intonation:
  - (i) Falling intonation [↘]
  - (ii) Rising intonation [↗]
  - (iii) Falling rising intonation [↘↗]
  - (iv) Rising falling intonation [↗↘]
- The falling intonation is associated with statements which are complete and definite:
  As in
  It was very good.
  I liked it very much.
- The rising intonation is normally used at the end of a question which does not begin with an interrogative word, as in
  Are you ready? You like it?
- The falling rising intonation involves the glide down followed by glide up
- The rising falling intonation involves the rise of the voice above normal and falling below normal, as in
  I said I could not hear you.

Rhythmic Pattern

The word *rhythm* refers to a strong, regular repeated pattern of sound. It involves the measured flow of words and phrases in verse or prose, as determined by the relation of stressed and unstressed syllables. Within a word group there is at least one stressed syllable which may have one or more unstressed syllable before it. They are articulated very quickly. As unstressed syllables are short and stressed syllables are long, there is a great difference of length between them. The stressed syllable may be followed by one or more unstressed syllables. A unit of this kind, with a stressed syllable at its centre and some unstressed syllables occurring before or after it form a rhythmic unit. We may look at the rhythemic units in the following extract:

> In the great city of Bhagavati | lived once upon a time|| a young Prince|| called Raja Ram.|| He was fond of hunting ||dicing|| sleeping by day|| and drinking at night|| in idleness.|| But he was adored|| by his children|| because he took the trouble || to win their hearts.||

In the passage given above, each rhythmic unit has been marked by '||'.

In a poem, the rhythm may be marked by its rhyme scheme, i.e., the correspondence of sounds between words, especially at the end. For instance. we may look at the following nursery rhyme:

> Mary, Mary | quite contrary||
> How does your | garden grow||
> With silver bells | and cockle shells||
> Any pretty maids | all in a row.||

As children sing the nursery rhyme in chorus, they pick up its natural rhythm. We may look at one of the 'Nonsense Alphabets' by Edward Lear:

> C | was a cat||
> Who ran | after a rat||
> But his courage | did fail||
> When she seized | on his tail.||

The teachers may reproduce such poems and nursery rhymes in his/her class; they will make students feel what a rhythmic unit is. Once their ears get attuned to the rhythm, they may be asked to repeat them aloud.

Modulation[1] of Voice

It is not enough to know how sounds are articulated and how stress, tone, pitch and intonation work. One should be able to note the modulation of the speaker's voice. We have already mentioned that a statement has a falling intonation, as in

> I liked it very much.

1. The act of varing the strength, tone or pitch of one's voice.

If it is spoken with a rising intonation, it becomes a question, as in

You like it very much?

A person can modulate his/her voice to indicate his/her intention; it may betray his/her emotion as well. That is why one should note the various ways in which one's utterance can be modulated. Then only one will be able to modulate one's own speech and make it clear and effective. The teacher can draw the attention of his/her students to a recorded nursery rhyme to note the modulation of the voice. He/she may expose them to dramatized dialogues in television broadcasts to motivate their efforts to enunciate them clearly.

Skill Development Activity

Since the objective of this unit is to enable elementary school children to understand and communicate orally in English, all skill development activities will aims at it.

The teacher may start with the *self-identification programme* by students. He/she may initiate the dialogue by asking questions, such as

What is your name? (My name is ________.)
What is your father's name? (His name is_____.)
What does he do? (He is______.)
What does your mother do? (She is_____.) etc.

The questions may be passed on to all students in the class. After one student answers them, he/she will ask the same question to his/her neighbour who will respond and repeat the question to the student sitting next to him/her. The process will continue till all students have responded. Meanwhile the teacher will note whether mistakes have been committed in pronouncing the words while using them. For instance, they might have said/nem/for/neim/ 'name',/pʰarmer/for/faːməː/'farmer'/apʰiser/or/afiser/for/ɒfisəː/'officer' and/klərk/for/klaːk/'clerk'. The teacher will make them aware of the difference between/e/and/ei/,/pʰ/and/f/and/ə/and/a/. He/she will improvise a practice drill in which students will participate, first collectively and then individually. He/she can use minimal pairs such as the following:

met-mate, tell-tale, fed-fade, less-lace, etc.
pair/p?eəː/-fair, peel-feel, pun-fun, pit-fit,
lodge-large, cough-calf, cot-cart, dock-dark.

he/she will point out how /ei/, /ɒ/ and /f/ are produced and how they are different from/e/,/aː/and/pʰ/.

Practice in Sound Contrast

These are examples of what may go wrong in this exercise. If some other sounds are mispronounced, they should be pointed out by demonstrating the difference between the mispronounced sounds and the required sounds. The teacher will have a list of contrasting sounds ready with him/her which he/she will use when needed. The point is to let the students pronounce the mispronounced sounds correctly as and when they make mistakes. He/she should make them aware of the difference between what they have articulated and what ought to have been articulated. In short, the phonetic drill programme should be gone through in a natural context so that students do not find it boring. If drills are based on the actual problems students have faced in the class on previous/relevant days, they will realise their mistake and will willingly go through the exercise.

Conversation may involve *identification of the objects* in the classroom and elsewhere in the school campus. Such identifications will increase their vocabulary and provide them with the opportunity to practise their names correctly. Such activities may be complemented by playing the recorded voice in the classroom or the language laboratory, if the school has it.

Exposure to Nursery Rhymes

We have already pointed out how nursery rhymes can be used to expose students to the concept of rhythm in a natural manner. They can listen to the taped voice or to the oral presentation by the teacher. They can sing or speak aloud, first in chorus and then individually. The events described in the poem can be enacted. The dramatization will make the poem more meaningful. These acts can be followed by questions and answers based on the poem. Again, the teacher will take note of the errors committed by students and present their correct forms. Instead of criticising students for their errors or censoring them, they should give them correct options. Elementary school children love to imitate and dramatize and they will pay attention to the correct forms.

After a few sessions, when students have acquired a reasonable stock of words and structures, they may be told stories by the teacher. They may be asked to tell stories they knew already. They should be encouraged to retell them in English. Later on, they may be asked to narrate similar events or experience of their lives. It is desirable that the teacher does not stop a student to correct his/her expressions, takes note of them and speaks about them casually. At the end of every exercise (whether it involves a nursery rhyme, a story or a narrated event) the teacher should present the correct forms of what was said inaccurately. Corrections, both grammatical and of pronunciation, should be made but not at the cost of fluency. The content for the presentation by the teacher should be based on the activity students have gone through earlier. Then only it will be meaningful to them. Such a procedure is likely to lead them to self-correction which is a very effective pedagogical process.

From Listening to Speaking

Teachers know that preparation for listening paves the way for concentrated listening by children. It means that they should be provided with conditions conducive to good listening. As a psychologist reports, children have desire to listen and understand. It is for the teacher to fulfil their desire by talking about something which they find interesting. Listening to stories may interest them and so can listening to their favourite radio programme or viewing it on a television. If they are going to listen to a prerecorded programme, the teacher can prepare them mentally by giving them a few tips. He/she should not interrupt them while they are listening but he/she must intervene if they are distracted or disturbed.

An act of listening may be followed by talking about what they have heard (and seen). It should not be an act of random talking. It should involve a real interaction, a tossing of the talk back and forth. If the teacher handles the situation properly, what begins as a casual conversation may lead to a meaningful discussion. It may provide them with an opportunity to express their own creative thinking. The goal is to let students use a clear and intelligible language fluently and confidently. The teacher should not expect every child to express himself/herself the same way. Children are interested in colourful language and they should be encouraged to make their expression not only clear but also colourful. The primary objective of the oral language teaching should be to let the child have freedom of expression so that he/she talks easily and confidently.

Main Objectives

The main objective of practice in listening is to enable students to listen with understanding which can be evaluated by planning listening-cum-speaking activities in the class. The teacher may narrate a story and ask a series of questions based on it. The response of the learner will point out how much they have comprehended and how well they can express what they have comprehended. Such an exercise will help the teacher in planning future exercises keeping in view the proficiency of students and their level of difficulty.

In short, listening and speaking exercises are complementary to each other and should be treated as such in the classroom. Only then, the desire to make students fluent in English will be fulfilled. It can be ascertained if every lesson in listening is followed by exercises in speaking. Whether these exercises involve questions and answers, word games, dialogues among students or open discussion should be left to the teacher's discretion.

To sum up, listening and speaking are two aspects of the same exercise; oral articulation.

- Students should be trained to listen to and speak sounds, stress and intonation of English correctly.
- They should be attuned to intensive and extensive listening.
- They should be shown how different sounds of English are produced, how consonant clusters are simplified and the difference between some nouns and verbs are indicated by change in stress.
- They should be familiarized with the reduction of vowels in speech.
- They should be taught how to recite nursery rhymes to practise proper training in rhythm and intonation.
- Emphasis should be put on sound contrasts to be able to differentiate between related contrasting sounds.

Remember

Listen to others as you would have them listened to you.

— A common saying.

To speak and to speak well are two things.

— Ben Jonson.

UNIT III: LANGUAGE SKILLS: READING AND WRITING

8

Reading

Reading has become an absolute necessity for any kind of satisfactory life in society. There are practically no jobs that can be carried on successfully without reading. Even a peon can perform better if he/she can read addresses, notices and titles of files. A person who does not read cannot claim to be literate. Parents are deeply concerned if their child does not learn to read. There is so much knowledge available in print but it is of no use to a person who cannot read.

Meaning of Reading

To 'read' means to look at and comprehend the meaning of written or printed matter by recognizing and interpreting the characters and symbols of which it is composed. The reader must be able to recognize the symbols which represent speech. However, they cannot be interpreted unless they are deciphered i.e. unless meaning is infused into them. The reader must relate them to what he/she knows about the language in which it is written. It is difficult to imagine what a person could do with reading before he/she had enough experience with language to understand how it operates. Besides, he/she must have a repertoire of words and their meanings.

Learning to Read the Mothertongue

By the time a child is ready to learn to read in his/her mothertongue, he/she has acquired some knowledge by listening and speaking it. It is the development of language in him/her that makes him/her ready to read. He/she has the knowledge of the sound system of his/her mothertongue. He/she knows reasonable number of words and some grammar. He/she knows how to put words together to frame phrases and sentences. All he/she has to learn is the writing system of the language so that he/she can establish a relation between the sounds he/she knows and the symbols which represent them. As children know their mothertongue by the time they start learning to read, it is not a difficult task for them to pursue reading.

Reading in the Second Language

Reading in one's mothertongue involves 'reading to understand' and 'reading to learn'. The first is a process which involves perceiving the internal meaning of what is written or printed; it may be known to the reader from beforehand. The second process leads to the acquisition of knowledge. When one intends to learn to read the second language, one has the same goals; one aspires to understand and gain knowledge. However, there is a difference. The second language learner does not have the same language resource which he/she had when he/she started learning to read in the mothertongue. He/she does not have the ability to listen to or speak the second language. He/she does not have any knowledge of its grammar or vocabulary. Only if a child comes from a family where English words are freely used in everyday conversation in the mothertongue, he/she may have some limited vocabulary and if he/she has been to a nursery school or kindergarten, he/she may be familiar with some English sounds, their combinations and sentences. Likewise, if the child is growing up in an English-speaking neighbourhood, he/she may have picked up some spoken English.

Letter-Sound Correlation[1] of English Consonants

The student is first taught the letter of the alphabet of English. After that, the first task in teaching class I students how to read is to make them aware of the relation between the letters of the English alphabet (i.e. its graphemes) and its sounds (phonemes). The task is a little difficult because one letter or a group of letters of English can represent various sounds and one sound can be represented by various spellings. Sounds such as/b, d, f, j, k, l, m, n, p, r, t/are easy to comprehend because each one of them is represented by one letter of the alphabet. For example, *big, dog, fan, jar, kite, lamp, man, nose, pen, rat* and *tree* are words in which the letters stand for the sounds represented by these symbols. The letter *v* and *w* stand for the sounds/v/and/w/respectively as in *van* and *wall*. The letter *x* stands for the sounds/z/, as in Xerox, and for *ks*, as in the last sound of *Xerox* and *box* or the first sound of *X-ray*. The letter *j* is pronounced as the sound/dʒ/and the letter z (zeal) as/z/. The letter c is pronounced as/s/, as in *ice*/ais/, and as/k/as in *cat*/kæt/. The letter g is pronounced as the sound/g/as in *goat*/gaut/and/dʒ/as in *gym*/dʒim/and *general*/dʒenərəl/. The letter s is pronounced as/s/as in *miss*/mɪs/, as/z/as in *nose*/nəuz/and/ʃ/as in *sugar*/ʃugə:/.

The combination of *c* and *h*, is pronounced as/tʃ/as in *child*/tʃaild/, as /ʃ/as in *challis*/ʃælis/and as/k/as in *chaos*/keias/. The combination of *p* and *h* is pronounced as/f/, as in *phone*/fəun/and that of *t* and *h* as/θ/as in/θiŋ/*thing* or /

1. Mutual relation between the two.

ð/as in *they*/ðe/. The combination of *n* and *g* is pronounced as/ŋ/as in *sing*/sɪŋ/. The combination of *k* and *n* is pronounced as/n/as in *knee*, and so is the combination of *g* and *n* as in *gnat*/næt/. The combination of *p* and *n* is/n/as in *pneumonia*/njuməun?ə/and that of *p* and *s* is/s/, as in *psalm*/saːm/and *psychology*/saikɒlɒdʒi/. The combination of *s* and *ch* is sometimes/sk/as in *scholar*/skɒləː/ and sometimes/ʃ/as in *schedule*/ʃedʒuːl/. The combination of *w* and *r* is pronounced as/r/as in *wrong*/rɒŋ/. The combination of *w* and *h* is pronounced either as/hw/as in *when*/hwen/or as *h* as in *who*/huː/or *whole*/həul/.

Vowels

English has only five vowels among its graphemes but 12 vowel and 8 diphthong sounds. The table 8.1 gives a list of all of them.

Table 8.1: Relation between English Phonemes and Graphemes

Vowel sound (Pronunciation)	*Letters (spelling)*	*Examples*
iː	ee	tree, free
	e	be
	ea	leaf, sea
	ei	receive, deceive
ɪ	i	rich, with
	y	lily, pity
	e	pretty, wicked
	ie	ladies, cities
	a	village, private
e	e	bed, red
	ea	dead, head
	a	many
æ	a	rat, sat, hand
	ai	plait
ʌ	u	sun, fun
	o	son, one, colour
	ou	country, enough
	oo	blood, flood
	oe	does
aː	a	pass, mass, father
	au	laugh
	ear	heart [haːt]
	er	clerk [klaːk]
	al	calm [kaːm]
ɒ	o	dog, gone

Vowel sound (Pronunciation)	*Letters (spelling)*	*Examples*
	a	was, watch, want
	ou	cough, cause
	au	all, talk door, floor
ɔː	aw	saw, lawn
	ou, au	baught, cause
	a	all, talk
	oor	door, floor
ʊ	u	put, full
	o	woman, wolf
	oo	good, book
	ou	could, should
uː	u	rude, crude
	oo	food, spoon
	ou	soup, group
əː (ɜ)	ir	girl, bird, first
	er	her, heard, earth
	ur	turn, nurse
	our	journey, courtesy
ə	i	possible
	e	gentleman
	a	woman
	o	oblige
	u	suppose
	ou	famous
	er	mother
	or	doctor
eɪ	a	late, make
	ai/ay	day, may, rain, aim
	ei/ey	eight, they
	ea	great, break
ai	i/y	time, write, try, dry
	(e)igh	high, height
	ie	die, lie
	ei	either
ɔi	oi	noise, voice
	oy	boy, toy
əu	o	home, old
	oa	road, soap
	oe	foe, toe
	ou	soul

Vowel sound (Pronunciation)	*Letters (spelling)*	*Examples*
	ow	know, blow
au	ou	house, mouse
	ow	cow, town
iə	ea	idea
	eir/ier	weird, fierce
	eer	deer
	ear	dear
ɛə	are	care, mare, rare
	air	chair, air, pair
	ear	bear, wear, tear
uə	oor	poor
	ure	pure, cure, sure
	ur	curious
	ewe	sewer
	our	tour

Based on Gimson 1965: 93-/94

The table given above illustrates the correlation between the vowel sounds of English and their spellings.

Word Recognition

Though sound recognition is the starting point, it is word recognition that is at the centre of reading fluency. In fact, the recognition of sounds and sound combinations is an essential step towards words recognition. Recent research suggests that it is slower in L_2 than in L_1. If both languages have identical or the same graphic systems (e.g. both use the Roman script), then the word recognition process of L_1 affects that of L_2. As most Indian languages have orthographic systems different from the system in English, this problem does not arise. It is a question of acquiring a new system without the interference of the practice used in the mothertongue. However, some tribal languages of the North-East India use the Roman script and they may show the influence of their system while reading English.

Spelling Games

In order to facilitate word recognition process, the teacher may organise spelling games. The teacher says a word and the student spells it out. If the student fails to complete the spelling or misspells the word, another student is given a chance. The process continues till the word is correctly spelt. The winner gets a point. The teacher spells another word and so on. A record is kept of success scores and the total is declared towards the end of the class.

Chain Spelling

Another game involves chain spelling. A student begins the game by spelling a word. The next student spells another word which begins with the last letter of the previously spelt word. Any student who begins his/her word with the wrong letter, misspells the word or mispronounce it is dropped from the game. If the game is divided into two opposite teams of students, it ends when one of the teams loses all of its members.

Drills and Dictation

Other steps which can be taken to consolidate word recognition are spelling drills and dictation. The spelling drill may involve practice to spell out words the spellings of which are tricky (e.g. *ei* vs *ie* as in *receipt, deceit, belief, achieve* etc) or word with double final consonants (as *begin* but *beginning, equip* but *equipped, control* but *controller, occur* but *occurred* or words where a *k* is inserted, as in *panic* but *panicky, picnic* but *picnicking, traffic* but *trafficking*, etc.). Dictation will force the student to give concentrated attention to both the sound and pronunciation of words.

Vocabulary and Reading Development

The knowledge of vocabulary plays a key role in developing the reading speed of the learner. That is why the teacher tries to increase the vocabulary of his/her students in several ways. The beginners are shown the pictures of objects and living beings that they denotate. Reading picture books is a very enriching exercise. One can show the pictures of shoes and ask students to name other items of footwear, such as *boots, chappals, slippers, sandals* etc. If they fail to name an item, its picture can be shown; most likely they will be able to name it. Likewise, objects in the classroom can be pointed out so that students can name them. Food items can be easily named. If the student does not know the name of an item in English, the teacher can supply it. He/she can name adjectives like *good, better, best; bad, worse, worst; big, small, nice, fair, clean, dirty, hot, cold, full, empty, long, short* and make them practise sentences such as,

This room is big/small, clean/dirty, hot/cold, etc.

The same sentences can be practised by adding intensifies to the adjectives, as in

This room is very nice/bad/dirty, etc.

It may be further increased in length, as in

My bedroom is very large.

My study room is relatively/rather small.
His blue shirt is very dirty.

The act of introducing various kinds of vocabulary items will have its impact on the reading speed of the child. It is essential that he/she is able to read pronouns such as *I, we, you, he, she, it, they* and their various forms, *this, these, that, those*, various forms of the verb *to be* (*am, is, are, was, were, been, being)* and to *have,* articles *a, an,* and *the,* prepositions such as *of, in, at, on, for, with, by, from,* conjunctions such as *and, or, if, which, that,* and, *but,* modal verbs such as *can, could, would, should, shall* and *will,* and the negative words *no* and *not*. According to the British National Corpus, they are among the most frequently used words. Vivian Cook (2009) gives a list of twenty most frequently used nouns, verbs and adjectives in English which are given in Table 8.2.

Table 8.2: 20 Most frequent nouns, verbs and adjectives in English (Taken from Vivian Cook (2008:48)

Position	*Nouns*	*Verbs*	*Adjectives*
1.	time	say	new
2.	people	know	good
3.	way	get	old
4.	year	go	different
5.	government	see	local
6.	day	make	small
7.	man	think	great
8.	world	take	social
9.	work	come	important
10.	life	use	national
11.	part	give	British
12.	number	want	possible
13.	children	find	large
14.	system	mean	young
15.	case	look	able
16.	thing	begin	political
17.	end	help	public
18.	group	become	high
19.	woman	tell	available
20.	party	seem	full

Guessing the Meaning

It is not suggested that these words should be passed on to the beginners in one go. However, they may be made familiar with them in writing/print and have the ability to pronounce them because it will help them in increasing their reading speed. Nation (2008) argues that a typical language learner can comprehend a text only if he/she knows 98 per cent of the words appearing on the page. His assertion implies that the learner should be able to expand his/her stock of words as fast as he/she can. One sure way to do so is to read more even if he/she does not know all the words he/she comes across. As he/she reads, he/she develops his/her ability to guess the meaning of words he/she does not know. As one goes on reading, one becomes aware of the context in which words and sentences occur which makes the task of guessing the meaning relatively easy but it is risky. The contextual guessing may sometimes lead one to the miscomprehension of the text. Even if the guess is correct, it may not lead to its retention. There is enough research evidence to suggest that guessing word meaning from context is neither very accurate nor very effective Nevertheless, guessing word meaning while acquiring adequate comprehension is strategically significant. If the learner has multiple exposure to such words while reading new material, his/her vocabulary is enriched.

Three Approaches to Reading

1. The Basal[1] Reading Programme

American pedagogues favour the *Basal reading programme* for elementary school children, after they have gained a clear concept of reading and have a fund of words they recognize with ease. The programme rests on assumption that a set of essential and fundamental skills are generally known to the learner. The programme provides essential prerequisites to successful growth in word comprehension, interpretation and all aspects of reading. By and large, the child learns what he/she is led to learn in response to the content and structure of teaching materials. It implies the careful planning of reading materials in terms of (a) the values of sounds and letters that represent them, (b) the practice to recognise a word as a whole unit and, (c) the grasp of their meaning, both of single words and larger units such as phrases and sentences. Besides, one should develop the suitable habit to adjust to reading in the light of one's purpose for reading. The Basal programme is essentially eclectic; it is designed to develop readiness of vocabulary, word recognition and word perception and comprehension skills.

1. Forming or belonging to the bottom layer or base.

2. Phonic[2] Method

The Basal reading approach puts emphasis on reading for meaning. Its alternative is the *phonic method* which encourages learning to read with the help of phonic clues. The work starts with consonant and vowel sounds and covers all the basic sounds and spelling patterns of English. Attention is given to structural analysis such as 'read', 'reads', and 'reading'. Some people pay special attention to phonics in the first grade and ignore reading as a thought-getting process. The critics of the method say that because of heavy emphasis on phonics at the beginning, the child becomes slow in deciphering what he/she reads. Besides, he/she does not get accustomed to reading for comprehension because his/her reading is centred mainly on letters.

3. Linguistics Approach

A third approach is the *linguistics approach* which was initially championed by C.C. Fries (1963) a structural linguist. He said that learning to read something is not meant to know something but to do something. By 'something' he meant high speed recognition of letters and sequence of letters in words. He claimed that the recognition results in getting the meaning of what one reads. The approach advocates introducing the child to consonant vowel consonant combinations first, as in *cut, hat, pin, not* etc. It then leads to the blend of consonants like *spin, skin, stand* and *then* to other modified words. As it relies solely on the printed letters, its books have no illustrations.

Reading English in Indian Context

In all the countries where English is the mothertongue, a child brings to school his/her oral knowledge of English. All he/she has to do initially is to acquire the knowledge of the letters of Roman alphabet which is used to write English utterances. The first step is to learn them and then to learn how they represent sounds of English. As soon as he/she starts reading words, he/she associates them with objects he/she recognizes. In India, that is not the case. Children have to learn the letters of the alphabet and how they are combined to form words. They have to learn what the words mean in isolation and in sentences. English-speaking children have a reasonable stock of words in English at their disposal when they learn how to read; Indian children have to learn all words and their meanings afresh. They must know the meanings of words they learn to read. They must read easy and interesting reading materials so that they encounter newly acquired words again and again. That is how they can recognize them instantly and accurately. Some Indian children learn to read a word letter by letter and some syllable by syllable but eventually they learn to read word

---

2. Relating to 'phones' or 'speech sound', a method of teaching to read by correlating sounds with symbols in an alphabatic writing system.

by word. If the teacher reads the material phrase by phrase, using proper pause and intonation, children get used to them. Besides, their experience of reciting nursery rhymes in chorus or alone comes to their help. The success that a child attains in learning to read is closely related to the satisfaction he/she finds in his/her experience with reading. Some teachers put children to read the passage again and again to enable them to gain rapid recognition of words but it tires them. Some teachers report that they find children learning better when they are given new contents with the same words to read in various contexts. The teacher may use flash cards with the words written/printed on them to renew the contact of children with words they have recently come across. He/she may ask children to work with workbooks for reforcement. The child begins to recognize a word from a context or from its similarity with another word (e.g. he/she guesses the meaning of *cleanliness* on the basis of his/her knowledge of *clean*). The child arrives at the initial stage of independent reading when he/she begins to recognize the word from its context or from its similarity with other known words. Given a suitable book to read, the child may make rapid progress in independent reading. It is the duty of the teacher to give guidance and suggest suitable reading material at that stage.

Disadvantaged Children

The same set of reading material may not be suitable for all children of the same class or age group. A special set is needed for those children who come from a disadvantaged family or social background. If the teacher keeps an eye on each student in the class, he/she may find ways to help deprived children as soon as they face problems. Children with special vision and hearing problems need compensatory aids to function adequately.

Slow Readers

All children who come from a similar socio-cultural background are not equal in picking up the same speed to read. Some are fast readers and some are slow learners. Even the slow readers are not necessarily slow speakers. They mix with and listen to their peers, watch television and pick up new expressions from their surroundings. Their reading speed may be slow because of which they read letter by letter or sound by sound. They may be encouraged to read as fast as they can, if necessary, ignoring correct pronunciation. As soon as they pick up an average reading speed, they may pay attention to their pronunciation.

Reading Aloud

While children practise oral readings, they read aloud. They enjoy it. It is a great fun. In order to practise reading aloud well, they should listen to the teacher reading aloud. That way they get a good practice in listening. If the teacher reads properly, modulating his/her voice to emphasize the elements of stress and intonation, he/she inspires the learner to read like him/her. It may be concluded that good teachers inspire their students to be good speakers.

Silent Reading

Reading is closely associated with comprehension. A good listener follows what is read out to him/her. But how will the teacher know that the student has followed him/her? By asking comprehension questions in a simple, straight forward language. The best way for the teacher is to read aloud, ask students to read slowly and then answer questions put to them. If the child has been going to an English medium school in India where English is used to teach other content subjects, they are used to silent reading. Other students may not be used to this practice. The teacher needs to tell them about the significance of silent reading. When students read silently, they have to concentrate on comprehension of what they read. Thus, silent reading is an useful mental exercise.

Improving Reading Speed

Recent research works suggest two alternative ways of improving learners' reading proficiency.

(i) The language threshold hypothesis, and
(ii) The linguistic interdependence hypothesis.

The Language Threshold Hypothesis

The word 'threshold' refers to a point of entry or beginning. It also means the magnitude or intensity that must be exceeded for a certain result. The language threshold hypothesis suggests that some minimal threshold of proficiency in the second language must be attained in order to enable the reader to transfer his/her first language reading skills to reading in the second language. In other words, L_2 reading development must take place in a learning context that promotes overall L_2 language proficiency. It is essential for the learner who belongs to the lower level (i.e. primary) classes.

The Linguistic Interdependence Hypothesis

It maintains that learning to read is accomplished only once. Once the learner has matured in his/her ability to read in the first language, his/her awareness of the reading process can be automatically applied to the second language. Thus, the reading programme in the second language is supposed to share a common underlying efficiency with reading ability in the first language. (Cummins, 1974).

Research has been conducted on these lines of thought and their results have been compared. It has been found that general proficiency in second language is a better prediction of second language reading than first language reading ability. It implies that the threshold hypothesis is more reliable than the linguistic interdependence hypothesis.

The controversy is relevant if second language teaching starts later than the first language learning. Since our proposal is to start teaching both the languages from class 1, it is not so relevant in Indian context. However, it does point out the need to prepare students who want to learn to read prior to the start of reading exercises. In other words, exercises in listening and speaking must precede exercises in reading for they will enable students to have some language proficiency in general when they start reading. It may be pointed out that this is not the practice in most of the schools in India, they start with the reading lessons and come to listening and speaking later. Recent researches suggest that the priority must be changed.

Reading Strategies

A good reader varies his/her reading strategies according to why he/she is reading. The following are the main strategies:

a) *Intense Reading*— It is for detailed information. It involves reading the whole text very carefully to understand every point mentioned in the text.
b) *Extensive Reading*— It is practised with a view to getting the gist of what one reads. For instance, the rapid readers prescribed in the course are meant for practising extensive reading.
c) *Scanning*— It implies having a point in mind and looking for it in the text. It may mean looking quickly, but not very thoroughly through a text in order to identify relevant information.
d) *Skimming*— It involves reading a text quickly just to understand the main idea or important points. For instance, one usually skims through a newspaper to get the important news.

Research on reading points out that readers can be successfully trained in the use of strategies. One should develop strategies not only for word, sentence and discourse analysis but strategies to improve semantic mapping. As these skills may be taught, the teacher should give suitable instruction in this sphere on right occasions. One can think of using more than one strategy to improve one's reading comprehension.

In short, students practise reading English aloud to practise speaking their sentences properly, with correct pronunciation, stress and intonation as well as to comprehend what they read.

- For an Indian child learning to read involves establishing a correlation between the letters and sounds of English. It is a complex task because there is no one to one correlation.
- It also means to acquire the ability to read clearly with proper stress, intonation and rhythm.
- As the main aim of reading is the comprehension of the reading material; one has to practise it.
- The main hurdle in the process of comprehension is the meaning of what one reads. The learner has to have a reasonable vocabulary. The native children come equipped with it but most Indian children have to acquire it from scratch when they learn English.
- The meaning of words can be had from the knowledge of what they stand for in isolation as well as from the context in which they occur in the text. Sometimes meaning can be guessed from the text but guesses are not always reliable.
- There are several ways to practise reading: the Basal reading programme, the phonic method and the linguistic approach. A teacher may have an eclectic approach.
- Indian children start reading letter by letter or syllable by syllable. They should have word recognition to enable them to read word by word, or better, by rhythmic units.
- The teacher should pay special attention to slow readers. If they are physically handicapped, their problem should be reduced by medical care. If they are socially backward or psychologically withdrawn, special attention should be paid to bring them at par with average students.

9

Writing

Writing Skill

Of all the four language skills, writing is the most difficult to acquire. Many people who speak well and read with ease are not good writers and some people who can write well do not enjoy writing. It is because writing involves a synthesis of several separate skills which the writer has to use in an orderly sequence almost simultaneously. A writer has to make up his/her mind about what to write and arrange his/her ideas in sequence in which he/she wants to produce them. He/she has to put his/her ideas into words and words into sentences to say what he/she intends to say. Not only that. He/she has to organise his/her sentences in a well-knit paragraph and arrange paragraphs coherently in a larger unit. He/she has to decide how to start, how to develop his/her ideas and how and when to stop. These are the processes through which even a well-established writer passes. Even a child attempting to write something for the first time has to go through these processes. The child has some ideas which may be laughable to a grown-up person but he/she is eager to express them. The experience of the child may be meagre in the eyes of others but they are interesting enough to keep him/her absorbed and inspire him/her to share it with others. They will get interested only if they find it worthwhile and the child does his/her best to make it so. In other words, to write is to communicate something worthwhile in an effective manner.

Steps in the Growth of Writing Skills

Before the child decides to share his/her ideas or experience with others in writing, he/she has to learn the basic writing skills. A proper training in these skills has got to be sequential, as given below:

(i) Learning letters and how to combine them into words.
(ii) Copying familiar texts
(iii) Writing dictation
(iv) Writing controlled composition
(v) Writing original free composition.

Learning to Write

Even if the child knows to speak the language, he/she may not be able to write in it if he/she does not know how to write the letters of its alphabet. An Indian child learning English as L_2 will not be able to write in English unless he/she learns the Roman alphabet.

The first step is to learn how capital and small letters are written in English. He/she should have a workbook and practise cursive writing by trying to write the way it is written in it. While teaching the writing skills, the teacher should remember that letters *i, t,* and *ı* belongs to the straight line group and *n, u, m, w* and *s* to the curve line group. Letters *a, o,* and *e* belong to the circle group while *f, p* and *z* belong to the hanging loop group. As soon as the student has practised writing the letters separately, he/she should be encouraged to write them in combination such as *am, be, mn, wh, qu* etc. As the next step, he/she should practise how to write words and then sentences. The mechanics of writing can be learnt by practising to copy sentences as written in the workbook.

Copying Familiar Texts

Children can begin to practise writing their own names. It will give them a level of muscular control and eye-hand-mind coordination. It is a gradual exercise. When they can write their names firmly in their notebooks, they can practise it on the books and notebooks they possess. That way they will declare their possession and learn to care for it. They can practise writing memorables to remind themselves what they have to take to school the next day.

Copying is an indispensable part of writing exercise. It provides practise in relating sounds to their graphic[2] representations. It is desirable that the student comprehends the sentence(s) he/she copies. It is a task which involves several sequential steps. While copying letters, students have to be careful that they are correctly ordered within a word and words are correctly ordered within a sentence. Apart from the word-order, the student has to pay attention to the spelling of everything he/she copies. Every sentence has to begin with a capital letter, should be well balanced and there should be proper spacing between words. The letters should be placed properly so that the handwriting is legible[3]. It must have a neat look.

Spelling

In the previous chapter we have briefly talked about the spelling. The teacher

1. Matters worth remembering
2. Relating to visual representation of sound, lettering.
3. Clear enough to read.

should choose only those words for the exercise in spelling writing which the student is familiar with. However, care should be taken to include the words which the student will need in writing exercises elsewhere. He/she could explain specific spelling patterns that permit generalization. For instance, the end consonants of certain verbs are doubled when they are in past tense, as in *drop-dropped, occur-occurred, equip-equipped.* They are doubled in words such as *red-redder-reddest.*

- It follows a simple rule. When words of one syllable and those of more than one accented on the last syllable ending in a single consonant are preceded by a single vowel, double the consonant before a suffix[1] beginning with a vowel is added to it. For instance,
  - begin, beginning, beginner
  - control, controlled, controller
  - drop, dropped, dropping
  - occur, occurred, occurring, occurrence
  - plan, planned, planning
  - refer, referred, referring
  - run, running, runner
  - swim, swimming, swimmer
- However, words ending in a consonant preceded by the vowel do not double their final consonant, as in
  - need, needed, needy
  - train, trained, trainer, training, trainee
- Likewise, words ending in two consonants do not double the final consonants, as in
  - bend, bending
  - turn, turned, turning
- Words not accented in the final syllable do not ordinarily double the final consonant, as in
  - happen, happened, happening
  - profit - profited, profitable
- Words ending in *y* preceded by a consonant usually change *y* to *i* before any suffix is added to it. Examples:
  - city- cities, sky-skies, fly-flies
  - beauty-beautiful, busy- business
  - easy-easier, easily
  - lucky-luckily
  - marry-married, marriage
  - merry-merrier, merrily

---

1. Morphemes added to the end of a word to form its derivatives.

- ➢ try- tried, (but trying)

words ending in y preceeded by a vowel do not change y to i before any suffix is added to it, such as

- ➢ baby, babyhood
- ➢ lady, ladylike
- ➢ shy, shyly, shyness

However, we have pay, paid; day, daily; lay, laid, etc.
Another generalisation can be made about final *e*.

- The final *e* is usually dropped before a suffix beginning with a vowel but it is retained before a suffix beginning with a consonant:

care- caring,	but bare- barely
come- coming	care- careful, careless
dance- dancing	hate- hateful
like- likable	safe- safely
love- lovable	excite- excitement

However, in some cases silent *e* is retained even if a suffix beginning with a vowel is attached to it, as in

here- herein	mile- mileage
there- therein	shoe – shoeing

People are often confused about words containing *ei* or *ie*. The generalisation given below is helpful:

- when the sound is/iː/, put *i* before *e* except after *c*, as in achieve, belief, brief
- when the sound is not/iː/, put *e* before *i*, as in eight, leisure, height

However, there are several exceptions to it.
Another helpful tip could be added about the *inserted k*. The letter *k* is generally added to a word ending in *c* before a suffix beginning with *e, i*, or *y* is added to it.

Picnic- picnicking
politic- politicking
traffic- trafficked

The spelling of English words is difficult because of many reasons. The main reason is that the sounds in English have changed in pronunciation in course of time but the writing system has remained unchanged. Not only that numerous words are not spelt as they sound, but many that sound alike are spelt differently. We have identical pronunciation for *no* and *know*, and for *cite, sight* and *site. Kernel* and *colonel* have the same sounds but are spelt differently. Hearing to spell may be treated as fun if we play word games. Besides, if one has discipline and concentration, one can acquire proficiency in spelling. Games like scrambles and anagrams (rearranging the sounds of a word to get another word) help one in improving one's spelling.

Punctuation Marks

The student should be told about punctuation marks. Every sentence ends with a period unless it is a question or an exclamation. If it is a question, it ends with a question mark '?'. If it is an exclamation or exclamatory sentence, it ends with a note of exclamation '!'.

1. 'What are you doing?'
2. 'I am writing a story.'
3. 'Oh! What a nice idea!'

The first sentence is a question. The second is the answer to that question, a statement of fact. The third sentence expresses surprise. Each type of sentence has its unique punctuation mark. They are like traffic signals. They signal writers to stop for a while and then move. A comma ',' indicates a very short break and semicolon ';' makes one stop for a little longer period than a comma does, however, it does not permit one to stop as long as a period (full stop) does. There are other signals but an elementary school child may not use them. However, if the child is telling a story, he should know what inverted commas "..." mean. When a character speaks directly in a story, one puts whatever he/she says within a quotation.

He said "I am not going to school today."

There are rules involving the use of a capital letter. The first letter of the first word in a sentence is written in the capital letter. The first word of proper names is also written in the capital letter. There are other occasions when a capital letter is used but they need not be mentioned to a child who has just started to write.

Dictation

In the beginning, a dictation exercise should be short. It may contain words, phrases or short sentences. As a student progresses, the teacher may dictate longer sentences. The sentences should be spoken or read at a normal speed. As a dictation is not a speed test, the teacher should allow enough time for the student to write the dictated material. If the student misses something to write, that portion should be reread at a normal speed. At the end of the exercise the teacher should check the paper and point out all errors of spelling, punctuation and capitalization. After this type of exercise is repeated several times, the student will get used to the mechanism of writing a paragraph; he/she will now be ready to write a piece of composition.

Controlled Composition

After getting used to dictation, students may be asked to write controlled composition. Initially they may respond to simple questions based on a story or an event the teacher has just narrated. After they have answered several questions covering the whole narration, they may be asked to write down all the answers in a paragraph. The success of this exercise will depend on the prior preparation on the part of the teacher. The questions he/she asks must be relevant and systematic. They may be simple so that students understand them and answer them without any difficulty. If students practise writing several pieces of the type, they will have some idea of what a paragraph is about.

Paragraph Writing

Another type of practice in paragraph writing is to give them the outlines of a paragraph. The students will have a clear idea of what the paragraph should contain. He/she will pick up the points one by one given in the order in which they are and write them in his/her own sentences. For example, students may be asked to write a paragraph on *A day* when *everything went wrong* on the basis of the following outlines:

> Got late, missed the schools bus, was late for the class...could not get the pen to take down notes-got out at the first ball in the game of cricket...got home late...found the house locked...

The topic[1] sentence indicates that the paragraph is about a day when everything went wrong in the life of the writer. The sentences that follow it specify what went wrong and how. Each student will read his/her paragraph aloud. The teacher will ignore their grammatical errors and concentrate on the structure of the paragraph. He/she will point out how the opening sentence starts the topic of the paragraph clearly; it signals what the paragraph is going to be about. Other sentences simply illustrate that point. The teacher will point out how the central point of the paragraph has been developed with the help of facts. He/she should keep the answers of students in view. If any student has digressed from the central point, he/she will point it out and ask him/her to delete it. He/she will try to convince the respondent that the sentence is irrelevant in the context. That is how students will avoid having pitfall in their writing. The objective of the teacher should be to create confidence in

1. Subject matter dealt with in a text.

Fig. 9.1: Picture of Two Dolls

his/her students so that they become gradually independent. Only when they have self-confidence, they will be in a position to write free composition.

Another way of encouraging students to write controlled composition is to show them a picture or a series of pictures. The students may be asked to look at it/them carefully and describe what they have seen. For instance, the picture in Figure 9.1 shows two dolls in a shop hanging up for sale. Students can describe what they look like, what type of customer is likely to buy them and for what purpose. The student may imagine buying them for himself/herself. What will he/she do with the dolls? Where will he/she keep them? Such questions will stimulate him/her to give vent to his/her imagination.

In Figure 9.2 (Page 84) we have a series of seven pictures which illustrate the story of 'The Stork and the Crab'. Children may be asked to look at them carefully and link up the scenes depicted in them; they will form a story.

Free Composition

As soon as the teacher is convinced that his/her students have gained self-confidence, he/she should encourage them to write whatever they feel on a given topic. However, they must be warned that they should not digress from the topic sentence. Though students will have freedom to write their composition without any outlines now, they will be restricted by the topic.

Initially students will be asked to write about themselves, their family members or school. They may be asked to talk about games, books, places, festivals or objects they like. A favourable topic will encourage them to express themselves well. However, the teacher should assign only such topics that they can handle grammatically. In other words, they are not expected to use structures that they are not familiar with. They should be sufficiently equipped with the vocabulary and basic structures that they are expected to use while writing. They should get all the help they need to handle a topic.

Creative Writing

Children love to listen to nursery rhymes and stories. At least some of them want to tell stories. A child learning English as a second language may be

Fig. 9.2: Some Connected Pictures Involving a Story

encouraged to tell a story in English which he/she has heard in his/her mothertongue. The teacher may encourage them to tell a story orally and then write it down. If a child needs some words to express himself/herself, the teacher should help him/her promptly. He/she may be encouraged to write imaginary stories as well.

Main Objectives: The main objectives of the teacher should be

- To develop the concepts of sentences and paragraphs in students,
- To teach them to use punctuation and capitalization properly and to develop a style of their own,
- To create interest in students to write what they feel like writing,
- To encourage them to express themselves.

All children imagine and think. If they gain confidence to write what they imagine and think, they will be moving in the right direction. They may not know rules of grammar adequately but they can learn it gradually. The teacher should not let their imagination be constrained simply because they cannot express correctly.

Strategy for Writing Free Composition

Apart from the level of acquisition of grammar and vocabulary, the difference between L_1 and L_2 writing is largely a matter of degree.

A basic concern is free composition is the logical construction of form. The skill to write a paragraph around a topic sentence is a basic requirement. Once this skill is developed, one should think of developing a text (an essay for example). It should have an introductory paragraph pointing out the subject of the text. The next point is to develop the topic in several ways, each forming a separate paragraph. Once it is done, the writer could write the concluding paragraph.

The teacher's concern should be to make students aware of the structure of a piece of composition, to show how the components of introduction, development of the main idea and conclusion are connected and how they all lead to the conclusion. In short, the piece of writing should be a cohesive whole. The style of the writer will depend on whether the topic is descriptive, narrative, discursive or exploratory. At the primary school level, it should be mainly descriptive or narrative but if a student wants to explore a new ground, he/she should be encouraged. Instead of having a conventional structural approach, the teacher should adopt a vibrant approach involving fresh ideas and outlook.

10

Teaching Grammar

In *Grammar* we learn and teach the followings:

i. Part of speech: Nouns, Adjectives, Pronouns, Verbs, Adverbs
ii. Kinds of sentences and their formation.
iii. Constituents of a sentence, Noun Phrase, Verb Phrase, Prepositional Phrase.
iv. NP: Determiner, Adjective, Head Noun
    VP: Verbs, Object, Complement, Adjunct, Tense, Mood, Verb types, Auxiliary, Model Verbs
    PP: Types and Usage
v. Agreement: Subject—Verb, Pronoun-Antecedent, Tense Agreement
vi. Narration
vii. Word order

Opinions differ in regard to the teaching of grammar in elementary classes. Experts such as Krashen and Terrell (1983) hold the view that children learn the grammar of a language subconsciously when they are exposed to the text, while linguists such as Norris and Ortega (2000) believe that it must be taught explicitly. Followers of Chomsky believe that the task of the teacher is to help students in developing their grammatical sensitivity. He/she should encourage students to process sentences consciously. They may start with simple sentences and gradually be able to handle compound and complex sentences. However, it is not so easy in practice. Sentences may be easily discussed out of context and isolated grammatical patterns may be rigorously practised. Students may do it mechanically but it does not guarantee that they will be able to handle them aptly in communicative interaction. As the goal is to enable students to express themselves fluently and confidently, a suitable method of exposing them to the grammar of English in a context must be found out.

However, there are problems. At a very initial stage students may come across a sentence which demands the knowledge of many rules of grammar.

For instance, in an introductory class on spoken English, a student may be asked:

1. What is *your* name?

To which he/she may say.

2. *My* name is Aparna.

Sentences (1) and (2) have possessive pronouns. *your* and *my* respectively. If the student has to answer:

3. What is *his/her* name?

He/she may say:

4. *His* name is Rakesh, or
5. *Her* name is Rita.

These sentences presuppose the knowledge of possessives such as *my, our, your, his, her* and *its*. In order to understand them, students need to have the concepts of singular and plural number and of masculine, feminine and neuter gender. Besides, they need to know how indicative and interrogative sentences are formed. Should the teacher use such sentences after discussing these concepts? If so, should he/she discuss them in English or use the mother-tongue of students? The teacher is not supposed to use a language other than English if he/she is supposed to follow the direct method of teaching English. These are difficult questions to answer. Without pondering over them, the teacher should begin the spoken English class, as suggested earlier.

Similar problems arise while dealing with the recommended text books which he/she is supposed to follow. Here again, the teacher need not wait till the grammar of all structures that the first lesson contains is discussed. It is true that the learner of English as L_1 does not face such difficulties. He/she knows quite a bit of his/her mothertongue, but the learner of English as L_2 does not have that advantage. Even then, he/she can be safely exposed to conversational English without being exposed to the subtlety of its grammar. Students may be exposed to them in course of time. Of course, the teacher need not postpone a grammatical query made by a curious student. His/her curiosity must be satisfied immediately; otherwise he/she will become indifferent to what the teacher says.

These are pedagogical questions which arise in the mind of every language teacher. From a practical point of view, we keep them aside and move to the aspects of English grammar every teacher is supposed to be familiar with.

SENTENCES

Types of Sentences

When we speak in a language, we use sentences to communicate with our listeners. We make statements to exchange information or to convey our view. Most of our sentences express simple statements of facts. They are called *indicative* or declarative sentences. However, all our sentences are not of this type. Sometimes we ask questions to get some information from our listener. Sometimes we express surprise when we hear his/her answer. Sometimes we ask him/her to do something and sometimes we invite him/her to do it together with us. We use *interrogative* sentences to ask questions and *imperative* sentences to ask the listener to do a job. We use *optative* sentences to express our desire or wish to get something done and *exclamatory* sentences to convey our remarks expressing surprise, strong emotion or pain. Every sentence we use is of one of these types:

1. Indicative/Declarative
2. Interrogative
3. Imperative
4. Optative
5. Exclamatory

Basic/Simple Sentences

Components of Indicative Sentences

Even elementary students know what a sentence is. It is a group of words that expresses a complete thought. The minimum requirement is that it should have a *subject* and a *predicate*. Both of them may have one word each, as in

6. *Amit* came.
7. He *cried.*
8. She *laughed.*
9. They *quarrelled.*

Subject

Sentence (6-9) have a one-word subject and predicate. The subject of the sentence is that part about which something is said. The predicate is that part which says something about the subject. (6) answers the question:

10. *Who* came?

(7) answers the question:

11. What did he do?

The subject may consist of more than one word, as in (12-14)

12. *The boy* came.
13. *The young boy* came.
14. *A very young boy* came.

If the subject is neither the name of an individual nor a pronoun, it may have an article before it. *The* is used as a definite article; *a* and *an* are used as indefinite articles.

A subject is a *Noun Phrase* which may be a group of words, as in (13), *the young boy* or a single noun [as in (6)] or pronoun [as in (7)]. The head of a noun phrase is a noun. For example, *the young boy* is a noun phrase the head of which is *boy*. In (6) and (7) the head of noun phrase is *Amit* and *he* respectively. (We may note the phrase is like a family which has a head. Even a one man family has a head.)

Predicate

Just as a subject is called a Noun Phrase, a predicate is called a *Verb Phrase*. A verb phrase may be a verb or a group of verbs. In (6-12) the verb phrase has only one verb, in (15-17) there are more than one verb.

15. She is *crying*.
16. She *has been crying*.
17. She *may have been crying*.

In (15) *is* helps the verb *crying*; it is a *helping verb*. In (16) *has been* and (17) *may have been* are helping verbs. Helping verbs are called *auxiliary verbs*.

The head of the noun phrase tells us whether it is singular or plural, masculine, feminine or neuter. It also tells us whether it is in the first, second or third person. In (6), (12-14) the head of the noun phrase is in the third person, it is masculine and singular. In (8) it is third person, feminine and singular. In (9) it is third person plural. We do not know whether it is masculine or feminine. It is because *they* is the plural form of both *he* and *she*.

It is easy to find the subject of a sentence. In English it is usually in the beginning of the sentence, as in (6-14). But it is not a reliable criterion. In (15), the first phrase is not the subject.

18. *Right now* he is crying.

However if we ask, (19) *who is crying*?
Its answers will point out the subject, i.e. *he*.

In a sentence with a subject and a simple predicate, the question with *who* or *what* tells what the subject is.

19. The glass broke.

(19) is the answer to the question. (20) *What broke*?

Intransitive Verbs

If the predicate (i.e. the verb phrase) does not need anything to complete the sense of a sentence, it is headed by an *intransitive* verb. *Be, become, walk, run, jump, fly* are intransitive verbs. So are *fall, lie, rest, sleep, die*. However, we can add additional information by adding an Adverb Phrase, e.g.

20. She ran *fast.*
21. He was walking *slow.*
22. They cried *aloud.*
23. They danced *in the class.*
24. They sang *in a group.*
25. They sang *in a group in the class in the morning.*

Fast, slow, aloud are adverbs which modify the verb. An adverb tells us *how* something was done (or happened). It tells us *where* it happened, as in (23) and how it happened as in (24). All these can be added to a verb. (25) tells us how they sang, when and where. Just as adverbs are attached to a verb to expand it, an adjective is added to a noun to tell us more about the noun, as in (13) and (14). Thus, the teacher can tell students how to expand a sentence with an intransitive verb and a bare subject.

Transitive Verbs

There are verbs which cannot complete the sentence without a noun phrase *complement.* They are called *transitive* verbs. For instance,

26. I *know you.*
27. She *got the book.*
28. He *made a cake.*
29. *They found him.*
30. She *helped me.*

Such complements are *object* complements.

Some verbs need two object complements, as in the following:

31a. He gave *me* a book, 31b. He gave a book *to me.*
32a. She told *him* a story, 32b. She told a story to him.

When a sentence has two object complements, one which is directly affected by the verb is called the *direct object*; the other Noun Phrase is the indirect object. In (31) *a book* is the direct object and *to me* is the indirect object. In (32) *a story* is the direct objet and *him* is the indirect object. Even transitive verbs can have additional information, as in (33).

33. He gave a book to me *in the class last evening.*

Here *in the class* is the adverb of place and *last evening* is the adverb of time.

Linking Verbs

Some verbs are *linking verbs*; they link the subject Noun Phrase to the other part of the sentence, as in (34-37).

34. He *is a doctor.*
35. The room *is quiet.*
36. She *is out of the room.*
37. Her husband *is in Chennai.*

In (34), *a doctor* is a Noun Phrase, in (35) *quiet* is an adjective, in (36) *out of the room* is a prepositional phrase and in (37) *in Chennai* is a prepositional phrase.

In all these sentences the linking verb *is* connects the subject Noun Phrase to the complement which is not an object. Even a sentence with an object NP can have such complements, as in (38).

38. He put the book *on the table.*

Here *on the table* is an essential part of the sentence just as the italic expressions are essential to complete the sentences in (34-37).

To summarise, we have discussed the following types of sentences.

- with intransitive verbs: subject NP + Verb
- with transitive verbs: subject NP + Verb + Object NP
- with linking verbs: subject NP + Link Verb + Complement

All these sentences can have an optional element, i.e. an adverbial phrase. Adverbial phrases are adjuncts; they are not essential for the completion of the sentence.

Such sentences are called *declarative* sentences.

Formation of Various Kinds of Sentences

We have already discussed what:

- declarative,
- imperative,
- optative,
- interrogative, and
- exclamatory sentences are. Some declarative sentences are
- existential. Besides, we have
- compound and complex sentences. To recapitulate,

A declarative sentence markes a statement: It declares whether something is or is not the case.

All sentences, when spoken, assume that there is a speaker and a listener; when written, it assumes that, beside the writer, there are readers. In declarative sentences both parties are presupposed. A sentence in which the listener is directly addressed and is given a command or made a request is called *imperative*, as in (38) and (39):

38. Please sit down.
39. Get out.

Both these sentences have only predicates which are explicitly mentioned. The subject, *you*, is understood. In other words, (38) means (38′) and (39) means (39′)

38′. You sit down, please.
39′. You get out.

A sentence that expresses wish or desire and may be addressed to anyone including the speaker and listener, is called *optative*. In (40) the speaker includes himself; (41) is addressed to a third party.

40. Let us go there.
41. Let him do it.

A sentence which asks a question is an *interrogative* sentence, as in (42) (43) and (44):

42. Is he coming?
43. Does he come here every day?
44. Why does he come here?

Questions (42-43) can be answered in '*yes*' or '*no*'. All such questions have an underlying statement; they seek its assertion or denial. The other type of question seeks new information. The type of information it asks for is indicated by a question word. For instance, *who* suggests that the question is about a person, *what*, that it is about a thing. *when* asks for time, *where* for place and *how* for the manner in which something was done (or happened). *Which* is used when the answer is to be selected out of more than one (explicit or implicit) option.

A sentence which expresses surprise, pain or strong emotion is called an *exclamatory sentence*, as in (44-46):

44. How nice it is!
45. What a wonderful house it is!
46. How painful it is!

Some declarative sentences do not have the subject in the initial position. Instead, they have *there*. The subject comes later, as in (47).

47. There was *a lion* in a forest.

In (47) the *lion* is the subject of the sentence but it is not in the subject position. Such sentences are called *existential* sentences. The existential *there* has no meaning. similarly, the existential *it* has no meaning, as in (48):

48. *It* rained last night.

(47) means (47′) and (48) means (48′)

47′. A lion was in the forest.
48′. The rain fell last night.

We may point out of that all the sentences that we come across are not simple sentences. Some of them are compound and some, complex sentences.

Compound Sentences: A compound sentence is a combination of two or more clauses, as in (49).

49. He came in and she went out.

CLAUSES

A clause is like a sentence. It is a group of words containing a subject and a predicate. The only difference is that it is a part of a larger sentence.

When a clause expresses a completed thought and is capable of being independent, it is a *main clause.* In (21) both clauses: *he came in* and *she went out* are independent. If they are separated, they are full sentences. In such a construction, the first clause is the main clause and the second clause is the *co-ordinate clause.* The conjunction *and* is used to combine them. They can be combined by *and, either...or, neither...nor, but, or, either, or, neither nor*. For instance

50. He came in *but* she went out.
51. He came in *or* she went out.
52. *Either* he came in or she went out.
53. *Neither* he came in *nor* she went out.

Complex Sentences: When a clause does not express a complete thought, it is not an independent clause. In that case, it is attached to the main clause. Such a clause is a *subordinate* clause, as in (54).

54. This is the cat *which caught the rat.*

The clause *which caught the rat* has a subject (*which*) and a predicate (*caught the rat*) but it is not independent. Because the interpretation of *which* depends on *the cat*, it is a *subordinate clause*. It is called a *dependent clause* as well.

There are three types of subordinate clauses.

(i) An *adjective clause* modifies a noun or pronoun. It is like an adjective. In (54), it modifies *the cat*; it tells us what kind of cat we are talking about.

The clause that begins with a relative pronoun such as *who*, *which* or *that* is called a *relative clause*, as in (55-58).

55. The man *who* came to see you is my friend.
56. The book *which* I needed was not available.
57. The medicine *that* he needed was costly.
58. The man *about whom you rang me up* came to see me this morning.

(ii) A *noun clause* is a subordinate clause that is used as a noun phrase, as in (59-61).

59. *What he told you* is false.
60. This is *what I need most.*
61. I remember *what you told me.*

In (59) *what I told you* is the subject of the sentence, in (60) *what I need most* is a nominal complement and in (61) *what you told me* is the object. These are the positions which are occupied by NPs.

(iii) The subordinate clause that is used like an adverb is an *adverb clause*. (62-65) provide examples of *adverb clauses*:

62. He ran away *when it started raining.*
63. He ran *because he wanted to run.*
64. He ran away *as if he was scared.*
65. He ran *as fast as he could.*

In (62) the subordinate clause indicates an adverb of time, in (63) of reason, in (64) in what condition and in (65) in what manner.

An adverbial clause starts with a subordinate conjunction such as *when*, *because*, *as if*, *as*, *if*, *since*, *unless*, *until*, *where*, *while*, etc.

- When two or more clauses of equal status are combined, we get a *compound* sentence.
- When a sentence has a main clause and one or more subordinate clauses, we get a *complex* sentence.
- When a complex sentence is combined with a compound sentence, we get a *mixed* sentence.

A mixed sentence has both coordinate and subordinate clauses attached to the main clause.

Agreement Rules

Subject and Verb Agreement Rules

An English verb agrees with its subject in number. When the head of the subject noun phrase is singular, the verb is singular, as in (66); when it is plural, the verb is plural, as in (67).

66. A small *child is* running in the lawn.
67. Several small *children are* running in the lawn.

In (66) *child*, the head of the subject noun phrase, is singular; therefore, the verb is singular. In (67) *children* is plural; it is followed by a plural verb.

The agreement is with the head of the noun phrase and not necessarily with the last noun in the subject noun phrase, as in (68).

68. *The performance* of the children *was* very funny.

Here the head of the NP is *Performance,* and not *children.*

When the subject NP comes after the verb, as in a *there* construction, the verb agrees with it, and not *there.*

69. There *is* a *frog* in the room.
70. There *were* three frogs in the room.

Most compound subjects are joined by *and* take a plural verb, as in (71-72).

71. John and Judy *are* married.
72. The truck and the bus were in the ditch.

However, some compound nouns are treated as one unit and take a singular verb, as in (73).

73. *The sum and substance* of his speech is not clear.

Singular subjects take a singular verb when they are joined by *or*, *neither... or*, *neither... nor*, as in (74-76).

74. Neither Ramesh nor Amar *is* coming.
75. Either he or his friend *is* guilty.
76. Either a cow or a buffalo *has* been sold.

When two subjects are joined by *or* or *nor* and one of them is singular and the other plural, the verb agrees with the nearest subject, as in (77-78).

77. Either the students or the teacher is wrong.
78. Neither the Principal nor the teachers *are* absent.

Some nouns have no plural and do not need plural verbs e.g. news, maths, gyms.

- *Proper nouns*, are names of single entities and are singular. They are names of people, places and events, such as Radha, Shamim, the Taj Mahal, Agra, the Second World War.

- *Nouns which are not countable are singular*, such as age, anger, beauty, education, fun, freedom, peace, poverty, pride, sickness, sleep, trust, truth

- furniture, baggage, information, evidence, homework, knowledge, luggage, machinery, money
- rice, milk, sugar, water, coffee, tea, juice, soup.

They are mostly *abstract* and *mass* nouns and are singular.

Some of them indicate amount (involving money, measurement, weight, volume, etc.)

- Common nouns are singular and need singular verbs. They can be made plural by adding –s or –es (pronounced as |s|, |z|, or |iz|, as in *books*, *bags* and *dishes*, respectively.) They are countable nouns.
- However, some countable nouns have the same form both in singular and plural, such as *sheep*, *deer*, *fish*, *aircraft*, *fruit*, *series*, *species*, etc.
- Some nouns ending in –s are uncountable and singular, such as *physics*, *mathematics*, *classics*, *electronics*, *politics*, *mechanics*, *statistics*.
- A collective noun is the name of a group and is counted as singular, as in (79). However, when we think of individuals in the group, we need a plural verb, as in (80).

79. The *crowd* was quiet.
80. The *crowd* were fighting among themselves.

When a noun is preceded by *every* or *many* a, it takes a singular verb, as in (81-82).

81. Every student and teacher was asked to attend the parade.
82. Many a student wants more holidays.

Agreement Rules involving a Pronoun and its Antecedent

A pronoun agrees with its antecedent in number and genders, as in (83-86):

83. Anand did *his* best.
84. Gita gave me *her* books.
85. The city is proud of *its* metro service.
86. They demanded *their* share.

If a noun phrase has *each*, *everyone*, *everybody*, *nobody*, *anyone*, *someone*, *somebody* or *anybody* as its head, it takes a singular pronoun even if it is followed by a plural word in its extended form, as in (87-89):

87. Each of the boys gets his/her share.

88. Everybody in this room has his/her interest in this task.
89. If anybody calls up, tell him/her that I am not available.

(We may note that each of these subsequent words may be referred to as *him* or *her*. Some people use *them* in such a context)

The number of relative pronouns – *who, which, that* – is determined by its antecedents, as in (90-92).

90. This is the book *that* I bought yesterday.
91. The books *which* I bought yesterday are there on the table.
92. The men *who* are working there are temporary employees.

Agreement Rules involving Nouns and their Modifiers

When the modifier of a noun is a qualitative adjective, it remains unchanged irrespective of the noun being singular or plural, as in

a brave boy, brave boys, a nice plant, nice plants

Quantitative adjectives which indicate number can be used only with count nouns, such as *five boys, many girls, several schools, many/few books.*

Quantitative adjectives which indicate amount can be used only with mass nouns, such as *much water*, a *little milk, very little sugar*.

The quantitative *some* can be used with both countable and uncountable nouns, such as *some* books, *some* milk.

PRONOUNS

Case Forms of Pronouns

English has the following pronouns:

I, we, you, her, she, it, they, who, what, and *which* of these, *what* and *which* remain unchanged in all cases. The rest change their forms depending on whether they are nominative, objective or possessive case. The following is the list of all forms of personal pronouns:

Singular

	Nominative Case	*Objective Case*	*Ge-nitive Case*
1st person	I,	me,	my, mine
2nd person	you	you	your, yours
3rd person	he	him	his
	she	her	her, hers
	it	it	Its

Plural

1st person	we	us	our, ours
2nd person	you	you	your, yours
3rd person	they	them	their, theirs

The subject of a verb is in the nominative case.

93. I/we/you/they go home on time
94. He/she goes home late.

The nominative that follows the verb is also in the nominative case, as in (95-96).

95. Are you sure it was *she*?
96. It might have been *he*.

The object of a verb is in the objective case, as in (97-98).

97. I saw her on the road.
98. She greeted me.

The object of a preposition is in the objective case, as in (99-100)

99. This letter is from him.
100. It is addressed to you/them.

When a possessive precedes a noun, it is in the form of *my*, *our*, *your*, *his*, *her*, or its, as in *my* book, *our* house, *your/her/her bag*, *its* contents.

When the possessive is used predicatively, it is in the form of *mine*, *ours*, *yours*, *theirs*, as in (101). *His*, *its* remain unchanged as in (102).

101. This book is mine/yours/ours/theirs/hers.
102. That book is his.

Who is a relative and interrogative pronoun in the nominative form. It becomes *whom* in the objective case and *whose* in the possessive case, as in (103-105) respectively.

103a. *Who* has come?
b. The man *who* has come is late.
104a. *Whom* did he call?
b. The man to *whom* he gave the book is here.
105a. *Whose* book is this?
b. The girl *whose* book has been stolen has complained to the teacher.

It is to be noted that now a days *who* is used in place of *whom*, as in (106).

106. *Who* did you call?

Reflexive Pronouns

A singular reflexive pronoun is formed by adding *self* to the possessive form of the pronoun, as in *myself* and *yourself.*

In most cases, a plural reflexive form is created by adding *selves* to the possessive forms, as in *ourselves* and *yourselves*.

The reflexive of a third person pronoun is formed by adding *self* to its objective form in singular and *selves* in plural; as in *himself, herself, itself, themselves*.

If a personal pronoun in the subject position occurs again in the object position in the same sentence, its reflexive form is used, as in (107).

107. I hurt *myself* and she hurt *herself.*

Here *myself* refers to 'I' and *herself* refers to 'she'.

When the subject of a clause and the object of a preposition refer to the same person or object, we use the reflexive after the preposition, as in (108).

108. I am ashamed of *myself.*

However, if the clause has a direct object, a personal pronoun is used, as in (109).

109. He slammed the door behind *him.*

A reflexive pronoun is used for emphasis, as in (110-111).

110. Chandrika *herself* said so.
111. He is not a punctual person, *himself.*

Demonstrative Pronouns

This, *that*, *these*, those are demonstrative pronouns which are used to refer to entities, as in (112-113).

112. *This* is a book.
113. *That* is the blackboard.

This refers to something that is closer to the speaker, *that* refers to something that is more remote in place. Thcy are deictic[1] pronouns.

These and *there* are used with reference to countable plurals as in *these* books, those tables, etc.

This, *that*, *these* and *those* can be used in place of the definite article *the*. In *that* sense, they are determiners.

Determiners

The is a definite determiner which is used before a definite noun, as in (114-115).

114. *The* man you told me about has come here.
115. *The* man sitting in the car is a doctor.

---

1. whose meaning is determined by its closeness to or distance from the speaker.

When a noun refers to one thing or person that is not definite, *a* or *an* is used.

A is used in an indefinite noun phrase when the head noun begins with a consonant sound; *an*, when it begins with a vowel sound, as in a horse, *an* ox, *a* European, *an* honest man, *an* hour. Though the word *European* begins with a vowel in spelling, it is pronounced as Ju, a consonant and so it takes *a*, and not *an*.

When a noun is preceded by an adjective the choice of *a* or *an* depends on the pronunciation of the first sound of the adjective. Though *honest* begins with a consonant, its sound begins with a vowel and so it takes *an*.

Besides *a* and *an*, *another*, *some* and *any* are also used as indefinite determiners. They are used with countable nouns. *Some* is used for quantity of something e.g. *some chocolate* or a number of things or people. some books/men Like, *some*, *any* is used with both quantity and number as in *any* liquid/book.

The determiner is first word in a noun phrase. However, some words may occur before determiners. They are called pre-determiners, as in *all* the boys, *all* is a pre-determiner.

In *both the friends*, *both* is a pre-determiner. So are *double* and *quite* respectively in *double the amount* and *quite a surprise*.

Now we have a complete picture of a possible noun phrase:

Pre-determiner	*Determiner*	*Adjectives*	*Head noun*	*Relative Clause*
both	the his John's	young	children	[who, where in school]

ADJECTIVE

Comparison of Adjectives

Some adjectives are used as qualifiers and may be used for comparison. When an adjective denotes the simple quality and no comparison is made, it is in the positive degree. When the entities are compared and are found similar in quality, the adjective is in the positive degree; as it is (116).

116. This chair is *as* comfortable *as* that one.

When two entities are compared and one is found better than the other, we use the adjective in the comparative degree, as in (117-118).

117. This boy is *smarter* than that one.
118. This flower is *more beautiful* than that flower.

When more than two persons or things are compared to point out which of them has the highest degree of quality, we use the superlative degree, as in (119).

119. This tree is the *tallest* in the park.

Most adjectives which are of one or two syllables form the comparative degree by adding – *(e) r* to their positive forms, and to their superlative forms by adding – *e(st)*

Positive	*Comparative*	*Superlative*
tall	taller	tallest

If an adjective has more than two syllables, we add *more* or *most* to indicate comparative and superlative degrees, respectively.

Positive	*Comparative*	*Superlative*
beautiful	more beautiful	most beautiful
obstinate	more obstinate	most obstinate

It we want to suggest degrees of inferiority, we use *less* for the comparative and *least* for the superlative degree.

Positive	*Comparative*	*Superlative*
peaceful	less peaceful	least peaceful

Certain adjectives have only one quality and cannot be compared, e.g. round, triangular, rectangular, unique, dead, etc.

A few adjectives have irregular forms in comparative and superlative degrees:

Positive	*Comparative*	*Superlative*
good	better	best
bad	worse	worst
little	less	least
much	more	most
old	elder	eldest
	older	oldest
late	latter	last
	later	latest

We must remember that in a noun phrase

(i) a pre-determiner precedes a determiner;
(ii) possessive adjectives (like *his*) and genitives (like *John's*) are used as alternatives to determiners. If we use a possessive or a genitive, we cannot use a determiner;
(iii) there is no bar on the number of adjectives to be used. [However, they must be used in an order, *a nice little young child*, *an old round mahogany table*.
(iv) the relative clause is added after the head noun and;
(v) so is the prepositional phrase which qualifies the noun.

VERBS

Verb Forms

A verb found in the dictionary is in the present tense plural indicative form. It is changed in present tense third person singular by adding the suffix-*s* or *es* to it, as in *eats* and *goes* respectively.

The citation form of verb is changed according to person, number, tense, mood and voice. In most cases, person is indicated by the subject of the verb. The verb is in the first person if the subject of the sentence is the speaker. It is in the second person if the subject is the person spoken to and it is in the third person if its subject is the person or thing spoken about.

120. First person: *I see you* (singular).
121. *We see you* (plural).
122. Second person: *you see him* (singular and plural)
123. Third person: *He/she/it sees the star* (singular)
124. *They see the star* (plural)

Number is the property of the verb which is indicated by the singular or plural nature of the subject. Only a third person singular verb changes its form to indicate number.

Mood is the property of the verb which shows the manner in which the speaker or writer thinks of the action or state.

The *indicative mood* indicates the action or state expressed by the verb as a fact or in close relation to reality.

When the action does not refer to reality but mentions a possibility, probability, desire, demand or condition, it is in the *subjunctive mood.*

125. He comes here every day. (fact) indicative mood)
126. He may/might/should come (probability/possibility).
127. He would prefer to do it (wish).
128. If I am late, he would not do it (condition).

(125). is in the indicative mood whereas (126-128) are in the subjunctive mood.

Imperative sentences are in the imperative mood, they express command or requests, as in (129) and (130).

129. Come here.
130. Kindly open the window.

• *Tense* is the property of verb which indicates the time of occurrence. *Aspect* indicates whether the action is complete or in progress. There are three tenses in the indicative mood, present, past and future and each of them is of four types:

(a) simple, (b) progressive, (c) past and (d) perfect progressive.

- '*Progressive*' and '*Perfect*' indicate *aspects*.

Auxiliary Verbs

Verbs *be*, *have* and *do* are most frequently used verbs. They are main verbs in (131-133) because they are the heads of the Verb Phrase.

131. He is a doctor.
132. He has a car.
133. He does it regularly.

Be and *have* play the role of helpers to mark the tense forms of verbs, as in (134-135). They are called *auxiliary verbs* in that capacity.

134. He *is* running.
135. He *has* gone home.

In (134) *is*, together with the *–ing* form of the main verb (which is called, present participle), forms the present progressive tense. In (135) *has*, together with the past participle form of the main verb, forms the present perfect tense. The past tense of *be* is *was* (for first and third person singular and *were* in all other cases). *Do* acts as an auxiliary verb when we form a negative or interrogative sentence, as in (136-137):

136. He *does* not come every day.
137. *Does* he come every day?

In such cases, *do* carries the tense of the main verb and changes its form accordingly. Its past tense form is *did* in all cases.

To be is the infinitive form. In the present tense, it becomes *am* in first person singular and *is* in third person singular. For all other persons, its present tense form is *are* (e.g. we/you/they are).

To have is the infinitive form. In the present tense, it becomes *has* in third person singular. In all other cases, it remains have (as in I/we/you/they have). Its past form is *had.*

To do is the infinitive form. It becomes *does* in the present tense in third person singular. For all other persons, it remains *do*. Its past form is *did.*

There are two types of verbs: *regular* (also called *weak* verbs) and *irregular* (also called *strong* verbs).

The past tense of all regular verbs are formed by adding the suffix *–ed* to the verb and so is the past participle form, e.g. walk – walked – walked.

The irregular verbs have fixed forms which do not fall in line with this rule, e.g. *eat – ate – eaten.*

The present participle form of all verbs – regular or irregular – are formed by adding the suffix – *ing* to the verb, e.g. walking, eating, etc.

In brief,

- *am* – in first singular, *is* – in third, singular, *are* in all other cases in the present tense; *was* in the first and third person singular and *were* in all other cases in the past.
- *has* in third person singular, *have* in all other cases, in the present
- *had* in all cases in the past.

The future is formed by adding *shall* or *will* to *be* and *have* respectively, i.e. shall/will be; shall/will have.

Some Irregular Verb Forms

Present	*Past*	*Past Participles*
*become	became	become
*begin	began	begun
bite	bit	bitten
blow	blew	blown
break	broke	broken
bring	brought	brought
catch	caught	caught
choose	chose	chosen
*come	came	come
do	did	done
draw	drew	drawn
drink	drank	drunk
drive	drove	driven
eat	ate	eaten
fall	fell	fallen
*find	found	found
fly	flew	flown
freeze	froze	frozen
get	got	got/gotten
give	gave	given
go	went	gone
grow	grew	grown
hurt	hurt	hurt
know	knew	known
lend	lent	lent
lose	lost	lost
ride	rode	ridden
rise	rose	risen

run	ran	run
*say	said	said
*see	saw	seen
set	set	set
shake	shook	shaken
sing	sang	sung
sit	sat	sat
speak	spoke	spoken
steal	stole	stolen
swim	swam	swum
*take	took	taken
tear	tore	torn
*tell	told	told
understand	understood	understood
wear	wore	worn
write	wrote	written

* The starred verbs are among the most frequently used verbs in English.

TENSE FORMS

Present Tense

Present Simple	he/she/it/goes	I/we/you/they go
Present Progressive	I am going	we/you/they are going
Present Perfect	he/she/it has gone	we/you/they have gone
Present Perfect Progressive	he/she/it has been going	I/we/you/they have been going

Past

Simple Past	I/we/you/he/she/it	went
Past Progressive	I/he/she/it was going	we/you/they were going
Past Perfect	I/we/you/he/she/it/they	had gone
Past Perfect Progressive	I/we/you/he/she/it/they	had been going

Future

Simple Future	I/we shall go	you/he/she/it/they will go
Future Progressive	I/we shall be going	you/he/she/it/they will be going
Future Perfect	I/we shall have gone	you/he/she/it/they will have gone

Future Perfect Progressive	I/we shall have been going	you/he/she/it/they will have been going

- We may point out that in modern English *will* is freely used in place of *shall*.
- Sentences with future perfect progressive are rarely used.
- If one wants to suggest that something will happen fairly soon, one has *am/is/are going to* preceding the main verb form; as in (138).

138. I *am going* to tell you a story.

Tense Usage

The *simple present* is used to—

- express one's thoughts and feelings at the present moment, as in (139)

139. I feel sleepy.

- suggest general present state of affairs, as in (128)

140. He works in the State Bank of India.

- regular or habitual action.

141. I do not smoke.

- describe an event on radio or television as a commentary

143. Kohli scores a boundary

- talk about a scheduled event in the future

144. My plane leaves for Kolkata tomorrow morning.

- It is also used to express general truth.

145. The earth goes round the sun.

- Regular action

146. We meet every weekend.

Present Progressive is used to—

- express the action in progress

147. He is speaking right now.

- emphasise the development of an action/event at present moment.

148. I am working on the project.

- report a frequent action.

150. It is always raining in Cherapunji.

Verbs which express a situation, rather than describing a definite action, are not usually used in the progressive.

We do not use the progressive with the following verbs: *agree, be, believe, deserve, disagree, hate, haves, know, like, love, mean, need, prefer, remember, recognise, want, understand and wish.*

The *Present Perfect Tense* is used to—

- talk about something that happened in the past but has its impact on the present.

151. He has gone to Mumbai. (He is not back to the place yet).

- suggest that something began in the past and has continued up to now.

152. I have lived in Delhi for thirty five years (I still live in Delhi).

Present Perfect Progressive is used to—

- talk about something which had continued to happen for a period of time in the past and is still happening.

153. She has been learning English for ten years. [Note: Verbs which are not used in the progressive tense are not to be used in the perfect progressive]

The *Simple Past* is used to—

- report an action which has happened in the past and is finished.

154. He broke the glass last night.

Usually there is a time gap between the occurrence of the event and the time of its reporting. We use an adverb of time to emphasise when it happened.

The *Past Progressive* is used to—

- talk about something which continued to happen during some period of time.

155. I was reading when he came.

The *Past Perfect* is used to—

- talk about a past action which took place before another past action.

156. By the time I came here, she *had* already *left*.
157. Suddenly I remembered that I *had forgotten* my identity card at home.

The *Simple Future* tense is used to—

- express an action (or state of being) at some time in the future.
  It is expressed by adding *will* or *shall* to the bare infinitive form of the verb. Generally *shall* is used with the first person and *will* with the second or third person subject, as in (144) and (145).

158. I *shall* not go there.
159. He *will* come soon.

We use *will* with the first person and *shall* with the second or third person if we wish to convey intention, promise, willingness, inclination or determination.

160. I *will* keep my promise.
161. She *shall* have whatever she wants.

Shall is rarely used in this sense in American English.

Future Tense is expressed by using *be going* to or *about to* as well.

161. He is *going to* come in an hour.
162. He is *about to* come shortly.

The *Future Perfect tense* is used to indicate an action or a state of being which will be completed in the future before some other future action or event.

163. By the time the school closes for vacation, I *shall have worked* for six months.

Future Progressive is used to indicate action in progress in the future.

164. I *will be leaving for* office at 9 a.m.

The Subjunctive Mood

All sentences we have discussed under TENSE so far have been in the indicative mood. They have been used to assert or deny a statement or ask a question. However, all the sentences that we come across in the real world are not in the indicative mood. Some of them are in the imperative (e.g. come here) and some are subjunctive.

Subjunctives are used to give a contrary to fact statement, as in (165).

165. If I were you, I would not do it.

They are also used to express wish, as in (166).

166. I wish I were taller.

They are used to offer suggestions as well, as in (167-168).

167. I suggest that he be admitted to the club.
168. I move that he be censured.

Modal Verbs denote the mood of a verb. They are used before the basic form of the verb (i.e. bare infinitive).

Permission

Can, *may*, *could* and *might* indicate permission.

169. You can leave whenever you like.
170. You may have the book.

Could is a polite way of seeking permission.

171. Could I open the window?

Might is very formal. It is rather old-fashioned.

172. Might I do it?

Obligation

Must suggests obligation and so does *have to.*

173. I *must* do it on time.
174. I *have to* do it.

Intention

Will and *shall* indicate intention.

175. I shall do it.
176. Will he come today?

Ability

Can and *could* indicate ability to carry out an action.
Can is stronger than *could* in this context.

Both *could* and *be able to* express ability. If someone managed to do something in a particular situation, we use *was able* to rather than *could.*

177. He *could* do it.
178. He *was able to* do it in spite of hurdles.

Possibility

Can or *may* can be used to suggest possibility. Of these, *may* is more polite and formal than *can.*

179. You can go by bus.
180. You may go by bus if you so like.

If an event is less likely to happen, *could* or *might* can be used.

181. We *could/might* go by bus if it is available.

Probability

When we want to say that something is likely, we use *should* or *ought to*, as in (182).

182. We *should/ought* to be there before 6 p.m.

Desirability

If we want to say that it is good if something happened, we use *should* or *ought to.*

183. We should not speak like that.
184. You ought to pay attention to my advice.

Necessity

If we want to say that something is necessary to happen, we use *must.*

185. I must meet you soon.

Certainty

If we are sure that something is true, we use *must.*

If we want to express the opposite of it, we use *need not.*

186. I *must* reach there on time.
187. You *need not* worry about it.

[Note: *must not* suggest obligation]

Prediction

If we think that something is going to happen we use *shall* or *will.*

188. He will come on time.
189. I shall meet him.

While giving information, we use modal verbs to show our attitude towards it. Since they are used to produce a particular effect, we have to be careful in our choice.

FINITE AND NON-FINITE VERBS

A verb may belong to any of the two categories; it is either finite or non-infinite. The finite form of a verb carried specific tense, number and person on it. For instance, *goes* is the third person, singular form of *go* in the simple present tense. As opposed to it, the non-finite form of the verb does not carry any of these features.

The three non-finite forms of a verb are: the infinitive, the gerund and the participle.

The *infinitive* is the basic form of a verb without any inflection binding it to a particular subject or tense when used in a sentence, it is generally preceded by *to*, as in (190).

190. He moved to help her (here *to* means *in order to*). Sometimes the infinitive can be used without *to*, as in (192). It is then called a *bare* infinitive.
192. I watched him *go*.

Infinitives can be used as nouns, as in (193).

193. This is the *go* of the world.

The –ing form of the verb is called present participle. It can be used as a noun, as in (194) or an adjective (as in 195).

194. *Walking* is a good exercise.
195. He is a *promising* candidate.

When used as a noun, it is called a *gerund.*

Passive Forms of Verbs

A transitive verb can be changed in the passive form by turning it into its past participle form preceded by an appropriate form of *to be*. Thus the past participle form of *do* is *is done* or *are done* and of did, *was done* or *were done.*

When an active sentence is changed into passive, we use the passive form of the verb. (196b) is the passive of (196a).

196a. *The boy* hit *the dog.*
196b. *The dog* was hit by *the boy.*

We get a passive sentence by

(a) moving the subject of the active verb to the end of the sentence, and putting *by* before it;

(b) moving the object of the sentence to the subject position; and

(c) by changing the verb form into the passive (i.e. by adding an appropriate form of the verb to *be* before the past participle of the verb). The object of (196a) has become the subject in (196b). The subject of (196a) is moved after the verb in (196b) and *by* is inserted before it. The verb *hit* of (196a) becomes *was hit*. In (196b), following the same rule, becomes (197b):

197a. Lewis Carroll wrote *Alice in Wonderland* in the nineteenth century.
197b. *Alice in Wonderland* was written in the nineteenth century by Lewis Carroll.
197c. *Alice in Wonderland* was written in the nineteenth century.

(197c) is the short form of (197b). Most passive sentences are shortened by deleting the *by NP*. Sometimes the subject is deleted and the predicate is used as a past participle phrase, it is added to a noun phrase, as in (198).

198. *Alice in Wonderland*, written by Lewis Carroll, is a famous children classics.

NEGATIVE SENTENCES

When we want to say that something is not true, we use a negative sentence. It contains a negative word like, *not*, *never*, etc.

We get a negative sentence out of a positive sentence by adding *not* between its auxiliary and the main verb, as in (199b).

199a. He was sleeping.
199b. He was *not* sleeping.

If the positive sentence has no auxiliary, we add an appropriate form of verb *do*. It carries the tense of the main verb, as in (200b.) and (201b.).

200a. He *comes* every day.
200b. He *does not come* every day.
201a. She *came* yesterday.
201b. She *did not come* yesterday.

In (200a) *comes* is in the simple present tense, in (200b) do becomes *does*, its simple present form.

If a statement denies the existence of something, we add *any* before the noun that indicates it, as in (202b) and delete the quantifier such as *some*, *many*, *much*, etc.

201a. He has some money.
201b. He does not have any money.

Not... any can be replaced by *no*, as in (201c).

201c. He has no money.

We may note that *not anyone* may be replaced by *no one*, *not anywhere* by *nowhere*, not *anything* by *nothing* and *not anybody* by *nobody*.

If the main verb is *is, are, was* or *were* we do not add *do* before it, we simply add *not* after the verb.

202. He is/was not known.
203. They are/were not poor.

If the verb is *have*, we may or may not add *do* before it, as in (204a, b):

204a. a. He *does not have* any money.
204b. b. He *has not* any money.

When *not* is used with an *–ing* form or a *to* infinitive form of a verb, it is placed in front of it, as in (205-206).

205. *Not* taking a chance to wait, he got into a crowded bus.
206. I try *not* to worry.

The contracted form of *not* is *n't*, as in *isn't*, *aren't*, *wasn't*, *doesn't*, *didn't* etc.

Very is often used before *not* to make the negative more polite, as in (207)

207. He was not a very good teacher.

Never is used to suggest that something was not or will not be the case, as in (208).

208. I never trusted him and never will.

None is used to suggest 'not a single'.

Words beginning with *no* (such as *nothing*, *nobody*, *nowhere*) are used for absolute denial.

Neither... nor is used together to say that the two given alternatives are not possible, as in (209).

209. He is neither my friend nor my neighbour.

Neither of suggests the same sense, as in (210).

210. Neither of them knows him.

Barely, *hardly*, *rarely*, *scarcely* and *seldom* are used to suggest a broad sense of negation.

INTERROGATIVE SENTENCES

There are two types of questions:

(i) Some questions can be answered by saying *yes* or *no*. They are called yes/no questions, as in (211-212)

211. 'Have you seen her?' 'No'.
212. 'Will you like to see her?' 'Yes'

(ii) Some questions begin with a question word (e.g. *who, what, which, where, whose, which, why, how*); they are answered by a statement containing relevant information. They are called *wh-questions*.

213. Who is he? (an enquiry about a person)
214. What is it? (about an object)
215. Which is it? (about the choice out of two or more)
216. Where is he? (about the place where he is)
217. When will he come? (about the time of his arrival)
218. Why will he come? (about reason)
219. How will he come? (about the means of transport he will use)

Yes/No Questions

An interrogative sentence is derived out of a positive sentence.

(i) If it is a sentence with a main verb and an auxiliary verb, the auxiliary is moved to the initial position of the sentence and the full stop (.) is replaced by a question mark '?'. That is how (220a) is a positive sentence and (220b) in its interrogative counterpart.

220a. He is going home.
220b. Is he going home?

If the positive sentence has no auxiliary verb, we add verb *to do* as its auxiliary and move it to the beginning of the sentence; it carries the tense of the main verb.

221a. He dances well.
221b. Does he dance well?
222a. He danced well last night.
222b. Did he dance well last night?
(221b) and (222b) are yes/no questions.

wh-Questions

If it is a *wh*-question, the relevant *wh*-word replaces the word about which the inquiry is made and it is moved to the beginning of the sentence. It is followed by the auxiliary verb and the rest of the sentence, as in (221-227).

221. When did he dance? (about time)
222. Where did he dance? (about place)
223. Why did he dance? (asking for the reason)
224. How did he dance? (asking about the manner in which he danced)
225. Who danced?
226. Which of them danced?
227. What happened?

We may note that we do not need to insert *do* as an auxiliary if the question is about the subject of the sentence; *who, what* or *which* is inserted in place of the subject, as is appropriate in the context.

Question Tags

A question tag is added to a declarative sentence if we want the confirmation of a statement. The rule is very simple, if the statement is positive, the question tag is negative. If the statement is negative, the question tag is positive.

A positive question tag is formed by taking the auxiliary verb out of the sentence and add a tag (i.e. an appropriate pronoun for the word concerned) to it, as in (228a, b).

228a. He is not coming, is he? 228b. he did not came, did he?

A negative question tag is formed by taking the auxiliary verb and adding *not* followed by the relevant pronoun to it.

229a. He is coming, is not he? 229b. He came, did not he?

Shifts in Verb Forms

- We should try to avoid unnecessary shift from one verb form to another within one sentence.

(i) Shift in voice of verbs

If there are two or more clauses in a compound or complex sentence and they are about the same subject, an unnecessary shift in the voice form of the verb means an unnecessary shift in the subject of the clause. Both should be avoided. In (230a) there is a shift from one voice (active) to another (passive), resulting in a new subject in the second clause. (240b) avoids that shift and is a better sentence.

230a. I read the newspaper from beginning to end but the story I wanted *could not be found.*
230b. I read the newspaper from beginning to end but *could not find* the story I wanted.

For the same reason (231b) is better than (231a).

231a. Although I could not see the plane, its sound could be clearly heard.
231b. Although I could not see the plane, I could clearly hear its sound.

(ii) Shift in the tense of verbs

An unnecessary shift in the form of the tense should be avoided. Suppose I start narrating a story in the present tense, I should stick to the use of the present and should not shift to the past. (232a) is an instance of such an unnecessary shift which has been avoided in (232b) or (232c).

232a*. He reads a prepared statement but refused to answer the questions.
232b. He read a prepared statement but refused to answer the questions.
232c. He reads a prepared statement but refuses to answer the questions.

The verb form is changed in the indirect (or reported) speech.

INDIRECT SPEECH

When we report directly what somebody said in the written form, we put the exact words of that person within the quotation marks ("..."). However, we do not use the direct quote all the time. Very often we use he/she said or told and report what he/she said indirectly. It is called Indirect Speech or Reported Speech. We do not use the quotation mark in the Reported Speech.

As we begin reporting by using the reporting verb in the past tense, we have to change the verb form of the direct speech in the following manner:

(i) The simple present is changed to the simple past (as in 233b).
(ii) The simple past is changed to the past perfect (as in 234b).
(iii) The present continuous is changed to the past continuous as in (235b).
(iv) The present perfect is changed to the past perfect, as in (236b).

233a. He said, 'I *am* all right'.
233b. He said that he *was* all right.
234a. He said, 'You *scared* me'.
234b. He said that he had scared him.
235a. He said, 'I *am* coming'.
235b. He said that he *was* coming.
236a. He said, 'We *have* eaten'.
236b. He said that they *had* eaten.

There are some other changes in the verb forms. For instance, *shall* becomes *should* and *will* becomes *would. Can* and *may* change to *could* and *might* respectively.

237a. He said, 'We *shall/will come* on time'.
237b. He said that they *should/would go* on time.
238a. She said, 'We *may be late*'.
238b. She said that they *might be* late.
239a. She said, 'We *cannot* find it'.
239b. She said that they could not find it.

We may note that the change in the Reported Speech follows a fixed pattern.

Besides these, there are some other changes in the Reported Speech. For instance, *here* becomes *there*, *today* becomes *that day*, *tomorrow*, the *next day* and *yesterday*, *the day before.*

Indirect commands needs verbs like *order*, *command*, *ask*, *warn*, *beg*, *advise* and *instruct* according to the context.

240. The police asked me to stop.
241. His mother warned him not to tell lies.
242. My friend advised me not to go there.
243. The commandant ordered/commanded the cadet to march.
244. The girl begged her mother to forgive her.

When we ask a yes/no question in the Reported Speech we use *ask* or *inquire* as the reporting verb and *if* or *whether* after the reporting verb.

245. He asked me whether I was going to school.
246. She inquired whether he would go to the party.

A *wh*-question is asked by putting the wh-word after the reporting verb.

247a. He asked me how to start that machine.

The change from direct to indirect speech entails the shift in the form of the personal pronoun as well. For instance, the first and second person pronouns of the quoted speech become the third person pronouns of the in the reported speech. We may note that '*I*' of (233a) and '*you*' of (234a) have become '*he*' in (233b) and (234b) and '*we*' of '236a' *they* in (236b). If the speaker of the reporting verb is '*I*' or '*You*', it remains unchanged in the reported speech, as in (247a, b, c)

247b. I told you that *you* need not worry.
247c. You told me that *you* would help *me*.

PREPOSITION AND PREPOSITIONAL PHRASES

We have already discussed that a simple sentence consists of a noun phrase and a verb phrase. We have also seen that a verb phrase may consist of a simple verb, as in (6-9), a verb and a noun phrase, as in (26-30) or a verb and two noun phrases, as in (31-30) or a verb and two noun phrases, as in (31-32). When a verb takes two noun phrases, usually the first noun phrase is a direct object which does not need any element to connect it to the verb, as in (31a and 32a) but the second noun phrase needs an element to connect it to the verb, as in (31b and 32b). The additional noun phrases in the sentence (which are called *adjuncts*) also need an element in each case to connect the noun phrase to the verb. In (33) the additional element is an adverb of location which is connected by *in.*

The grammatical element that connects a noun phrase to the verb and precedes it is called a *preposition.* For instance, in (248) *to*, in, *at and in* are prepositions.

248. She gave the book [*to* me] [*in* the class] [*at* 10 o'clock [*in* the morning].

Here *to* connects *me* to the verb, *in* connects *the class* to it and *at* connects *10 o'clock* to it, *in* connects *the morning* to the preceding phrase *at 10 o'clock.* It means that a preposition can connects some constituent other than the verb to another constituent. For instance, in the expression *the man on the platform, on* connects 'the platform' to 'the man', it tells us that the man is on the platform. In short, a preposition connects a noun phrase to the verb or to some other constituents in the sentence. The whole unit, i.e. a preposition followed by a noun phrase is called a *prepositional phrase.*

In English the subject noun phrase is never preceded by a preposition, nor is a direct object noun phrase. Other noun phrases are usually followed by a preposition in each case, as in (249).

249. He bought a book [*for* her] [*for* Rs. 500] [*from* the bookstore] [*on* the college street [in Kolkata]].

Since prepositions play a vital role in making a sentence well formed, it is essential to discuss their functions.

According to the British National Corpus of a hundred million words, the prepositions among one hundred most frequently-used words in English are—*of, in, to, for, with, on, by,* at, *from.*

If we take other corpuses into consideration, we can have some other prepositions as well such as *into, inside, over, above, across, under, below, etc.* Besides, there are some *complex prepositions* such as by *means of, on account of, inspite of, instead of,* etc. Some complex prepositions are combinations of a noun and prepositions (such as *away from*) adjective and preposition (such as *owing to*) and two prepositions (such as *out of, off of, etc.*). We purpose to discuss some of them.

- **Some prepositions *are preposition of location.*** For example, *at* locates where (i.e. at what point in space or time) something is, as in (250a, b)

250a. He is *at* the gate.
250b. They were *at* a party *at* night.

There are many such expressions such as *at home, at work, at school, at the station, at an airport.* We have sentences like (251-253):

251. I was *at* university till 5 P.M.
252. I rang you up *at* 5 P.M.
253a. He came home late *at* night.

At in (251) indicates the location of an institution in space whereas that in (252-253a) indicates a point of time. When we talk about an address and give the house number, we use *at.*

253b. I live *at* 54 Uttaranchal Apartments.

At can be contrasted with *on* because in Hindi and many other Indian languages we have the same word for both. That is, speakers of some Indian languages do not differentiate between *on* and *at.* However, in English they have their distinct uses.

- **Whereas *at* refers to a distinct point of place or time, *on* is used when something is in contact with and supported by a surface.** We may contrast *on* with *at,* as in the following:

254. The dog is *at* the gate.
255. The cat is *on* the gate.

(254) indicates that the dog is close to the gate whereas (255) indicates

that the cat is sitting on the railings of the gate.

257. The meeting was scheduled to start *at* 4 P.M. and started exactly *on* time.

• In (257) *on time* is used because the meeting started as scheduled. *On* is used with days (e.g. on Monday, on Saturday), special days {*on* Republic Day, *on* his birthday, *on* Krishnasthami) and dates (*on* 1 st of May, *on* 25th of December). **With reference to location of place, *on* stands for 'on the surface of,** as in (258-259)

258. He sat *on* the sofa and I sat *on* the floor.
259. I put my cap *on* the top of the bookcase.

• ***In* is used when we refer to something that is enclosed or surrounded by something else.** For example,

260. My pen is *in* the drawer of the table.

(We may compare it with "My pen is *on* the table").

261. There were some chairs *in* the corner of the hall.

We use *in* when we talk about a place as an area.

262. I was *in* the USA for ten years.
263. I have been *in* Delhi since 1981.

When we want to talk about people or things inside a building, we use *in*, as in (264).

264. I was *in* the Tagore Hall at that time.

Sometimes *in* refers to language or medium, as in (265)

265. He spoke *in* Urdu and I put everything he said *in* writing.

In time means 'in a period slightly less than the scheduled time'.

266. He reaches home *in* time, though he was delayed on the way.
267. He reached home *on* time.

In time in (266) is used almost in the sense of *on time,* but not exactly.
• Sometimes we use *inside* in the sense of *in.*

268. He was *inside* the bathroom.
269. The radio was playing *inside* the car.

• Here *inside* means *within* the confines of the bathroom or the car. *Within* means in the boundary of something (e.g. some enclosed space or fixed time).
It also means not further than something, as in (270)

1. The man is at the gate.
2. The monkey is on the tree.
3. The cate is in/inside the compound.
4. The dog is under the tree.
5. The bird is flying over the house.
6. There is a tree by the side of the house.
7. There is another tree behind the house.
8. The car is coming out of the compound.
9. The house is across the road.
10. A squirrel is going up the wall.
11. A lizard is going down the wall.
12. There is nothing between the house and the road.

Fig. 10.1: Illustrations of Some Locational and Directional Prepositions

270. Greater Noida is *within* four kilometres of Delhi.

- In so far as the opposite of *in* is concerned, we use *out of,* as in (271).

271a. The car *in* the garage.
271b. The car is *out of* 'the garage.

- However, *out of* can also indicate *direction* in which something is moving, as in (272).

272. The car was *moving out of the* garage.

- The prepositions *across* and *over* can also be used in both contexts, as in (273, 274, 275, 276)

273. The river is just *across* the playground (place).
274. I went *across* the river last night (direction).
275. We live in the house *over* the bridge.
276. The thief escaped *over* the compound wall (direction).

- Prepositions such as *into, from, to, up, down, through, towards* and *back to,* basically refer to *direction,* as in (277-283)

277. *He jumped* into the river,

278. Rakesh *comes from* a remote village.
279. The man went *to* Bhubaneswar.
280. I went up the hill but came *down* with difficulty.
281. This train passes *through* Patna.
282. This river goes *towards* the Bay of Bengal.
283. He came back to his town after a few weeks.

- *For* indicates *duration* of time, i.e. a period of time, as in (284-285).

284. I was absent from office for a week/two months.
285. I lived in this house *for* eleven years.

We use *during* to suggest when something happened.

286. I fell asleep *during* his lecture.
287. I made many American friends *during* my stay in Chicago.

It is obvious from (286-287) that *during* means "throughout the course or duration of period of time". It may also refer to a particular time in the course of an action, as in (288).

288. He got bored *during* the heated arguments in the meeting.

- *Since* is also used in the context of time, but in a specific sense. It is used to refer to a particular time when something started and continued till the time under consideration (e.g. the present), as in (289)

289. It has been raining *since* morning.

- *Above* means higher than the specified plan, amount, rate, norm, etc., as in (290-291)

290. He has a scar above his left eye.
291. The boy is *above* the average students of his class.

- *Over* means 'above so as to cover or protect', as in 292.

292. He had an umbrella *over* his head.

It also means 'higher than', as in (293)

293. The temperature is *over* 40° centigrade today.

Below is the opposite of *over,* it means 'at a lower level than specified.

294. The ship is 50 feet *below* the surface of the sea. It also means 'lower in rank'.
295. The junior engineer is ranked *below* the assistant engineer.

- *Under* is the opposite of *above.* It means 'extending or directly below something', as in.

296. The ancient city of Dwarka is now *under* the sea.

It also means 'lower than' the specified amount, rate, or norm, as in (50).

297. The rate of last year's growth of Indian economy is just under 7 per cent.

• *Beneath* is 'extending or directly under'. It conveys the sense of 'hidden behind', as in (298).

298. *Beneath* the glamour of success was hidden a tragic life.

• *Underneath* means situated' directly below something' (so as to be coccealed), as in (299)

299. The money changed hand *underneath* the table.

• *Between* means 'across the space separating two objects or regions', as in (300).

It also means 'a period separating two points in time', as in (301)

300. The border *between* India and China is under dispute.

301. Winter falls *between* autumn and *spring*.

• *Among* indicates differentiation involving three or more parties, as in (302)

302. The opposition in Parliament are divided *among* themselves on this issue.

It also means situated (more or less centrally) in relation to several other things, as in (303).

303. He was *among* the best performers on the stage.

• *With* means 'accompanied by a person or thing', as in (304-305).

304. He came to the *party with* his wife.

305. He came to the meeting *with* a large bag.

With also indicates an instrument for the performance of an action.

306. He cut the apple with a knife.

It also indicates a material used for a purpose, as in (60).

307. He filled the container *with* milk.

• *By* identified the agent who performs an action, as in (308)

308. This stonework was done by artisans from Rajasthan.

It also indicates a term to which an interpretation is assigned, as in (309).

309. *By* 'scam', we mean 'a dishonest scheme, a fraud'.

Sometimes it means, 'a deadline', as in (310)'.

310. This work is to be finished *by* the end of this month.

By is also used with reference to some means of transport, as in (311).

311. He came *by* car/train/plane/boat/ship/bicycle/bus.

It is also used to show the route that someone takes, as in (312)

312. He came *by road/by sea.*

We always say (313-314) to suggest the means of movement/transport.

313. He came *on* foot. We also say,
314. I came *on* my bicycle/scooter/the bus/the horse back.

In 313-314 *on* is used in place of *by.*

Though *of* is the most frequently used preposition, it does not connect the NP with the verb.

• *of* shows the relationship between a part and a whole, as in *this chapter of the book.* Here *this chapter* is a part of the *book.* The same relation is established in *the pocket of the jacket, the back of the bus, the first day of the week, a piece of the cake, a series of the programme,* etc.

• *of* expresses the relationship between a scale or measure and a value, as in *an increase of 10 percent, a height of six feet,* etc. It expresses the relationship between two entities, as in *the government of India, the daughter of my friend, a photograph of the scene, a colleague of mine.* It shows the relationship between an author and his/her work, e.g. *the novels of* Premchand.

• While establishing the genitive relationship, we mostly use *'s* for people and animals, and *of* for thing and ideas. For example, *Ramesh's father, Ritu's computer, a bird's nest* but *the door of the flat* (but not* *the flat's door*), *the name of the box* (but not* the book's name) *the beginning of the year* (but not* *the year's beginning*), However, we do use expressions such as *yesterday's newspapers, the city's park* and *next week's meeting.*

• In some cases, the compound noun may be used instead of the genetive form, e.g. *the restaurant owner* (for the owner of the restaurant). If compounding is not permitted, the NP_1-NP_2 relation is indicated by NP_2 of NP_1.

of is also used to show the relationship between a direction and a point of reference, as in *the north of Delhi.* It also indicated a mental state, e.g. tired *of his behaviour, cause of aging,* etc. It is because of its multifaceted roles that *of* is used more frequently than any other preposition.

Some prepositions are used in fixed association with certain words, but almost all prepositions have subtle nuances of meaning. They are not used arbitrarily.

Word Order

We have already discussed that a declarative sentence consist of a noun phrase (subject) and a verb phrase (predicate):

An extended noun phrase has the following word order:

Pre-determiner + determiner + adjective phrase + head noun + relative clause

For example, let us look at the noun phrase in (315):

315. All the intelligent students who have applied for admission.

In this NP, *all* is the pre-determiner, *the* is the determiner, *intelligent* is the adjective phrase and *students* is the head of the noun phrase, and 'who have applied for admission' is the relative clause which defines *students.*

Order of Adjectives in an Adjectival Phrase (AP)

If we have two or more adjectives modifying a noun in an NP, we have to think of the order in which they have to be used. The following pattern seems to work:

316.

	The Speaker's Qualitative	*Size*	*Age*	*Shape*	*Colour*	*Where the Head is from*	*The Material of which the head noun is made*	*(Head Noun)*
a.	nice	small	–	round	black	American	Mahogany	Table
b.	beautiful	big	new	L-shaped	brown	Indian	Plastic	bench
c.	horrible		old		dark	–	Marble	Stool

It is because of such preference in the word order of adjectives we can say *new Mumbai metro* (but not* *Mumbai new metro*) a *broken teak chair* (but not* *a teak broken chair*), *the entire local team* (but not* *the local entire team*).

An extended verb phrase has the following word order:

317. *head of the verb phrase*	*direct object*	*indirect object*	*complement/ adjunct*
gave	the book	to me	last evening

A simple sentence may have the subject NP followed by the verb, which may be followed by the object, NP if the verb is transitive, as in (318).

318. Ratan gave the book to me.

- The basic word-order of a declarative sentence in English is: s(ubject), v(erb), o(object).
- The basic word-order of an interrogative sentence is:
- Question + Auxiliary Verb + Subject NP + Main Verb + Object NP + Indirect NP

319. What did he give you?
320. Who did he give the book to?
321. Who gave the book to you?

- IF a sentence begins with a main verb, it is an imperative sentence.

322. *verb* + *direct object* + *indirect object*
Give the book to her

In short, the basic word-order of a declarative sentences in English in SVO. An imperative sentence has the order VO and an interrogative sentence: Auxiliary verb followed by the questions word which is followed by the rest of the sentence. If the main verb is *be* or *have*, the order is VSO, as in (323).

323. Have you any chocolate?

In imperative sentences, *never* and *always* are sometimes used in the beginning of the sentence.

324. Always drive carefully.
325. Never look at the sun directly.

Adverb phrases may come in the beginning of the sentence.

326. Early morning he went to the garden.

Adverbs do not come between the verb and the object, as in (327).

327. (i) I like Chinese food very much. (but not *I like very much Chinese food).
(ii) a model verb and a main verb, as in (328).
328. I can cook Chinese food quite well. (but not *I can quite well cook Chinese food).

As a modifier of an adjective *too* occurs before it but *enough* after it.

329. He is too young to do it.
330. He is old enough to do it.

When an interrogative sentence is used in a reported speech, it becomes a declarative sentence and ends with a full stop, and not a question mark. However, it is connected with the main clause by *if* or *whether* and not *that*, as in (331c).

331a. He asked her, 'Do you want to eat?'
331b. He asked her *whether* she wanted to eat.
331c. * He asked her that she wanted to eat.

In conditional sentences, usually the conditional clause comes before the main clause (as in 332a) but sometimes it can come after it (as in 332b).

332a. If you come on time, I will go with you.
332b. I will go with you if you come on time.

If a compound sentence has several clauses which report actions in sequence, they should be ordered in that sequence.

333. He woke up, had a bath and a breakfast.

Sometimes, the word-order is deliberately changed to bring some constituent in focus, as in (334a) or (335b).

334a. Those days are gone when we always played at home.
334b. Gone are the days when we always played at home.
335a. I like bananas; I do not like apples.
335b. Bananas I like, apples I do not.

There are some other instances of change in the word-order but they are not ordinarily used.

The teacher of English may not need to use all these rules in elementary classes but his/her awareness of these phenomena may be of help.

UNIT IV: LESSON PLANNING AND MATERIAL DEVELOPMENT

11

Lesson Planning

While commissioning National Knowledge Commission (2005), the Government of India laid down certain terms of reference, one of which was to "build excellence in the academic system to meet the knowledge challenges of the twenty first century and increase India's competitive advantage in the field of knowledge." The report of the Commission (2007) emphasized the importance of an inclusive society as the foundation for a knowledge society. It felt that an understanding and command of the English language is a most important determinant on access to higher education. It argued that the highly unequal access to English, as it exists today, should be done away with. Therefore, it recommended that the teaching of English as a language should be introduced, along with the first language of the child, starting from class I in schools.

While recommending the teaching of English from class I, the Commission has two objectives in view:

(i) It should create a meaningful learning experience.
(ii) It should be used to teach some non-language content subjects, starting from class III in schools.

Thc Commission wants government schools to become multi-media schools. It hopes that such an arrangement will reduce the gulf between English medium schools and regional language medium schools. While planning lessons to teach elementary English, this broad objective must be kept in view.

Objectives of Micro[1]-Lesson Planning

Any micro lesson planning for teaching English in the first two classes (i.e. standard I and II) should prepare students to follow a non-language content subject through the medium of English from class III. In other words, by the end of class II, students should be able to follow the lessons on a content subject in English. It means they should acquire enough knowledge to listen to the teacher speaking in English to

1. Small, of restricted size.

- answer questions orally in English,
- read textbooks in English,
- do written home assignments in English.

Priorities in Lesson Planning

Since the priority is the development of listening skills, the following components of the skills will get special attention:

- To have auditory perception of all vowel and consonant sounds of English,
- Ability to discriminate between sounds,
- Identify stressed syllables in words and sentences,
- Identify the pattern of intonation in sentences.
- Recognise frequently used simple words.

We have already talked about the differences between sounds of English and the letters of its alphabet on pp. 66-68. The teacher should keep the point in mind and point out how different sounds are pronounced in isolation and in words. For instance, he/she may speak *pun* and *fun* distinctly and let student pronounce them as /pʰʌn/and/fʌn/. He/she may have several contrasting pairs (such as *pat* and *fat*, *pig* and *fig*, and *supper*/sʌpər/and *suffer*/sʌfər/. In the sentence, *what is your name*?, there are four words. In isolation, they are *what*/hwɒt/or/wɒt/,/ɪz/,/jɔəː/or/jɔər/and/neim/but when they are spoken in a sentence, it is spoken as/*hwɒt's jɔər neim*/.

The teacher will tell children that in a connected speech/ɪz/becomes/s/. He/she will also tell them how and when a sentence will be spoken with rising intonation. Without explaining the concept of rising intonation in technical terms, he/she will demonstrate how it is spoken. The teacher will ask Ramesh, a student. *What is your name*?

In response to this question, a student will respond, '*My name is Ramesh*'.

Ramesh will ask the same question to the boy sitting next to him who will reply and repeat the question to the next boy. That is how the whole class will be involved in both listening and speaking. The next questions could be:

What's your father's name?
What does he do?
Where do you live?

Each of these questions should be asked and answered in a proper manner. The sentences should be correctly pronounced. If a word is mispronounced by a student, it should be corrected as soon as the respondent finishes his/her sentence. However, he/she should not be interrupted in the middle of his/her speech.

Telling a Story

Since speaking and listening are closely connected events, the two exercises should be taken up together. After children get used to listening and responding to simple questions, they could be exposed to listening to a short story or a poem. It should be a story with which they are familiar. Most likely they have heard it from their parents or grandparents. For instance, the teacher could tell the story of "The Stork and the Crab". At the end of the story, he/she could ask questions such as:

> What did the stork tell the crab?
> What did the crab tell other crabs and fish?
> Did they agree to the proposal of being taken to another waterpool?
> What did the stork do when he carried them one by one in his beak?
> What did the crab do when the stork carried him?
> How did the crab reveal the truth to other crabs?

Since the children have heard the story in the mothertongue, they will find it easy to follow it in English. They will have little difficulty in answering questions. In case a child does not have suitable words to speak, the teacher may help him/her with the required expressions.

In case students have learnt the alphabets and can read, the teacher could modify his/her method. After telling the story orally, he/she could ask them to read it silently. Then he/she could ask them questions. If this method is adopted, three types of communication skills will be covered: listening, reading and speaking. In case they can write as well, the teacher could ask them to rewrite the story in their own words. That way, all the four skills will be covered.

In order to put the suggestions given above into practice, the lessons will have to be sequentially planned. First, the teacher will read the lesson aloud. Second, children will read the same story quietly. Third, they will answer questions asked by the teacher. The answers will indicate how much the students have comprehended. If something is not clear to them, the teacher will rephrase that part of the narration. This method of comprehensive, rather than fragmented, teaching has been found useful. It is the major trend in the English curriculum which has been in practice in the USA for several decades. The programme can be further enriched by adopting a short course in spelling and vocabulary development involving items in the context of the integrated comprehensive lesson programme.

In short, the goal of the lesson planning should be to have an integrated view of oral and written communication. Each lesson should have a discernible unity. It should represent a balanced study with listening, speaking and reading. It is important that this balance is maintained so that students are ready to develop the ability to study a content subject through the medium of English.

In other words, the first two years of teaching of English should enable students to use English as a tool to acquire knowledge.

Unit Planning

The term 'unit planning' involves 'unit teaching'. It implies search for unity in the English teaching programme. It is central to the teaching process.

There are three types of units: (a) the *subject matter* unit (b) the *activity unit* and (c) the *idea-centred* unit. The subject matter unit seeks unity by concentrating on a story prescribed in the text or a unit of grammar (e.g. the use of the simple past tense), or some other aspect of the prescribed text. It is a pedestrian programme which tries to present many things in somewhat unrelated fashion. The activity unit finds its unity in language activity. The subject matter of this type of unit may vary. The unity is found in the process of skill development. The idea-central unit takes its unity from an idea or theme. The thematic unit permits the unity of an idea pursued through various selected pieces or through the oral discussion of the idea. However, these three types of units are not mutually exclusive; a given unit may combine all the three approaches. For instance, the story "The Stork and the Crab" can be used for an exercise in speaking, listening and reading and even writing. With a little imagination a teacher can convert it into an imaginative and significant presentation. One of the students can play the role of the crab; another, of the stork. There may be some dramatic activity by the stork of carrying fish out of the waterpool one by one to the back of the stage (or the classroom) and finally the crab killing the stork. Thus a little effort to dramatize the story can make it more unified and significant.

Of course, there is no magic inherent in any type of unit; the teacher is the most significant factor in successful teaching. However, there is a significant advantage of idea-centred unit; it offers the most vital context for the teaching of skills and content. Many English classrooms have the same atmosphere of boredom, the same emphasis on items of grammar and vocabulary, as if the content is merely a vehicle to carry them around. It does not activate the mind of students. If the unit plan is an effort to turn this routine affair into something engaging and exciting, the atmosphere will change and students will take more interest in what they go through. The unit must provide some vital context for the teaching of English.

Steps in Planning a Unit

Select Specific Objectives

As soon as the teacher has selected the theme of the unit, he/she should plan it specifically. The teacher should ask the following question to himself/herself. "What skills should the students develop as a result of this unit?" In other words, he/she should lay down the specific objectives of the lesson that will provide the guidelines for him/her.

Put Selected Items in Sequence

After deciding on the specific objectives, the teacher will decide what activities students should engage in to bring about the expected result. Every activity-reading aloud the text, class discussion, dramatization of the dialogues, if any, question-answer session, the reading and writing assignment—, should aim directly at the objectives of the unit. It is not necessary that all the four skills are emphasized all the time, sometimes only one or two of them may be stressed.

After choosing the activities, the teacher should decide their *sequences.* They should be logically organised. If possible, each activity should develop out of the previous one. *Materials* needed for the activities (i.e. teaching aids) must be planned for in advance. At the end of the exercise, the teacher should determine to what extent the objectives have been fulfilled. It may be in the form of an objective or subjective test or in the form of a group discussion. Whatever the form, there must be definite evaluation.

Recent research has emphasized the fact that there should be a sequential and cumulative programme from standard I to the end of the higher secondary school. It leads to a more systematic development of skills in learner than an unplanned development of the curriculum. It is, therefore, necessary to have a planned approach to the teaching of English right from standard I, making room for flexibility to develop the skills of the learner.

Components of a Good Plan

A good plan should have—

- suitable teaching material ready for the target levels;
- stages of the lesson in logical order;
- preventive steps ready if something goes wrong;
- provision for checking whether students have comprehended what was taught;
- provision for feedback;
- measures to consolidate what was taught.

The lesson should conclude within the allotted time.

PRESENTATION OF A LESSON PLAN

General objectives: Focus on listening

- To enable students to listen to various sounds of English.
- To encourage them to hear the difference between contrasting sounds.

Specific Objectives

To enable students to hear the difference between:

(i) /p/, /p^h/ and /f/
(ii) /b/, /v/ and /w/.

Teaching aids needs

- A piece of chalk, duster, blackboard.
- Diagrams showing the articulation of
  (i) /p/,/p^h/and/f/
  (ii) /b/,/v/and/w/.
- Slides showing the point and manner of articulation of each of these sounds.

Previous knowledge assumed

- Familiarity with sounds/p, p^h/and/b/and/w/among Hindi speaking children and all these sounds among Urdu-speaking children.

Introduction

The teacher introduces the topic and talks a bit about the sounds of Hindi-Urdu (or whatever is the mothertongue of the majority of students) and tells them which sounds of English are new to them.

The teacher produces the sounds /p/, /ph/ and /f/ and tells students how to produce them by referring to the diagrams which show the points and manner of their articulation. He/she shows them slides and charts to illustrate the points further.

Presentation

The teacher produces the sounds/p/,/p^h/and/f/and tells students how they are produced by referring to the diagrams showing the points and manner of their articulation. He/she shows them slides and charts to illustrate the point.

- The teacher raises his/her soft palate (i.e. top part of the front part of the inside of the mouth) and provides the obstacle to air stream by the closure of the lips. The lung air is compressed behind the closure and the vocal cords are held wide apart to produce the sound/p/but they vibrate to produce the sound/b/. Aspiration is added to produce /p^h/.
  In order to produce/f/, the teacher raises the soft palate and lets the inner surface of the lower lip make a light contact with the edge of the upper teeth such that the air that escapes produces friction. For/f/, friction is voiceless but for/ʋ/it is voiced.
- The teacher shows slides or charts to incorporate the following points:

Table 10.1: Some Consonants Sounds

sound	*voicing*	*duration*	*Articulation*	*Point of articulation*
p	Voiceless unaspirated	Stop/ plosive	Lower lip	Upper lip
p^h	Voiceless aspirated	plosive	Lower lip	Upper lip
f	voiceless	Continuant (fricative)	Lower lip bottom	Upper teeth
ʋ	voiced	Continuant	Lower lip	Upper teeth bottom
b	voiced	plosive	Lower lip	Upper lip
w	voiced	Continuant	Lower lip (Lips are tightly rounded)	Upper lip

Note: The description given above is to enable the teacher to produce these sounds and not to pass on the description to students.

- The teacher asks students to listen to the sound/p/in the following words:
  spit/spɪt/, *speak*/spiːk/, *start*/staːt/, *stick*/stɪk/, *station*/steiʃn/, *stamp*/ stæmp/, *Spanish*/spæniʃ/, *stone*/stəun/, stand/stænd/.
- He/she asks them to listen to the sound/p^h/in the following words: *pit*/p^hit/, *pill*/p^hɪl/, *pig*/p^hig/, *pat*/p^hat/, *pile*/p^həɪl/, *pan*/p^hæn/, *pair*/ p^heəː/, *pal*/p^hæl/.
- He/she draws their attention to the pronunciation of/f/in the following words:
  fit/fit/, *fad*/fæd/, *fill*/fil/, *feel*/fiːl/, *fig*/fig/, *fail*/feəːl/, *file*/fail/.
- He/she draws their attention to the contrasting sounds, such as in *pit* and *fit*, *pad* and *fad*, *peel* and *feel*, *pig* and *fig*, *pile* and *file*, etc.
- He/she asks them to note the sound contrast in sentences such as,
  He *faints* when he *paints*.
  The *chief* wants it *cheap*.
  His *cuff* fell in the *cup*.
  I *praised* his *phrase*.
  Her *pun* was a *fun* to hear.
  His *plight* was miserable during the *flight*.
- After they hear the sentences, the teacher wants to know whether they can hear the difference between/p/and/f/. He/she reads the following lines and ask them to pick up words which have contrast between/p/and/f/.

The teacher recites:

The boy did *leap*
To get the *leaf*,
But fell in the *pit*
Though could not *fit*.
He crawled to the *pool*,
The silly old *fool*.
It was not a *prank*,
I must be *frank*.

Contrast

(He/she remarks before stopping.) There is a contrast between *prank* and *frank*.

Can you find any other contrast between/p/and/f/?

Student 1: Yes sir, between *pool* and *fool*.

Teacher: Very good. Any other pair?

Student 2: Between *pit* and *fit*.

Teacher: Nice. Any other pair?

Student 3: Between *leap* and *leaf*.

Teacher: If we look at these pairs, we find a common point. What is it?

Student 4: There is a contrast between the sound/p^h/and/f/.

Teacher: Excellent. These contrasting sounds are in the initial positions of words, except in one case. Can you give me an example in which they are in final position.

Student 5: Yes, sir, between *leap* and *leaf*.

Student 6: Between *tip* and *tiff*.

Student 7: Between *cup* and *cuff*.

Teacher: Excellent. Can you find such contrast in the middle of the word?

(Silence)

Teacher: Between *copy* and *coffee*.

Student: Between *puppy* and *puffy*.

Teacher: Yes, You are right. Now listen to the contrast between/b/and/v/. *Bat* and *vat*, *ban* and *van*, *bail* and *veil*, *boat* and *vote*, *bow* and *vow*. And listen to the contrast in the following sentences:

He did *vote* on the *boat*.
There was a *bent* on the air *vent*.
The *base* of that *vase* is broken.
That piece of *marble* is a *marvel*.
There is a *curb* on the *curve* of the road.
They are *vying* for *buying* these cars.

Teacher: In the following pairs the sound /v/ contrasts with the sound /w/:
wine and *vine*, *west* and *vest*, *want* and *vent*.
wail and *veil*, *worse* and *verse*, *wow* and *vow*.
Now listen to me and tell me which sound is there in the first word.
His verse is getting *worse*.

Student 1: 'v'

Teacher: That is correct.
He looked in the *west* for his *vest*.

Student 2: 'w'

Teacher: Correct.
That *vine* produces grapes for good *wine*.
Which sound is there in the last word?

Student 3: 'w'

Teacher: very fine.
The *viper* was sitting on the *wiper* of the car.
What is the first sound in the second word?

Student: 'v'

Teacher: That is fine.

In this lesson we have learnt to hear the difference between

(i) /p/, /p^h/ and /v/
(ii) /b/ and /v/
(iii) /v/ and /w/

Now listen to the tapes at home and try to produce these sounds correctly.

12

Approaches to the Teaching of English

There are three ways of looking at the process of language acquisition; philosophical, psychological and sociological. One's approach to the teaching of any language-first or second-depends upon how one treats the question of language acquisition. Before the growth of psychological study of human beings, philosophers like Decartes looked at the problem and considered language as 'the product of mind'. They analysed the relation between thought and language and thought the latter was the product of the former. Earlier psychologists looked at the problem the same way. This approach changed with the growth of behaviourism.

A. PSYCHOLOGICAL APPROACHES

Behaviourist Approach

Behaviourism considered all behaviours results of habit formation. It believed that man differs from other animals only in the types of behaviour he displays. **John Watson** (1924) considered 'language habits' a kind of behaviour which, was 'manipulative'. It begins with the unlearnt vocal sounds that infant makes at birth and afterwards. The verbal response to a stimulus given to a child consists of one word (e.g. *dada*) and later on two words or three words. The child forms the verbal habit of uttering "mama" when he/she (a) looks at the mother, (b) her photograph, or (c) listens to the sound of her voice or (d) the sound of her footsteps. Later on, when he/she learns to read and write, the sight of the printed or written word 'mother' becomes the stimulus for him/her to speak the word 'mother'. Watson believed that in bringing children up in our own verbal footsteps, we verbally condition them as we were conditioned both as to the word themselves (in a language such as English, for example) and their pronunciation and inflection. He observed that stimulus for pronouncing words comes from the way the child's parents and neighbours speak. A French child will speak an English word as if it is a French word but if he/she is exposed to the speakers of English, he/she will speak perfect English.

Watson also observed that it is difficult to learn a foreign language "if we start to learn that language late in life for the very same reason that a 40 year old blacksmith can never learn toe dancing (1924:232). He thought that it is so because habitual types of response rob the organism of its muscular flexibility. In his view, an adolescent trying to learn a new language will fail because his/her vocal organs have become less flexible, less capable of being shaped to utter new sounds. In short, Watson believed that word habits are built up like mammal habits and are organised around a series of objects. In verbal behaviour, the spoken words may act as initial stimuli and start the process of response. One's memory is nothing except the fact that when one meets stimulus again after an absence, one does the old habitual thing, i.e. say the old words.

Watson's theory of verbal behaviour in terms of stimulus and response was developed further by **Edward Thorndike**. His theory of learning was based on his experiment with an animal in a problem box, a situation in which a specific behaviour, like pressing down a lever, was rewarded with escape from the box and a bit of food. Initially the animal in the box acted at random, pressed the lever and received the reward. In subsequent trials, the period between the animal's being introduced to the situation and the pressing of lever decreased. Thorndike called it process of learning and evolved a theory of learning. He maintained that learning involved the wedding of specific response to a specific stimulus through a psychological bond in the neural system, such that the stimulus regularly calls forth the response. Thorndike believed that a satisfactory outcome of any response tends to 'stamp in' its connection with a given situation. He called it 'the law of effect'. He believed in its impact on pedagogical science. He observed that the clearest explanation and the best models for imitation fail often but the child learns something by doing it, even without his knowledge of what he is doing. It becomes the basis for his theory of connectionism and ultimately a comprehensive view of pedagogy.

In the functional analysis of verbal behaviour, **B.F. Skinner** (1957) identified stimulus, reinforcement and deprivation as factors which control verbal response. He felt that they could be manipulated to have a desired response. The behaviourist's schemata of language learning devices are given in figure 11.1

Stimulus *Response*

↑ ↑

$$S \rightarrow r \rightarrow s \rightarrow r \rightarrow s \rightarrow R$$

Reinforcement

Fig. 11.1 : Behaviourist language learning device

B.F. Skinner refined the theory further by emphasising the concept of 'stimulus control' and identifying the 'controlling stimuli'. He called 'response strength' the 'basic datum[1]'. He believed that the verbal behaviour occurring in a given situation is fully determined; at the same time he considered 'overall frequency' an important factor, which brings in the importance of reinforcement. The three concepts- stimulus, reinforcement and response-were taken to be fundamental and were applied to language teaching, including second/foreign language teaching. The pedagogical development based on the approach was called the *conditional development* or *operant behaviour.* The process which a person undergoes to deal effectively with a new environment is operant conditioning. Sometimes behaviourist psycholinguists are called environmentalists because of their belief that the environment in which a child learns a language is the strongest stimulus.

Developmental Approach

In 1959 **Noam Chomsky**, a theoretical linguist, published a detailed review of *Verbal Behaviour*, in which he observed that, in so far as language acquisition is concerned, "reinforcement, casual observation and natural inquisitiveness (couple with a strong tendency to imitate) are important factors, as is the remarkable capacity of the child to generate, hypothesize and 'process information' in a variety of very special and apparently highly complex ways" (1959 (1964:563). After providing convincing counterarguments against Skinner, Chomsky observed:

> It appears that we recognize a new item as a sentence not because it matches familiar items in any simple way, but because it is generated by the grammar that each individual has somehow and in some form internalized. And we understand a new sentence, in part, because we are somehow capable of determining the process by which this sentence is derived in this grammar.
>
> (*Ibid*, 576)

Chomsky's Claim: The fact that all normal children acquire essentially comparable grammar of great complexity with remarkable ease and ability suggests that human beings are somehow specially designed to do this, he argued. Chomsky called this ability to hypothesize and formulate utterance *innate*[2] and suggested that it be explored in order to understand the process of acquisition of language.

Chomsky argued that there is a special component of the human brain (he called it the language faculty) that is specially dedicated to language. Like other components of the body, it is genetically determined. The language faculty

1. a peace of reinforcement
2. inborn

changes from the initial stage to a relatively stable state at some stage of maturation. It is this period that the process of language acquisition (what many other call 'language learning') is at its best. Changes take place even after this period but they are marginal after puberty. By that time, the system gets stabilised. This steady state incorporates the generative power (or the computational system) which generates infinite possible expressions (called language).

This approach embodies many assumptions. First, the language faculty of the mind interprets signals independently of other features of the environment. Secondly, parsers are fixed. The changes that take place during language acquisition are because of the parsers. It is the generative procedure that distinguishes English from Hindi-Urdu (or any other language). They are very efficient and quick but not so easy. The theory of learnability assumes that natural languages are learnable under normal conditions.

Chomsky stated that children often hear incomplete or ungrammatical utterances along with grammatical input but ungrammatical input is not incorporated into their system. Besides, they hear only a finite subset of possible grammatical sentences but they are able to generate an infinite number of sentences which they have never heard before. It goes essentially against the stimulus argument of language learning.

The strongest argument offered in favour of Chomsky's innateness hypothesis is from Eric Lenneberg, a neurolinguist.

Key Issues in the Chomskyan Approach

This cognitive revolution involved a shift of perspective from the behaviourist approach to the study of the mind that entered into thought and action. It asserted that the study of language is not the study of its elements and their arrangement and the process to identify them. It is the study of linguistic intuition; a study of the process of language acquisition. Chomsky and Miller (1963) formulated these questions:

(i) What is the knowledge of language?
(ii) How does it arise in the human mind?
(iii) How is it put to use?

To these questions, a new one has been added:

(iv) How is the knowledge of language represented in the brain?

Psycholinguists have been trying to answer these questions.

Early developmental psycholinguistic research by David Mc Neill (1966, 1970), E. Klima and U. Belluchi (1966), Roger Brown (1973), Cazdan (1968), Jerry Brown (1973), Jerry Fodor, Tom Bever and M. Garrett (1968, 1974) proved that children do not learn by imitation. When exposed to utterances in a natural language, they formulate their own rules which may be wrong but they may resist any correction. For example, we have the instance of a child who used *childs* (instead of *children*) but was convinced that he was right. When the mother tried to correct him, he resisted.

Mother: say 'children'.
Child: childs
Mother: children
Child: childs

The process is repeated several time. The mother gets fed up and raises her voice.

Mother: Now listen carefully, say 'children'.
Child: o.k. childs, children.

The fact that the child keeps on saying *childs* points out that language learning is not an imitative act. The same point is illustrated below:

Child: My teacher *holded* the baby rabbits and we patted them.
Adult: Did you say your teacher *held* the baby rabbits?
Child: Yes
Adult: What did you say she did?
Child: She *holded* the baby rabbits and we patted them.
Adult: Did you say she held them tightly.
Child: No, She *holded* them loosely.
(Cazdan 1972:92)

The child is aware of the general rule and adds- *ed* to *hold*. The attempt to force the child to imitate the correct expression has failed in both the cases. Selinker (1971) calls such errors 'interlanguage'. Ravem calls them 'approximation'. Eventually both the children might have corrected themselves when they heard every normal speaker saying *children* and *held*. The implication is that the language environment plays a crucial role but not the coercion to imitate and repeat. Such examples prove convincingly that the behaviourist's insistence on the learner practising drills and repetition of structures was not natural and scientific. In other words, learning did not consist of a series of conditioned connections and the stimulus-response theory of learning was without any solid basis. Psycholinguistic research done within the Chomskyan framework encouraged new approaches to language teaching not only in the USA, but also in Britain and the mainland of Europe and other countries of the world. It has influenced both monolingual and bilingual approaches to language teaching.

The New Schemata[1] of Cognitive-Developmental Approach

The developmental approach assumes that the child has a general learning mechanism that enables him/her to recognise patterns in utterances and to

---

1. Plural of *schema*, outlines of a plan or a theory.

build rules for his/her own language. Based on this assumption, Dulay, Burt and Krashen (1982) suggested the following schemata for creative construction in language acquisition.

Fig. 11.2: Language Acquisition Device

According to Dulay, Burt and Krashen (1982) the *filter* is that part of the internal processing system that subconsciously screens incoming language based on learner's motives, needs, attitudes and emotional states. The *organizer* is that part of the internal processing system that is responsible for the learner's gradual organization of the language system. It functions subconsciously and is based on the language systems. It comprises principles and parameters under which they apply. The research on the functioning of the organizer reflect three phenomena:

(i) the systematic progression of changes in transit construction that the learner used before a structure is finally acquired;
(ii) the errors that systematically occur in the learner's speech and
(iii) common order in which mature structures are learnt.

The *monitor* is that part of the internal learning system that is responsible for conscious linguistic processing. When a learner tries to acquire a rule from a book of grammar or from a teacher in the classroom, it is conscious language learning. It is at the point that the monitor is used. The linguistic knowledge that one acquires through monitoring is used to correct one's own speech and writing. The degree to which the monitor is used depends on the learner's age, his/her formal education, the nature of and focus on the verbal task and his/her personality.

Some researchers have reported that conscious linguistic learning is independent of the linguistic system that is built up subconsciously. However, they also point out that young children are virtually unaware of linguistic rules. It implies that if Indian children are exposed to English as a second language, they will not face the problems that adults face when they try to acquire a new language. First of all, they will be psychologically in an advantageous position because of the plasticity of their language acquiring ability (see the discussion on critical period hypothesis on p. 13) and secondly, they will not have much gap between their learning complexity and linguistic complexity. The only difference they face is that they will not have the same amount of exposure to the language (e.g. English) outside the classroom that a native (English) child has.

---

1. Development of a skill or knowledge.

Krashen's Input Hypothesis: Krashen's distinction between 'acquisition'[1] and 'learning' has had enormous influence on the way a teacher (especially in the USA) thought how a second language should be taught in schools. He argued that it should have much less focus on grammar and much more emphasis on 'comprehensible inputs'. Krashen *et al.* who feel that the process of second language acquisition is not so much different from first language acquisition, argue that people do not learn language by talking about it (i.e. by studying the rules of grammar but by experiencing enough meaningful input and communication in that language). According to *Input Hypothesis* (Krashen 1985:100) the second language learner improvises and progresses a step beyond his/her current stage of linguistic competence if he/she is supplied more natural communicative inputs.

Developmental Approach in Europe

Piaget and Vygotsky are considered to be the founders of developmental psychology in Europe. Though they did not pick up any controversy against the behaviourists, they tried to offer an alternatives to them.

Piaget: Jean Piaget (1926) argued that development is a process of having equilibrium[1] between internal knowledge and input. He distinguished the two mechanisms of assimilation and accommodation. He stated that assimilation is the integration of external elements into evolving or completed structure of an organism and accommodation is the modification of an assimilatory scheme or structure by the elements it assimilates. He considered assimilation a conservative force which aims at keeping the system close to its present form while accommodation is a progressive force, which aims at changing the system through input. Assimilation of new input leads to more automatisation[2] of an activity, an increase in mastery, which implies a decrease in errors. Recent research claims that input is most effective in learning when it is a part of interaction and not when the learner is simply exposed to a spoken or written text.

By describing the mind as proceeding through a series of cognitive development, each being a prerequisite for the next and by making language acquisition an important part of its overall development. Piaget (1926) made an important contribution to the theory of language development. Many programmes have been undertaken with cognitive focus under his influence, particularly for the growth of vocabulary.

Lev S. Vygotsky

Piaget's concepts of assimilation and accommodation in the process of learning are closely related to Vygotsky's zone of proximal development (ZPD), Vygotsky defines ZPD as "the difference between the child's developmental level as

---

1. A state in which opposing forces are balanced.
2. automatic functioning

determined by independent problem-solving and the higher level of potential development as determined by problem-solving under adult's guidance or in collaboration with other capable peers" (1978:85). In other words, 'actual developmental level' refers to what a child can perform independently and ZPD to those functions a learner can perform with the help of someone else. He argues that optimal learning takes place when there is maximal accommodation.

Another key concept of Vygotsky is 'scaffolding'[1], a modified interaction between a native speaker and a non-native learner. It provides the learner with relevant and increasingly more precise information in the environment at the right time to help him/her to solve a particular problem step by step. In so far as the second language acquisition is concerned, Vygotsky would argue that learning will be fruitful if the learner interacts with the speakers of the language in their natural environments. Scaffolding is something that happens with a learner as an active participant.

Krashen considers the provision of 'comprehensive input' the most fundamental pedagogical principle. However, he does not discuss what the processes of decoding these inputs are. As Vivian Cook (2003:133) points out, this notion is "too simplistic and too all-embracing" to produce anything but general guidelines on what a teacher should do. However, Krashen's approach has given impetus to Vygotsky's acculturation theory[2] of second language acquisition. Research is going on the role of input and interaction in second language acquisition. Though their role is considered to be crucial, we have yet to have a comprehensive account of these processes to understand them better.

Connectionist Approach[3]

Another psychological approach to language learning is connectionism. It is also called 'parallel distributing processing'. Just as multiple connections of nodes have a massive interactive network in computers, human brain has cells with a network of multiple connections all interacting simultaneously, it has a network of mental lexicon which connects words and phrases in a complex manner. For instance, the word *colour* belongs to various networks. It reminds us of colours such as, *red, yellow, green, blue, purple, black, white, violet* etc. and their various shades. It also reminds us that an object could be *colourful* or *colourless*; it could have *bright, dark, dim* or *light*. If we can colour something, it is *colourable.* If it has been *coloured*, it is *coloured.* We think of people who are *white* or *coloured.* Non-whites are sometimes colour-barred.

1. Literally, *scafolding* refers to a temporary structure on the outside of a building made of wooden planks and metal poles. It is used by workmen while the building is being repaired or cleaned.
2. the way in which second language learner adopts to the life with two languages.
3. a theory that accounts for the way in which words are there in the interactive connective network; a new version of associationism.

At a metamorphorical level we *give* or *lend colour* to something to make it seem true or probable but it may *show its true colour.*

If we draw a line to represent colours, we will put black at one end and white at another; the rest of them are in between. (Figure 11.3).

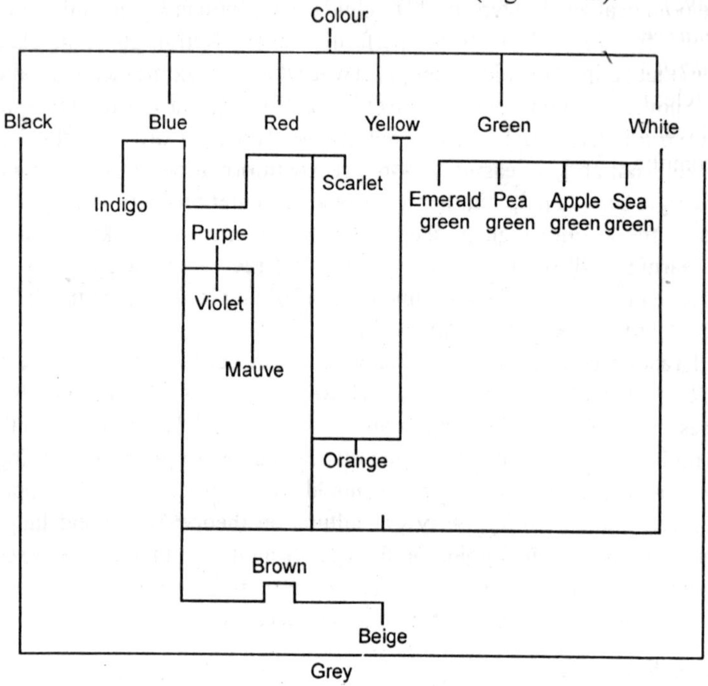

Fig.: 11.3: Hierarchy of Colours

Apart from J.J. McClelland and Rumelhart (1486), J. Elman, E. Bates, M. Johnson (1997) and A.W. Ellis (1980) are the main champions of this approach.

Rumelhart and McClelland (1986) applied the artificial neural model to the past tense of English verbs. It correctly predicted the past tense forms of regular verbs and some irregular verbs. Rather than associating a word, with another word, it associated properties of a word with the properties of another word. As Pinker (2000) argues "if an association between *bread* and nourishment is in fact stored in the brain as a set of associations between beigeness, sponginess, savouriness and nutrition then we encounter *cake* which is also spongy and beige. Our brain registers the fact that *bread* and *cake* are similar (p.104). Pinker thinks that connectionism is a theory of the mind.

Connectionism can be fruitfully used to increase the vocabulary of children learning English as a second (or even first) language but it has limited capacity to account for syntactic complexity.

Prototype Theory

Another type of associationism is based on the prototype theory (Rosch, 1975, 1976). If we have a hierarchy of 'birdiness' (features a typical bird ought to have), *robin* is a prototypical bird. If it is in the centre of a circle, *canary*, *sparrow*, and *dove* are in its nearest circle; *owl*, *pheasant* and *ostrich* and *parrot* are next in the second circle and *peacock* and *duck* are next in the third circle; *penguin* are on the periphery. This network is based on the similarity of features; the less are the similarlity features, the further is the bird's distance from the prototypical bird (see Figure 11.4).

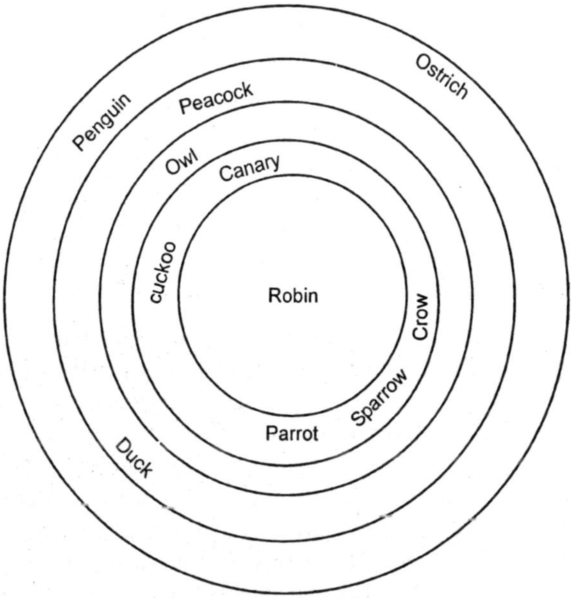

Fig. 11.4: Bird-like Features in Prototype theory

B. SOCIOLOGICAL APPROACH

Malinowaski-Firth

Anthropology and sociology are other related disciplines that have affected our approach to the study of language learning. Two British scholars of early twentieth century- B. Malinowaski (1923, 1935) and J.R. Firth (1951, 1957) focussed on the context of situation in the process of the analysis of language. Malinowaski maintained that language is an abstract universal entity which is actually manifested in different forms in different societies. Firth believed that a person is totally constrained in his/her utterance by a given social situation. The relationship of the sentence to its context of situation[1] is one of the key points in his attempt to understand its meaning. The other points are its phonetics, grammar and lexicon. While describing the 'context of situation' he thought of the socio-economic and religious settings of the society (or socities) in which the interlocutors[2] live, their age and sex and the type of speech function they indulge in. Although they did not speak anything directly about the second language learning, their implication was clear. The second/ foreign language learner has to understand the context of situation in which an utterance he has come across was made. As Firth was a professor of English phonetics and literature at Punjab University Lahore (at that time in India) for a decade (1928-1938), he must have incorporated this view while teaching in India. Though it had its impact on the teaching of English literature, the school teachers were, by and large, unaffected; they were under the influence of Henery Sweet and Harold Palmer. They believed in teaching structures and not in when to use them. While teaching literature in school, the context in which a poem or a story was written was hardly paid attention. The functionalists who follow Halliday adopted the socio-cultural approach in the UK.

Sapir-Whorf Hypothesis

In the USA, Edward Sapir (1931) emphasized that, while studying a language, one should pay special attention to the role of society in which it is spoken. It was further strengthened by the theory of linguistic determinism proposed by Benjamin L. Whorf (1956). While discussing the relationship of habitual thought and behaviour to language, he asserted that every language "is a vast pattern system, different from other, in which are culturally ordained forms and categories by which the person not only communicates but also analyses... Types of relationship and phenomena channel his reasoning and build the house of his consciousness" (1956:252). He thought that language influences unconscious habitual thought rather than limiting thought potential. Though Sapir-Whorf Hypothesis influenced language philosophers and pedagogues in the USA, it did not have much impact on language teachers in schools. The influence is obvious in the writings of Gumperz, Forguson, Berlin and Kay, Levinson, Lucy and Toley.

Language Deficit Hypothesis

In 1960s **Basil Bernstein**, a professor of Sociology of Education at the University of London, came up with the *Language Deficit Hypothesis*. He studied how class regulated the structure of communication within the family

1. The situation in which language is used.
2. The speaker and the listener, those who participate in verbal communication.

and the initial coding orientation of the children. The pre-school children of upper and middle class used *elaborate code*[1] and were more verbal and inclined to reason than the children of the working class. The latter were more restricted than the former in vocabulary, in sentence pattern and in the variety of use of conjunctions and prepositions. They were limited to a *restricted code*[2] primarily because of the subculture and role system of the family, community and work, he argued. For them, the school should induce a change of code so that their culturally induced backwardness transmitted through language could be reduced. However, these children displayed low performance on verbal IQ tests and had difficulty in improving their linguistic capability. Consequently, they had general difficulty in profitting from the school" (1971:151-152).

Charles C. Fries

In the USA Charles C. Fries, who was a pioneer of structural approach to English language teaching, came up with somewhat similar views on the "vulgar" English of the Black children[3]. In 1968, A.H. Jensen elaborated the view further. A number of investigations were conducted in the USA which found that there was language deficit among pre-school and school children from poverty stricken and disadvantaged population. Cazdan (1965) argued that environmental assistance could be provided to develop their syntax. A series of specific programmes were developed for the improvement of their language skills, not only in the USA but also in Britain. However, the implications of those investigations were not applied while teaching Indian children who were also environmentally deprived with reference to English. William Labov (1970, 1974) pleaded that Black children were not deprived. They had the power of creative expressions in their own variety of English (i.e. Black English vernacular) which should be encouraged. Variationists have argued for the recognition of native varieties of English outside the UK and USA and made a case for Indian English. However, it had little impact on Indian educationists. Those educationists who had sociological orientation ask language teachers to pay special attention to them but no specific items have been suggested in the curriculum of English for culturally disadvantaged Indian children. Efforts should be made to compensate for their environmental deprivation.

Communicative Competence

The growth of transformational generative approach to language laid emphasis on two aspects of language users: their competence (i.e. ability to produce, understand and discriminate the grammatical sentences of a language) and

1. Detailed and complicated verbal expressions.
2. Limited expressions
3. Those who believe that languages vary in use.

their performance (i.e. actual use). Dell Hymes (1974) came up with the theory of *communicative competence* which involved their ability to participate in the society "as not only a speaking but also a communicating member" (p. 75). He asked linguists to study 'the communicative means available in the relationship condition, its nature and outcome' (p. 76). In short, he asked them to study language discourse and explore the 'dimension of discourse' (p. 97), Hymes arguments were convincing and they influenced the method of language teaching both in USA and Britain. Instead of discussing the use of isolated sentences, experts decided to discuss language in discourse. Widdowson (1978, 1979) Sinclair, (1972, 1975, 1985) and Coulbhard the chief practitioners of this approach.

Discourse Analysis

The communicative competence approach encouraged language pedagogues to analyse how a language is structured in different contexts of use with a view to helping textbook writers to determine the underlying features of a text. It wanted language teachers to be more interactive with their students systematically. The **discourse[1] analysis** of students' performance (oral as well as written) is supposed to lead to a better evaluation of students' performance. It is also supposed to be more sensitive to different demands that speech and writing put on the learner. Coulthard (1985), M.J. McCarthey (1988, 1991, 2001) D. Tannen (1984) and Schiffrin (1994) have done pioneer work in this field. Recent development in critical discourse analysis[2] (as in FairClough 1995) views social context as dynamic and changing. It pleads that the text should not only be a reflection of social reality but also construct social reality.

To sum up, recent psychological and sociological approaches to language have influenced language teaching method. The social factors demand that the language to be taught/acquired must be relevant for a society in which the learner is to be active in life and bring him/her at par with other speakers of the language. The psychological approach helps the learner to obtain the desired objectives in a natural manner. Various developmental psycholinguistic approaches have been in search of such a method.

1. Oral or written communication.
2. An analysis involving merits and demerits of a discourse.

THEORETICAL APPROACHES TO LANGUAGE TEACHING

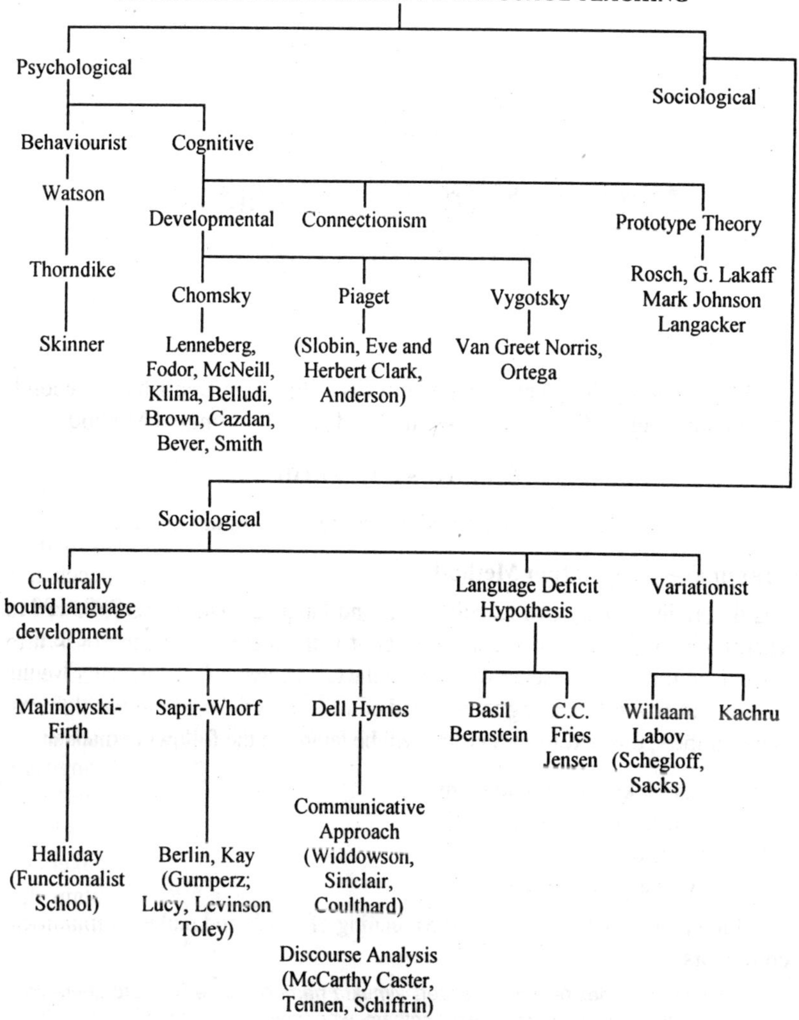

13

Methods of Teaching English and Developing Skills

Broadly speaking there have been two ways of teaching English as a second/foreign language: (A) Bilingual Method and (B) Monolingual Method.

BILINGUAL METHOD

The Grammar—Translation method is the oldest bilingual method.

Grammar—Translation Method

It is the traditional style of teaching a second language which was followed to teach Latin and Greek to British students. It is the method to teach Sanskrit to students in India. The teacher would read the text sentence by sentence, give the meaning of words occurring therein and comment on their grammatical forms. For examples, this text from Sanskrit will be taught in the following manner.

kāma krodh-vimuktānām
yatinām yata cetsām
abhito brahma-nirvana
vartate viditātmanām

First of all, the teacher gives the meaning of words and makes grammatical comments.

kāma- from desire, *krodh*- anger, *vimuktā nām*- of those who are liberated; *yatinām*- of the saintly person, *yata cetsām*- who have full control over the mind; *abhito*- assured in the near future, *brahmānirvanani* – liberation in the supreme; *vartate*- is there; *viditātmanām*- of those who are self-realised.

Then he/she translates it-

> Those who are free from anger and all material desires, who are self-realised, self-disciplined and always struggling for perfection, are assured of liberation in the supreme in the very near future.

The study of such a text, accompanied by its vocabulary and grammatical information, was supposed to help the learner understand the text. He/she could apply the knowledge of the language to the study of other texts with the help of a book of grammar and a bilingual dictionary. Attempts were made to write grammar textbooks for learning English on this pattern. The book included a discussion on the parts of speech and various types of declensions of nouns and conjugations of verbs. However, it was realised that such books were not appropriate for children learning English although this practice was followed to teach a second language throughout Europe.

When Johaan Franz Ahn wrote a book on teaching English to non-English-speaking persons, he followed this pattern. Instead of texts, he used ideal sentences and gave grammatical rules, followed by practice-sentences, Heinrich Gottfried Ollendorf wrote an English textbook for French speakers in 1848. His book included declensions such as

Nominate: John
Genitive: of John
Dative: to John
Accusative: John
Instrumental: with a stick
Locative: in London.

The examples of conjugation of a verb were like:

PRESENT INDICATIVE

First person	I go	we go
Second person	you go	you go
Third person	he/she/it goes	They go

These examples show that the grammar-translation method, which was helpful for heavily inflected languages like Greek, Latin and Sanskrit, was not helpful for a language like English.

Ollendorff wanted his method to be interactional and used question-answer sentences as examples of grammatical explanation. He graded his text materials though it is not clear what his basis of grading was. For instance, a lesson on imperative sentences came much after a lesson on passives. It was not based on the ease of construction.

John Miller's Bilingual Conversational Texts

It may be pointed out that much earlier than Ahn and Ollendorf, John Miller (1797), published the *Tutor or New English and Bengali Workbook* which he considered well adopted to teach the natives (i.e. Bengalis/Indians) English. His lessons comprised English sentences of functional value (e.g. about the sale and purchase of rice, the use of boats or bullock carts, etc). The left half of a page contained English sentences and the right half had their Bengali equivalents in Bangla script. Indeed the book was useful for Englishmen learning functional Bangla and Bengali learning functional English. It was like a bilingual tourist guide book but one had to learn the writing system of Bengali or English to use his workbook.

The Mastery System

Thomas Prendergast served in the Indian Civil Service in Madras and learnt Telugu and Hindustani. He was one of the individual reformers who reacted to the Grammar-Translation method. He came up with his own methodology and called it the *Mastery System* of learning languages. He was the precursor of the Reformist Movement. He observed that when exposed to a language, children learn a lot of chunks of expressions. They retain them and add some new words and phrases even when they do not comprehend them fully. They use them fluently in complete idiomatic sentences. He thought that since these children had mastered the use of these prefabricated chunks in simple sentences, they can be induced to use them in compound and complex sentences. That way Prendergast was a precursor of behaviourist-structuralist methodology. The other bilingual methods will be discussed later.

The Reform Movement

The Reform Movement, led by Wilhelm Viëtor in Germany, Paul Passy in France, Otto Jesperson in Denmark and Henry Sweet in England was a reaction against the Grammar-Translation method. Its methodology was based on three principles:

(i) the primacy of speech in language learning,
(ii) the centrality of the connected text in the teaching-learning process and,
(iii) the priority of the oral method in the classroom.

The primacy of the spoken language with correct pronunciation, stress and intonation gave a new direction to language teaching. It demanded the use of accurate phonetics of English and recruitment of properly trained teachers to carry out their assignment with students. The emphasis on the oral method took students away from the reading and translation of the text to listening and speech exercises in English. The children were kept busy with listening and speaking and there was a great demand for properly trained phonetician teachers. Getting such trained teacher was not so difficult in England but to have so many trained native speakers (or native-like speakers) was not easy in the colonies where the demand for the teaching of English was increasing fast.

The number of European immigrants to the USA was increasing and so was the demand for learning English to get them adjusted in a country dominated by its speakers. What was needed was a systematic method to teach normal English. It was at this point that Montaigne came up with his model, followed by Blackie, Sauveur, Heness and Berlitz. The natural method was considered to be the most serious attempt in language teaching development in the USA so far.

Berlitz: The Trailblazer of Direct Method

Though Berlitz was not an academic methodologist, the method he adopted was simple, systematic and ordered. He put strong emphasis on oral work and suggested that grammar be discussed much later in the course. The opening session used the verb *be* and most common adjectives (such as *big, small, think, thin, light, heavy* etc.). The learners' vocabulary was gradually increased by adding the names of parts of the body, cloths, common household things etc. The alphabet was introduced in lesson 8. The second section of the part 1 course introduced simple texts involving everyday dialogues and question-answers. Natural conversation followed these lessons.

The Direct Method/Oral Method of Practising Sentence Patterns

The grammar-translation method was bilingual; it used the mothertongue of the learner to introduce and explain the new language. Its exercises were focussed on translating from English to the mothertongue of the learner and vice versa. As against it, the reformists insisted on the exclusion of the mothertongue of the learner. They pleaded that English be introduced directly in the classroom. It was called the *Direct Method.* It was also called the *Oral Method* because of the primacy it gave to speech. Harold Palmer did research and experimental teaching according to this, on the bases of which he wrote *English through Action* (1925), *English for Children* (1927) and *English through Questions and Answers* (1930). The theoretical bases of these books were: The *Oral Method of Teaching English* (1921) and *Principles of Language Study* (1921). In order to guide the teachers of spoken English, Daniel Jones published *The Pronunciation of English* (1909) and *The English Pronouncing Dictionary* (1917). The collaboration of Jones and Palmer ensured the success of the oral method in Britain. Palmer devised various types of oral drills and exercises which were tried out successfully. Lawrence Fawcett, C.F. Eckersley and many others helped him in consolidating the Direct Method.

Harold Palmer: The Champion of Direct Method in Britain

Palmer provided a surface analysis of structures of English and stressed on their functional relations. His emphasis on learning the pattern of systematic structures was, in a way, a retrograde step, for it ignored the connected text which the reformists had emphasised. Often unconnected sentences were presented in substitution tables. Palmer emphasised the organisation of the curriculum in the following way. A typical course on teaching English would begin with students being familiarised with English pronunciation. At stage two, 'primary matters' would be presented in the form of oral exercises, drills and direct speech activities. Attempts would be made to let the students assimilate the structures accurately. At stage three, (i.e., advanced level), attention would be paid to reading, composition and conversation. It was hoped that students would form accurate language habit by repetition. His course design involved gradation, concreteness, proportion, the multiple lines of approach and a rational order of progression.

Objectives of the Direct Method

The objectives of the direct method were:

(i) to make students proficient in recognizing and producing the sounds of English,
(ii) to let them memorise a large number of sentences,
(iii) to let them have all types of sentences in their control and,
(iv) to let them learn how to have the words in the dictionary in their repertoire.

It was Palmer's experience as a native language teacher in the classroom which provided him with the necessary input to develop the direct method. The method was welcomed in the USA as well. However, its success depended on the availability of an energetic and enthusiastic native speaker teacher and suitable teaching aids. As the second language learning had to take place in total isolation from the native language of the learner, pictures of objects and events had to be presented to give them visual stimulus. Questions and answers had to occupy a large part of the direct method. For instance, the teacher would show the picture of a bird in flight and ask:

Teacher: What is this?
Student: It's a bird.
Teacher: What is it doing?
Student: It is flying.

A.S. Hornby: The Consolidater of the Direct Method

The second phase of the Direct Method began with the publication of *English Language Teaching,* a journal devoted to the teaching of English to non-native learners. It was edited by A.S. Hornby and published by the British Council, and later on, by the Oxford University Press. Hornby published *An Outline Guide for the Practical Study of Foreign Language* in 1942. It was supposed to have a general methodology of language teaching. The teacher was to ask students to practise certain sentence structures till they learnt them by heart and were able to use them in normal discourse.

C.C. Fries: The Father of Direct Method in the USA

What Hornby did for Britain, Charles C. Fries did for the USA. The technique of descriptive analysis of language given by Leonard Bloomfield (1931) was further developed by Charles Hockett, Bernard Bloch, A.A Hill and many others to apply it to analyse languages which were not described so far. During the Second World War, the US defence services organised Army Specialised Training Programme (ASTP) to offer short training courses in foreign languages. It is irreverently called the *G.I. Method.* It insisted on drills to memorize the patterns of language. The inventive nature of the new method, which emphasized the priority of spoken language, impressed Charles C. Fries. He championed the cause of direct method in the USA the way Harold Palmer did in the UK.

Michigan Oral Approach

Fries selected and graded the structures of English for pedagogical purposes. He proposed that the structures of the mother tongue of the learner of English be contrasted with those of English. He further suggested that the structures that were different from those of the mothertongue be sorted out, for they deserved special attention while teaching them. He called the method he had evolved the *Michigan Oral Approach.*

In many ways Michigan Oral Approach was similar to Harold Palmer's oral approach. Both adopted a sentence-based approach for the teaching of grammar. However, there was a basic difference. Palmer's generalization was based on his intuition and Fries' on the contrastive analysis of L_1 and L_2. *The Structure of English* (1952) by Fries was a definitive grammar of English from a descriptive point of view. The English Teaching Programmes in the USA were based on it. Its popularity got for it a high level institutional support. It was adopted by the State Department of the US for its Language Training Programmes. The method adopted by Fries was known as the *Structural Method* and that of Hornby, the *Situational Approach*[1] because he emphasised when a specific structures was to be used.

Like other twentieth century structural linguists, both Fries and Hornby believed in the supremacy of the sentence and made it the basis of linguistic analysis and language teaching. The focus on sentences became even more prominent when transformational generative grammar replaced structural linguistics.

---

1. The approach which believes that the use of human language is determined by surrounding circumstances rather than personal qualities.

The Audiolingual Method

Those who adhered to the principles of Direct Method for teaching English as L_2 outside the English-speaking world faced difficulty in finding suitable native speaker-like teachers. Even in Britain and the USA, the teacher found the process of drill practices in the class very time consuming and tiring. However, they found it advantageous to use audio equipment (such as gramophone records and audiotapes) in the class. The records and tapes provided students with ideal pronunciation of sounds, words and sentences which they were supposed to repeat. The tape would keep on repeating them as many times as needed for students to imitate them well and get habituated to use them freely. It was possible because of the use of electronic devices in the classroom or language laboratories. This direct/oral method was called the *audiolingual method.*

Various types of electronic device were made available:

(i) The *audio passive installation* where students could simply listen to prerecorded messages,

(ii) The *audio active installation* where students could listen to the message and respond to the questions posed on the mastertape.

(iii) The *audio-active compare laboratory* where the student could not only listen to the master tape and hear his/her own response to it over the headphone but also record questions and his/her responses. He/she could playback his/her own response and compare it with the correct response recorded on a different track on the same tape. Both the electronic classroom and language laboratory needed a teacher to keep a tab on what the students were doing. The teacher could monitor the students individually or collectively but that was a less exhausting duty than to help them practise orally.

The audio-lingual method was direct because it did not leave scope for the use of any language other than the target language. It was behaviourist because it believed in habit-formation among students. It was oral because it believed in the practice of the spoken forms of the language. It was effective but could not be implemented widely because most schools had paucity of funds and shortage of expert staff. The shortage of time and space in the school was also a problem. Besides there were problems involving their servicing and maintenance. As a consequence, even in the USA, many schools could not make use of audiolingual method.

Television

The audiolingual method enabled students to practise the ideal pronunciation regularly and help them in inculcating the habit of speaking well. However, the facility was rarely available in government-run schools in India. The situation became better when televisions became easily available. Apart from the language programme which some TV channels provide, all of them can be used to play videotapes. This audio-visual aid has become more effective than the audio aid because it could not only produce sounds but also show how certain sounds are produced. In India the recently launched Da Vinci Learning channel caters to a child's curiosity. It provides interactive fun knowledge learning programmes. It not only emphasizes knowledge dissemination but zeroes on its practical application. Its passage is not only educative but also entertaining and inspiring. Its contents are for children between six and twelve years. Its programme is launched in English and it hopes to overcome the initial inhibition of non-English audience.

Computer Assisted Language Learning (CALL)

The computer-assisted language learning programme (CALL) is also audiolingual in its orientation, as it emphases drills and pattern practice. The greatest handicap the audiolingual method suffers from is that it does not pay much attention to the way people usually use the language. Instead of having a communicative style, it is preoccupied with isolated sound patterns and sentence structures. It creates the impression that language learning is a mere physical activity. It makes students unanalytical. It has not succeeded in enabling them to speak fluently and properly in a normal speech act situation.

Contexual Method

The Situational Approach

The direct/oral method changed the orientation of second language teaching. Instead of written texts, which was taken from the writers of repute, it concentrated on sentences which were less bookish. They emphasized that students capture the linguistic features of the language in use. The idea appealed to the neo-Firthian linguists in Britain who had already talked about the language in use in their *Situational Approach.* Halliday (1985) called it a *functional* approach but Hornby and other neo-Firthians favoured Firth's term. They emphasized the verbal and non-verbal action of the participants in a speech act and its observable effect. The practical effect was to prepare 'special purpose courses' in 'restricted languages' i.e. specialized languages of the professionals (e.g. English for doctors, scientists, engineers). The focus on register studies led to the special purpose language teaching (ESP), such as in *Industrial English* (1975) by T.C Jupp and Holdin, *English in Education* (1977) by Elizabeth Laird, *The English Used by Teachers and Pupils* by Sinclair, Coulthard and others.

The Communicative Method

A major development in the field of language study and language teaching took place in the USA with the arrival of Noam Chomsky's approach. He severely criticised the behaviourist method of language teaching and emphasized the creative aspect of language use (see chapter 11, pp. 108-114). His emphasis on the difference between *competence* and *performance* of a language user caught the attention of Dell Hymes who came up with the concept of *communicative competence.* He asserted that one should pay attention to not only the speaker's potential and actual utterances but also to his/her communicative competence, i.e., "his/her ability to participate in society as not only a speaking but also a communicating member" (1974:75). His was another way of focussing attention on what British language pedagogues called functional English.

Hymes asserted the significance of the rules of language use "without which the rules of grammar would be useless". In other words, the rules should show how things are done with words, and how one interprets these utterances as actions. Widdowson (1974) distinguished between cohesion[1] of text and coherence[2] of discourse as communication. Such assertions gave new direction to language teaching. Candling *et al.* (1978) discussed how practical problems in developing study skills in English should be handled. John Sinclair suggested that it was not children's knowledge of English but their experience of using it that is restricted. The implication was that a new methodology should be evolved to increase this ability. In short, they should be enabled to develop workable strategies for language use. This idea has been further developed in *Communicative Syllabus Design* (1978) by John Munby. Wilkins *Notional Syllabuses*[3] (1976) recommends not only the study of semantico-grammatical categories of modality but also the category of communicative functions. The learner must know how to ask questions, make requests and express agreement and disagreement, etc. For instance, a language learner should know how people take turn in conversation, how they open and close conversation and how people launch new topics, close old topics and shift from one topic to another.

Discourse Analysis

The technique of discourse analysis developed because of the progress in the understanding aspects of communicative competence. It concentrates on the following points while discussing a text:

- Who are the participants in the discourse?
- What type of relation exists between them? (e.g., 'asymmetric power' or 'symmetric solidarity')
- What do we need to know about the context in which the discourse text has materialised?
- What does the language of the text reveal about the relation between participants?

1. The action of forming a united whole.
2. The quality of being logical and consistent.
3. Relating to an approach to languages which is dependent on notions

- What factors lead the reader of the text (or listener) to his/her conclusion?

The major contribution to the spoken discourse has been from the sociological point of view. Some linguists (e.g. Labov) have analysed the spoken text from the variationist point of view, i.e. how language varies from one linguistic style to another depending on its participants. Some people (e.g. FairCough 1992) have looked at it to understand the relation between language, ideology and power. They are not relevant for elementary school students but they are for teacher-trainees to understand the teacher-student relation in specific situations and also to prepare them for social interaction. Teachers could use their insight from such discourse analyses to evaluate their own students.

Discourse analysis is the study of language (used by individuals) in its social context. Discourse analysts are interested in the analysis of both spoken and written discourse. The difference between the two is very marked. While the written discourse is structural and grammatically correct, the spoken discourse is often formless and grammatically inaccurate. Its sentences are full of incomplete phrases and hesitation. Sometimes the speaker makes a false start, sometimes he/she is repetitive; as has been shown by Beattle (1983) and McCarthy (1991). Such a style of speaking is informal. A formal speech style, on the other hand, is better organised and focussed; it is grammatically correct and can be used for classroom discussion at a suitable level. Discourse analyses of the language used by hotel maids by Jasso-Aquilar (2010) and others, as given in Guy Cook and Sarah North (eds.2010), prove convincingly that they cannot be used as text for primary school children. They may be of interest to language variationlists and stylistitians but not to language learners.

The Cognitive-Developmental Method

In chapter XI, pp. 138-142 we have already discussed Chomsky's theory of language acquisition which asserts that the process of L_2 learning is not different from that of L_1 learning. Language experts such as Jakobovits (1968/1970), Owen Thomas (1974), Richard Omann (1970a, b), Kellogg, Hunt and Mark Lester implemented the cognitive developmental approach to language teaching following the *Aspect* model of linguistic analysis. As Chomsky revised his theory further in (1981), Burt, Duley and Krashen (1982) came up with new schemata, which we have already discussed on p. . We have talked about the *filter* and the *organiser* which work subconsciously and the *monitor* which works at the conscious level of L_2 learners. We have reported that exposure to natural communication in L_2 is necessary for the process to work well. Dulay, Burt and Krashen (1982) argue that the understanding of the second language will increase in proportion to the amount of exposure the learner has. They report that the silent phase in the beginning of language learning is helpful to most students in cutting down intralingual errors and in improving their pronunciation. They also report that the mothertongue of the learner has the least influence while he/she is learning L_2. He/she organizes subconsciously the words and phrases of L_2 that he/she hears and organises its structures in accordance with the principles of uniformity and predictability.

Burt *et al.* claim that conscious learning and application of grammatical rules play their roles in the production of his/her sentences; the subconscious learning makes him/her fluent. As primary school children will start learning English much before puberty, their process of language acquisition will be faster than of those students who start late. They can learn from their peers in the school environment. Dulay *et al.* add two notes of caution. Certain structures are acquired late by the learner and exposing them early to such structures is of little use. Secondly, correction of grammatical errors at an early stage is not helpful either. Their recommendations on the method of teaching are based on psycholinguistic research and teachers are expected to treat them as guidelines.

Essential Steps Recommended to the Teachers

Discussing on the basis of guidelines given above, the teacher may follow the following classroom techniques:

1. Initially the teacher should use simple sentences in English and allow students to listen and watch. They may act out their responses and try to respond in the target language, if they can. They should not be stopped from speaking and their expressions, if wrong, need not be corrected at that stage. This strategy will encourage students to speak fluently without any inhibition.
2. He/she should show concrete objects within classroom while speaking about them. He/she can use hand puppets and toys to act out scenes.
3. When the learners are ready to speak, the teacher may ask questions. Artificial questions are of no interest to students. It is either because their answers are already known or because no one cares about them.
4. The teacher should not insist on students' using complete sentences where a short answer is possible in a natural conversation.
   e.g. Teacher: Is that your book?
   Student: Yes.
5. When convenient, the teacher could talk about grammatical rules which are relevant at that point of teaching.
6. The teacher should create an atmosphere in which learners are relaxed and eager to learn.
7. The teacher should observe the most common social interaction in which students are interested and create a situation in which relevant, useful expressions are made available to them.

8. He/she should familiarize himself/herself with the general learning order in which structures should be presented in the class. For instance, a simple question follows a simple answer.

Teacher:	What is this?/	What is that?	What are those?
Student:	This is a book./	That is a pen	Those are pens.

After going through such introductory sentences, the teacher may explain the word-order in simple questions and their answers. While explaining the word-order in English, the teacher need not compare it with the word-order in the learners' mothertongue. Sentences with copula may be followed by sentences with other verbs in the simple present. They may be followed by sentences in the past tense using regular (weak) verbs. The next session may be devoted to sentences with most frequently used irregular verbs, such as *come, go, see, give, get, say, know, think, take, find, begin, become* and *tell* (which according to British National Corpus are the most frequently used verbs in English).

Important Points

1. By and large, the teacher is expected to follow the prescribed textbook. In case he/she feels that certain essential words/structures are missing that students need for conversation, he/she should introduce them early.
2. The teacher should encourage students to use their creative power in the English class. If need be, he/she could be unconventional in taking up an item that the students need but has not been provided in the curriculum at that stage.

Dulay, Burt and Krashen (1984, chapter X, Appendix A) include the teaching items in certain order. As it is based on the psycholinguistic research on the acquisition of L_2 by children, it should be paid special attention to. The goal of the developmental approach to language learning is to activate the learning device that is there in a child's mind. It should be the goal of the language teacher as well. However, he/she will be able to do so only when he/she is aware of the results of the research done in this area.

Developing the Four Skills

Of the four skills-listening, speaking, reading and writing- the development of listening skills should get the top priority. If a learner can hear and understand what is said, he/she gets motivated to learn the other skills much better.

Listening Comprehension

During the beginning stages of learning English, a new language for the non-native learner, listening exercises should be arranged in a planned manner. The teacher could begin with simple sentences (e.g. with copula verb *be: is, are, was, were*) and present sentences with English words which are familiar to students. Sentences with unfamiliar words and structures may be used in listening exercises much later. If the teacher is going to play a tape, he/she should make students familiar with the words they do not know. If they are going to see children's programme on television, the teacher may not know what words will be used. He/she should explain such words when the programme is over. Constant listening increases one's listening comprehension. Taped materials available for use are of limited value because very often they do not contain gradually developed interesting material and do not sound natural. Dialogues on televisions are more natural, though they may not be equally focussed. Ideally listening material would consist of highly interesting stories, nursery rhymes and poems that are graded. The existing material available on tapes or cassettes should be suitably adopted by the teacher.

Speaking Ability

Speaking requires the learner to retrieve precise sounds, words and sentences he/she has heard almost instantaneously. Initially the L_2 learner may articulate his/her sentences slowly and deliberately but he/she should remember that excessive slow delivery may make the listener uncomfortable. One can improve one's pronunciation, intonation and speed by producing sentences after listening to recorded messages. While the learner is speaking, there should not be any attempt to stop and correct him/her because overcorrection may produce hesitation or silence. Students trained in language laboratory learn to make a specific response to a specific cue but he/she may not respond instantaneously in a free conversation. The teacher should see to it that he/she learns to respond automatically. The audiolingual teacher tries to teach a controlled structure in advance so that the learner can apply the pattern accurately in a given situation. The developmental method asserts that if the student expresses his/her thought fluently; he/she will gain accuracy in course of time. The student does not learn to speak freely by listening to the tape or the lecture; he/she does so by conversing freely. The dialogue in which he/she is a participant must not have unnatural questions and answers.

The student should be introduced to the sounds of the language before their graphic-symbols (i.e. written forms). The teacher could begin with sounds that are relatively easy to pronounce and then concentrate on sounds that are difficult to pronounce (e.g./θ/,/ð/and/ʒ/for Indians learning to speak English). If training in the production of sounds does not precede learning to read, students may form the incorrect notion that letters of the alphabet represent the sounds. As it is widely assumed that graphemes represent sounds, students are likely to use incorrect sounds on the basis of the spelling of words. However, there is another point to note. Speaking becomes relevant only when the speaker knows the meaning of what he/she speaks. It is as true of primary school children as of advanced learners. One way of dealing with the situation is to explain the meaning of words they are going to use in advance. Some pedagogues believe that students should be familiarised with the letters in the very beginning of the programme. When most students have learnt the art of associating phonemes of the language with its graphemes, they are ready to learn to read.

Reading Ability

Except for some tribal languages in the north east of India which use Roman script, all Indian languages have their own scripts. Hindi uses the Nagri script and Urdu, the Perso-Arabic script. In all these languages a particular sound is represented by a particular letter of the alphabet. As this kind of sound-grapheme correlation does not exist in English, one's knowledge of the Roman script does not guarantee that one can read English correctly. It is a priority task of the teacher to enable his/her students to acquire the ability to associate graphic symbols with sounds (See pp. 65-68 for some useful hints). All Indian students, except the speakers of Urdu, have the habit of scanning sentences from left to right which is of advantage while learning to read English.

Trying to learn English from the very beginning of primary education has one advantage. The learner does not find attempts to learn very simple sentences such as *Look, Raman look* or *he runs fast* childish; they can take any sentence in their stride without feeling ridiculous about it. If reading is preceded by learning to listen and speak, students may come across sentences they have heard or spoken earlier. During the process of learning to read, the following procedure may be followed:

(i) Students may keep the book closed and listen to the teacher while he/she reads a paragraph.
(ii) Then they open the book and imitate the teacher aloud as a group.
(iii) The teacher asks some students to read the passage, one by one at random.
(iv) While students are reading aloud, the teacher follows their response. He/she reads the utterance correctly at the end.
(v) After students have learnt to read the passage in an acceptable manner, the teacher notes down on the black/white board words and expressions which are unfamiliar to them. He/she may ask students whether some more items need to be added to the list.
(vi) The teacher explains the expressions unknown to students.
(vii) He/she asks students to read the passage quietly once more.
(viii) He/she asks questions to find out whether students have comprehended the passage. If some students do not give the expected answers, others can, which will not go unnoticed in the class.

Acquiring New Words

While reading a new material, students will come across new words and expressions. They may infer their meanings from the context or guess them in a logical way. Even then they will have some words whose meanings they are not able to guess. At that point the teacher will put the unknown word in a relevant context with which students are familiar. If all efforts fail, he/she will rephrase the given expression in such a way that its meaning becomes clear. When students are advanced, the process of vocabulary building may be explained to them. Given a word, they may be asked to come up with other words derived by a similar process (e.g. adding a prefix or suffix).

Graded Reading Material

Advanced students may be exposed to graded reading materials. At every stage, efforts should be made to find out how much they have comprehended. The goal should be to have fully prepared students who can read and understand any text they come across in a subject of their interest.

Usually our language teacher asks all students of a specific class to read the same book at the same speed, chapter by chapter. This method is redundant for students with better reading ability. It is better to let such students read books of higher complexity and submit their reports to the class. It will make the atmosphere more competitive.

Writing Skills

At the initial level, writing in English involves the skills of writing in the Roman script. The first grade children should be taught to practise it well. Then comes the skills of writing words with correct spellings and sentences in correct word-order. Students will learn them by copying sentences from the workbook, practising dictation and learning how to put scrambled sentences in correct word order.

Copying and Writing Dictation

One can start with simple sentences which one has mastered while acquiring the skills of how to listen, speak and read. If it is practised properly, the writing exercise will reinforce these skills. After the student has finished the first act of copying, the teacher should check it carefully to see that each line has been copied well. He/she should check all punctuation marks and other orthographic features. Next is the task of writing dictation. The teacher should go through the dictated material to see whether punctuation marks have been used correctly and other requirements have been met. The student should copy the words from the book correctly and then practise writing them from memory. They may be asked to fill up the blanks in a given text. The teacher would check whether these assignments have been done correctly.

Writing Coherently

Once student has established control over the sound letter correspondence by means of using copying and dictation exercises, the teacher should encourage them to begin to work on self-expression. In the first phase they should learn how to combine and expand sentences. As soon as they have learnt them, they should be taught to write logically coherent sentences in a paragraph. For instance, the student could write a paragraph on *'My best friend'*. The teacher could help him/her by asking question such as:

> What is the name of your friend?
> How old is he/she?
> Where does he/she live?
> What things do you do together?
> Why do you like him/her?

The student could be encouraged to write the summary of a story he/she has read or heard. The teacher could help him/her by asking a series of questions. Such assignment will prepare the learner to write a piece of free composition. They could be given examples of personal and formal letter writing and asked to write their own letters on their patterns. Well-motivated students could be encouraged to try their hands at creative writing.

Enriched Vocabulary

One more point. The student should be constantly encouraged to increase his/her vocabulary. He/she should also pay attention to the basic rules of grammar while learning the four skills. The better vocabulary he/she has, the easier it is for him/her to make a productive use of the language. Their grammatical awareness means the ability to use specific types of sentences for specific purposes, whether in speech or writing. Words and forms of sentences are essential tools at one's disposal while one tries to express oneself. They must be enriched to develop communication skills.

Medium of Teaching English in India

Earlier in the chapter, we have referred to the Grammar-Translation method of teaching second language which was essentially bilingual. We have also pointed out that the Direct Method is primarily monolingual. In so far as India is concerned, John Miller's (1797) method was bilingual. He presented the material in such a way that Bangla speakers could use it to learn English and English speakers to learn Bangla.

Micheal West

Micheal West (1922-1934) was influenced by the Direct Method, as is obvious from his insistence on the technique of question-answer and substitution tables.

However, he recommended the bilingual method for teaching English in India, as is clear from *Bilingualism, with special reference to Bengal* (1926). Since most Indian children dropped out of school, and needed English only for reading for knowledge, he argued that bilingualism was needed in India "for the intellectual, emotional and moral development of the child". He wanted Indian children to acquire 'minimum adequate vocabulary' but it is not clear whether he wanted them to use a bilingual dictionary. However, teacher trainers in India were heavily influenced by Henry Sweet and Harold Palmer and favoured Direct Method. This continued even after Second World War and teacher training colleges emphasized the methodology developed by structural linguists. It was much later in 1980s that the communicative method became important. As all three methods favoured monolingulism, they kept on emphasising that only English should be used to teach English.

Sastri's Bilingual Method

In 1960s HNL Sastri of the Central Institute of English, Hyderabad came out in favour of bilingual method but he had very limited impact on the methodology of teaching English in India. However, bilingual approach continued as a method in schools in rural India, as a residue of the traditional Grammar Translation Method. Some Indian teachers use a regional language to explain the vocabulary of English and sometimes for grammatical explanations. More or less the same method continues in some schools even now.

BILINGUAL OR MONOLINGUAL METHOD?

The debate on bilingual vs. monolingual method has heated up recently. In Canada the Immersion Teaching Programme has been favoured whereby two languages-English and French-are used as media of instruction in schools. Under the programme some selected subjects are taught in French to English-speaking children in Onterio. The scheme has proved successful and been adopted to teach minority children in two languages- their mothertongue and the national language (e.g. French or German) in Europe. In some states in the USA, Spanish-speaking children have two languages as media of instruction: English and Spanish. As Cranston (1974) points out "both languages are used for the same student population-not as an isolated effort but as a key component of a programme embracing a total curriculum". (as quoted by Alatis (1975:3). The Knowledge Commission of India (2007) has adopted a similar scheme. It has recommended that a selected subject be taught through the medium of English from class III of the primary schools. In short, the primary education in India is going to be bilingual. However, it does not make the teaching of English bilingual at the primary level. For instance, it has not recommended that English be taught through the medium of Hindi or a regional language.

The question is: should Hindi or a regional language not be used at all in the English language classroom in India? The experts are divided on such an issue in the USA. Some linguists and educationist believe that, since the young children are so deeply under the influence of their mothertongue that no amount of Direct Method teaching can override it, it is better to capitalise upon their knowledge of the mothertongue. Not all methodologists would totally agree on these points. Some of them would be in favour of explaining the meaning of some expressions in the mothertongue. Such a technique is needed particularly in the beginning of the second language teaching. For instance, the meaning of some common verbs in English *come, go, get, use* can be conveyed by demonstration, but what about other common verbs such as *know, think, mean, seem* etc. which are also on the list of twenty most frequently used verbs in English. According to *Oxford Dictionary of English (ODE)* (2005) *know* means 'to be aware of through observation, inquiry or information'. Its Hindi equivalent is *jaannaa.* If it is used in the class, the child would immediately understand what it means. On the other hand, if the dictionary meaning is given to a first year primary school child, he/she may feel wildered. *Time, life, way, system* and *case* are some of the most frequently used nouns in English. *Life*, according to the ODE means 'the condition that distinguishes animals and plants from inorganic matters, including the condition for growth, reproduction…' or "the existence of an individual human being or animal". None of these explanation can be comprehended by the young learners of English. However, if the Hindi word *jeevan* or *zindagi* is used, they will get an idea of what the word stands for. Similarly, the use of the mothertongue is advantageous if the child's doubts are to be removed or some grammatical points are to be explained in the beginning of elementary classes.

Some experts are against the use of the mothertongue even in a case when grammatical explanation is to be given or a concept has to be explained. In view of the controversy surrounding this issue, we leave it undecided.

We conclude that genuine learning includes the ability to apply the target language to the world of reality and all methodologies must keep this objective in view. Learning the second language (i.e. English) as a fluent vehicle of expression needs a dynamic approach. We favour the developmental method of teaching how to generate them, the communicative method to understand their functions, and the audiolingual method to enable students to pronounce English expressions correctly. One may have a bilingual approach to let the second language learners have the meaning of words clearly understood.

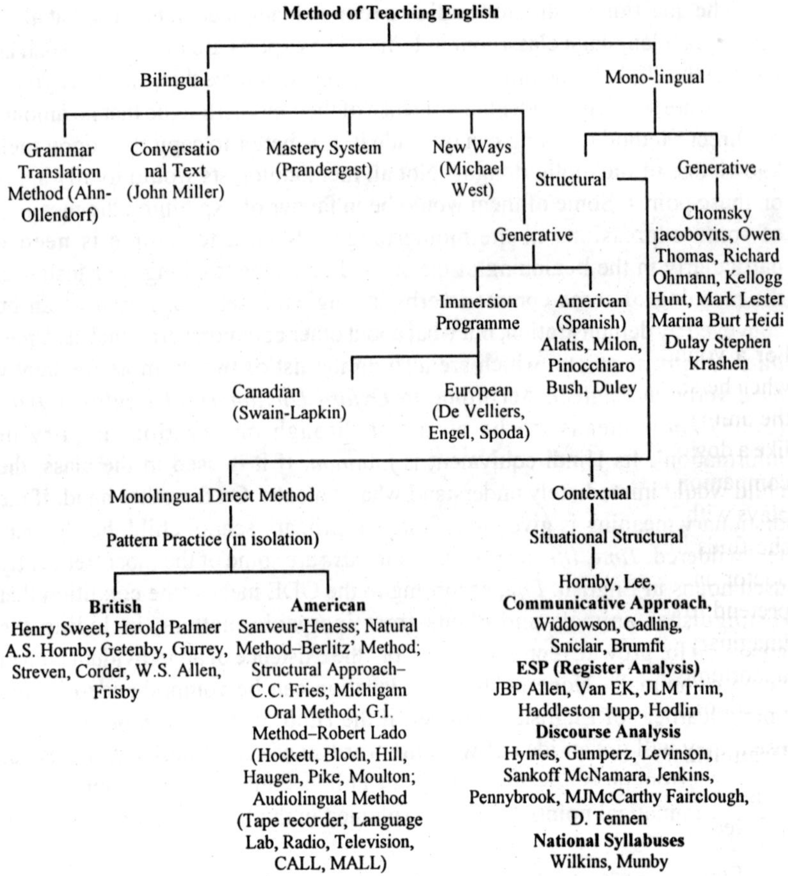
Method of Teaching English
Bilingual
Mono-lingual
Grammar Translation Method (Ahn-Ollendorf)
Conversational Text (John Miller)
Mastery System (Prandergast)
New Ways (Michael West)
Structural
Generative
Chomsky jacobovits, Owen Thomas, Richard Ohmann, Kellogg Hunt, Mark Lester Marina Burt Heidi Dulay Stephen Krashen
Generative
Immersion Programme
American (Spanish) Alatis, Milon, Pinocchiaro Bush, Duley
Canadian (Swain-Lapkin)
European (De Velliers, Engel, Spoda)
Monolingual Direct Method
Pattern Practice (in isolation)
British
Henry Sweet, Herold Palmer A.S. Hornby Getenby, Gurrey, Streven, Corder, W.S. Allen, Frisby
American
Sanveur-Heness; Natural Method–Berlitz' Method; Structural Approach–C.C. Fries; Michigam Oral Method; G.I. Method–Robert Lado (Hockett, Bloch, Hill, Haugen, Pike, Moulton; Audiolingual Method (Tape recorder, Language Lab, Radio, Television, CALL, MALL)
Contextual
Situational Structural
Hornby, Lee,
Communicative Approach,
Widdowson, Cadling, Sniclair, Brumfit
ESP (Register Analysis)
JBP Allen, Van EK, JLM Trim, Haddleston Jupp, Hodlin
Discourse Analysis
Hymes, Gumperz, Levinson, Sankoff McNamara, Jenkins, Pennybrook, MJMcCarthy Fairclough, D. Tennen
National Syllabuses
Wilkins, Munby

14

Developing Material Aids for Language Teaching

For a young child dramatization is natural and spontaneous. For instance, when he/she looks at a picture book, he/she likes to demonstrate what each of the animals in the book looks and behaves like. He/she likes to run or bark like a dog or move like a cat. A pre-nursery school child may have an imaginary companion if a real one is not available. He/she talks to that companion, plays with him/her, shows his pleasure or anger and does to him/her what he/she finds his/her parents doing to him/her. He/she may play the role of the doctor and examine a toy or any object as if it is a sick patient. He/she may pretend to be a shopkeeper and sell chocolates and other goodies to his/her imaginary customers. When he/she starts going to school, he/she misses the opportunity to play the role of his/her choice. If such opportunities are provided in school, going there will be a fun for him/her.

Dramatization in Grade I Classroom

"Baa, baa, black sheep" is a favourite nursery rhyme which can be easily enacted in the class. Two students can play the roles.

First student: 'Baa, baa, black sheep
Have you any wool?
Second student: 'Yes sir, yes sir
Three bags full.

The first student could be without any costume. The second could have a piece of black cloth over him/her. He/she may carry three bags and point at them while speaking 'three bags full'. He/she may point his/her finger at one bag and say,

'One for the master'

And shift the finger to another bag and say,

'And one for the dame'

He/she may finally point at the third bag and say,

'And one for the little boy'.

He/she may look at a distance while saying

'Who lives down the lane'

To enact Jack and Jill, the boys who play their roles could use crowns made of cardboard. Besides, they need an empty pitcher or bucket which they carry to fill up with water. Jack can fall down and break his crown, Jill may follow him clumsily and fall down all of a sudden. This dramatization is easy and makes the meaning of the poem clear to the beginner.

The children may enact the *Punchatantra* story "The stork and the crab". One boy will pretend to be the stork and the other, the crab. The stork will talk to the crab about the coming draught and the crab will convey the message to the assembly of fish and crabs. As proposed by the stork, each day a fish will come to him. The boy/girl pretending to be the fish will climb up the back of the stork who will carry him/her to an isolated place in the classroom and pretend to kill him. This act will be repeated and several students acting as the fish will be 'killed' Finally the crab will ride on the back of the stork and guess what was going to happen. He will strangulate the stork and carry his head to show it to other fish and crabs. Children will enjoy having a ride on the back of the child who acts as the stork. Likewise, all the stories narrated by the teacher to the class can be enacted. The children will not only have 'fun' but also a clear comprehension of what is narrated. The class may have a *costume box* to supply suitable apparel to children. It may have *makeup* box as well.

The teacher has to see to it that the story that is going to be dramatized is suitable for the children of a specific age group. The lower their age is, the simpler the story should be. We may point out that the children of eight to twelve years enjoy enacting a story as much as four to seven years. The children of the older age group are more interested in 'genuine' acting and need more time to prepare for dramatization. These children understand that they are playing roles of various characters whereas the younger children think they are the characters.

Dialogues

The teacher can arrange short dialogues among students. A dialogue may refer to an activity in their daily life or an event in a textbook. It could be based on an anecdote or a real or imaginary event. A child may pretend to be a fruit vender or a snack seller. Whatever the case may be, the act must appear to be realistic. The children should not be encouraged to memorize the lines and repeat them mechanically on the stage. They should be in their natural form and enjoy whatever they are doing.

Puppets and Marionettes

Young children of primary schools can handle puppets of various kinds. Puppets made of used bottles and cans can be pushed around on a table as though they are real characters. Their dialogue are spoken by the children who push them around. Such puppets cost almost nothing. Primary school children like to handle hand puppets. They may be made of paper bags or scraps of cloth. Alternatively dolls made of cloth or wood may be bought from the market and used. Senior children like to handle marionette (puppets which work by strings). They can be manipulated by hand to indicate their movement and action. They can produce a puppet play based on a story they have read in the class. Pantomime[1] and shadow plays can be better handled by children of senior classes.

A primary school teacher at Kakinada, Andhra Pradesh has used puppetry to attract students from fishermen hamlets to his school. He explains his lessons with the help of puppets in the form of conversation between two persons, two criminals or a man and an animal. He uses not only shadow puppets but also glove puppets, rod puppets and string puppets along with ventriloquial[2] puppets. He converts waste materials into attractive puppets and uses them to teach academic topics.

If children can dramatize what they read, they are 'doers' rather than mute observers. They absorb what they read but also entertain themselves by acting out whatever they have experienced while reading the story. Since, young children do not bothers about the setting on the stage and are happy to dramatize the event they have just read, their production costs almost nothing.

Songs and Choral[3] Readings

Young children like nursery rhymes and poems through listening. Tapes and cassettes can be used in the classroom to entertain and educate them. They are not very costly and are easily available. After listening to the tape/cassette, the children are in a mood to sing. If they are given a chance to get involved in choral singing, they feel great. Choral singing improves their voice quality. They learn how to articulate, enunciate and capture the rhythm and flow of what they are singing. Even inattentive children are swept into the experience when they participate in a group activity and share the enthusiasm of others. Timid children become enthusiastic and aggressive children submerge themselves in the group.

Comic Posters

Since children like to read comic books, they should be made available. Even very young children who cannot read like to have a good look at comic posters. The teachers may prepare his/her own posters by cutting them from old

1. A dramatic entertainment in which performers use gestures rather than words to convey meaning.
2. Whose voice appear to come from somewhere else.
3. Composed for or sang by a choir.

newspapers and magazines and pasting them in the classroom. Some comic books contain stories familiar to children. They may be displayed when such stories are likely to be read in the class.

Cartoons

A vigilant teacher can collect cartoons of children's interest and display them in the class. He/she can get photographs/pictures which are relevant to understand a prescribed text and use them on appropriate occasions.

Flash Cards

Cardboards can be used to make appropriate flash cards. For instance, a small flash card may contain a word on one side and its picture/sketch on the other. The teacher may show the picture/sketch to students and ask them to give its name. Another type of flash cards may have a word on one side and its meaning on the other. Flash cards may be used to teach correct pronunciation of words; such cards may have words on one side and their pronunciation on the other. They can be used to enrich the vocabulary of children.

Charts

The teacher may prepare charts to give relevant information on specific topics. Each chart may have a specific piece of information in attractive colour or print. A chart displays materials in a systematic manner and can be permanently on display in the classroom. Flow charts can be prepared to show the connection between different parts of a word formation system or between grammatical categories.

Pictures

Pictures depicting scenes of various phenomena can be collected and displayed to decorate the classroom. Each of them could be a theme for narrating its content orally or in writing. They can be topics for conversation. They can also be used for building vocabulary. Slides could be made to capture various scenes. The images of transparencies can be projected on the screen with the help of an overhead projector. The person who handles the projector can manipulate the projected material to highlight a point.

Language Laboratory

Language laboratory usually contains mechanical equipment to hear and repeat materials recorded in a language (e.g. English). Students can listen through earphones, repeat words and sentences through a microphone and record their own voice on a disc or tape. Later on, they can play back their own recordings and compare their voice with the model voice. An alert student can find out his/her own shortcomings and try to remove them. The teacher can monitor and hear his/her voice and suggest corrections. The laboratory may have a monitoring system which is centrally controlled. It gives students a chance to listen and speak in a systematic manner.

The student can benefit from practising in the laboratory if the tapes are of good quality and he/she practises regularly. It is necessary that the materials are varied and played at a normal speed. The laboratory provides regular practice in listening to model voices and enables students to reproduce them approximately correctly. However, recent research suggests that drilling sentence structures is not of much use. However, regular practice of sounds and words can not only improve his/her pronunciation and enrich his/her vocabulary but also his/her self-expression.

The situation in India is not very encouraging. Many schools cannot have language laboratory because of lack of infrastructure (e.g. space trained teacher and finance). In urban areas several neighbourhood schools can pool their resources and have a central laboratory. However, they need to coordinate the use of time and space and agree upon the proper maintenance of equipment.

Information and Computing Technology (ICT)

Recent advance in information and computing technology has made it convenient to arrange for Computer-Assisted Language Learning (CALL). It has made it possible for students to work on their individual computers at their own convenience. It has facilitated the incorporation of audio and video input in a learning programme. The best of the available programmes are interactive; they tailor their input and task to the progress of individual learners.

The computer has provision for programmed instruction which has the following characteristics:

(i) Each lesson has a precise description of the target language utterances.
(ii) The course content is divided into small, closely-knit units called 'frames'
(iii) The learner goes through the programme at his/her own speed.
(iv) The learner is immediately informed of his/her achievement after the completion of each unit.

The main thrust of the programme is on grammar and vocabulary of English. Recently programmes for listening comprehension and reading comprehension skills have been added. The initial programmes were based on the behaviourist theory of habit formation. Attempts are being made to make them communicative. However, there are problems. In a communicative situation, the reaction of the participants is not easily predictable. Nevertheless, some aspects of phonetics are programmable. They have been programmed.

Primary school children can use the programmes that aim at improving their pronunciation. The programmes concerned with vocabulary building and structure practices can be used in a limited way. The methodology has shifted from the *programme-assisted instruction* to *programmed instruction.*

Computer Assisted Language Learning (CALL)

Indian experts should pay attention to the kind of help computer can give to primary school students and come up with suitable programmed instruction. The goal of this instruction should be to help young children all over India to acquire pronunciation which is nationally acceptable.

Mobile Assisted Language Learning (MALL)

The next development in the ICT is the use of the mobile in language teaching/ learning. It is called *Mobile Assisted Language Learning* (MALL). So far, it has been used to produce materials that can be used at a higher level. This programme is interactive. It has produced connected material for use by advance learners. There is no reason why it cannot be done for beginners. Since, mobile is an instrument which everybody uses freely these days, children will be able to use it if suitable teaching material is available.

Multimedia Approach

Experts advocate a multi-media approach in second/foreign language teaching. However it will be successful at the primary school level only if the quality of the material improves. Sylvie Thouësny and Linda Bradley (2011) contains various articles involving the use of the computer for second language teaching. The book reports that the available CALL software enables learners of L_2 to be independent only to a limited extent. It also points out that suitable materials are not available for primary school children. We hope that there will be an improvement in the situation and new material will be available to be used successfully. Meanwhile teachers are expected to utilize all the aids available to them locally. It is necessary that the language classroom has all the necessary fittings to use the equipment properly.

In short,

- posters, cartoons, flash cards, charts and pictures could be prepared locally or arranged by the teacher as teaching aids.
- He/she can use puppets and marionettes for dramatisation of lessons. Students could play the roles of different characters. They should be provided with costumes and other objects for staging a drama.
- Language laboratory should be equipped with necessary materials.
- Information and computing technology should be made available. Besides, CALLs, MALLs could also be used.

UNIT V: ASSESSMENT AND EVALUATION

15

Assessment of Learners

Assessment/Achievement Test

To assess means "to evaluate or estimate the nature, ability or quality of a person or thing". Assessment is the action of assessing how much a candidate has achieved after going through a programme. We can call such a test *"achievement test"*. It is closely related to a curriculum. It evaluates how much has been acquired by students with reference to how much has been taught by the teacher. Thus, it determines the gap between an attempt to teach and what has been learnt. The pedagogues can find ways to fill up the gap by suggesting suitable remedial measures. An achievement test can be administered at the end of a course. It can be also be used to test a simple unit within a course.

Summative Test

Another kinds of evaluation that takes place at the end of a programme is called summative test. It evaluates the programme as a whole. 'Summative' means the 'process of adding things together'. It implies that a summative test covers testing everything that was discussed in a course designed for a specified period. It differs from the achievement test in the sense that it can only be administered when a programme is supposed to be complete whereas an achievement test can be organised at any time during the programme and also at the end.

Diagnostic Test

A diagnostic test gives much more information than achievement test. While the latter answers the question how much the learner knows, the former finds out what the learners knows or does not know. It suggest a programme of revising what the learner has failed to learn. We think the diagnostic test is most appropriate to evaluate the progress of students in a course.

Assessment of Listening Ability

The goal of evaluating listening ability is to find out whether the learner

- is able to hear meaningful sounds in English when they are spoken at a normal speed.
- is able to note all the changes in meaning caused by the modification of word-forms (e.g. between *class* vs. *classes,* or between *eat, eats, ate* and has *eaten*)
- understands words in normal, conversational context,
- discovers the meaning of an utterance in a specific context e.g. the difference between the indicative sentence *He will not come* and the question *he will not come*?

The student may be shown a clock on the wall or elsewhere and asked, 'what is it?' The teacher may note the response. If the student says/klɔk/, the response is correct. If he/she intends to say *clock* but says *cloak*/kləuk/, the response is wrong. It means, he/she is not able to listen to the difference between /ɔ/ and /əʊ/. Likewise, he/she may hear/t^h/ for/θ/, and/dʒ/for/z/, i.e. he/she hears/t^hænk/for/θænk/and/dʒest/for/zest/. Those students who fail to make phonemic sound contrasts can be grouped together for further practice.

At the morphological level the teacher may note whether the students differentiate between cats/kæts/, dogs/dɒgz/and churches/tʃəːtʃiz/with reference to the pronunciation of the plural marker –s. Likewise he/she may find out whether they differentiate between/t/,/d/and/ɪd/with reference to the past tense marker –d (as in *slept*, *dragged*/drægd/and *minded*/maindid/.

At the syntactic level, the teacher should find out whether the learner makes a tonal difference while listening to:

He is going home.
He is going home?

The listening comprehension of the children may be tested by telling them a very simple story in English which they might have heard at home in their mothertongue. The teacher may ask questions to test their comprehension. Alternatively, they may be asked to retell the story they have just heard. The responses of the children will point out whether they comprehended the story completely, partially or not at all.

Assessment of Speaking Ability

The teacher may ask simple questions about the student, his parents, home, neighbourhood or school. He/she should listen to the answer carefully with a view to finding out whether the student

- pronounces the sounds correctly.
- uses correct stress and intonation, and
- speaks at a normal speed (and does not halt unnecessarily)

Another way to test the listening and speaking abilities of the student is to engage him/her in conversation. The teacher will pay attention to his/her pronunciation, stress and intonation.

A third way is to ask the student to narrate a story or any anecdote of his/her choice. The teacher pays attention to his/her pronunciation and enunciation rather than to the content.

Yet another way is to show the students a picture or a series of connected pictures and ask them to describe what they have seen. Likewise, they may be shown the clip of a cartoon or a scene from a movie and asked to describe it.

Listening and speaking are two aspects of oral communication. The questions we have discussed involve one's ability to hear and speak. In the course of a mid-term evaluation the teacher may come across students who can-

- listen to and speak all sounds and their combinations correctly,
- listen to an utterance correctly but cannot speak it out well, or
- neither listen accurately nor speak correctly.

The class may be divide into three sub-groups if all the three types of students are there. Reinforcement practice may be done according to the needs of the sub-groups

Assessment of Reading Ability

The test on reading ability may cover two areas: (i) reading aloud and (ii) reading silently.

Reading aloud requires active manipulation of speech organ. When a student is reading aloud, the teacher should concentrate to find out whether he/she is producing the sounds of English accurately. During the first few years, the target should be to enable the learner to do so. If he/she can read short sentences correctly, with proper pronunciation, stress and intonation, he/she has considerable achievement to his/her credit. A student who has practised reading aloud, will not be hesitant to do so. He/she will not read letter-by-letter or word by word. He/she will have a pause only when it is needed. If he/she followed the intonation pattern of a sentence, he/she will succeed in conveying the intended meaning.

The teacher should try to access whether the student has developed ability to recognise:

- similarities and differences in sounds,
- the letter-sound correlation,
- similarities and difference in words,

- Similarities and difference in reading various types of sentences he/she has become familiar with,
- The significance of modulation of his/her voice while reading a dialogue.

Some experts think that, while listening to a student reading aloud, the teacher may be subjective and even arbitrary. He/she can avoid being so if he/she is guided by a clear criterion. A student who reads fluently with good pronunciation and enunciation could be awarded a 'good' grade, a student whose delivery is comprehensible but makes a few mistakes may be awarded a 'satisfactory' grade and the one who has a hesitant delivery and makes many mistakes should be graded 'unsatisfactory'.

Developing Reading Practice

The beginner should always be asked to read aloud, but at an advanced stage of primary classes he/she could be asked to practise silent reading. He/she could be given a short passage which he/she is able to read within a fixed time. The administration of timed test is justified because the ultimate goal of reading is to develop the ability to read rapidly and yet comprehend the meaning. A normal reading requires an instantaneous grasp of meaning by the reader. In short, the student who can comprehend most items in the shortest possible time is a good reader.

After the student has read a given passage within the fixed time, he/she should be able to answer short comprehension questions. In the beginning the teacher may ask such questions which may be answered in 'yes' or 'no'. It should follow with questions which contain the answer (e.g. is it Monday or Tuesday today?). Once the learner gets used to such questions, a questions-word question may be asked (e.g. How is the weather today?)

Vocabulary

A reasonable knowledge of vocabulary is needed to answer comprehension questions. The teacher should note whether there is a new word in the passage. He/she should pronounce it and explain its meaning before the student is asked to read silently.

If the student exhibits slowness in reading, the teacher should help him/her in the process of word recognition. He/she should show how a small word becomes large with the help of prefixes and suffixes. If a student displays faulty eye-movement and fails to recognize the word correctly, it may not always be because of lack of familiarity with the word; it may be due to his/her nervousness or unwanted self-consciousness. The teacher should diagnose the problem accurately and begin afresh with very simple reading material.

Assessment of Writing Ability

As the writing is the final stage in the four stages of language learning sequence, the student's ability to write depends on whether he/she can recall what he/she has learnt while learning to speak and read. As the writing system of English is different from the systems that various Indian languages have, the initial stage of testing involves finding out whether the student has learnt to read the printed words and whether he/she knows to what extent hand written letters are different from printed letters in words. If he/she does not know it, he/she should be shown the difference. He/she should practise *cursive writing*, first in isolation and then in words. Well-planned and controlled exercises help students to write correctly within a short period. Students may begin copying, writing dictation, writing simple structures and then writing a paragraph. The teacher can ask questions to find out whether the student has learnt correct spelling of words he/she already knows and whether he/she knows when to use capital letters and punctuation marks.

Dictation

As students progress, they may be dictated long and more difficult passages. While dictating the passage, the teacher may read it at a slow speed. As dictation is not a speed test, he/she may not read it at a normal speed. The idea is to test the ability of the student to write down the dictation correctly and the assignment should be looked at from that point of view. The teacher should correct the answers, note down the errors and comment on them at the right moment.

When students get used to dictation writing, they should be guided to write *controlled compositions*. They may be shown a scene and asked to describe it. The topic should be such that students do not feel helpless because they do not know the structures they need to use or lack the necessary vocabulary.

Fill in the Blanks

Another exercise that may be undertaken is to ask students to *fill in the blanks*. They may be given a familiar passage from which certain words are missing. They may be asked to supply appropriate words. They may be content words or functional words but in either case, they must be familiar to students. The students of upper primary classes may be administered a *Cloze Test.* This test provides a text from which every *n*th word (e.g. fifth or tenth word) is deleted. The students are supposed to supply the deleted words. The test is more a test of one's vocabulary and grammar than of reading comprehension.

Types of Test

For comprehension test at this level, objective questions may be asked. They are of three types: (i) *close-ended,* (ii) *restricted,* and (iii) *open ended.* The main characteristics of a close-ended test is that the student has to choose from among the given answers. One type of close-ended question is to find out whether a given statement is *true* or *false* (for example, there are 31 days in June; True/False). In all cases there is only one relevant answer. Another is *matching questions* in which correlation combinations have to be selected.

For instance

Match the following

1. Tomato	seed
2. Carrot	tuber
3. Peas	root
4. Lettuce	fruit
5. Potato	bud

For a *multi choice question* the learner has to select a correct answer out of four given alternatives (e.g. choose the correct answer by writing A, B, C or D.)

Birds are the only living creatures which____

(a) ______can fly.
(b) ______have two feet.
(c) ______have feathers
(d) ______cannot fly.

(*Ans. C*)

Evaluating the Child's Growth

Studying the language growth of an individual is a challenging affair. It cannot be done entirely through objective tests. The most that such tests show is responses to arbitrarily selected items of skills and that is usually based on the respondent's memory. For instance, a student can fill in blanks correctly but misuse the same item in practical situations. Studying the language growth of the child means finding his/her ability to handle the language in all types of situations. For instance, the teacher may keep an eye on how the student uses the language while speaking to other students. A child may be silent and withdrawn while he/she is with his/her peers. Another child may be very chatty but careless about the use of words. Yet another may be aggressive, unpleasant and over-assertive.

Portfolios

The teacher can keep *anecdotal records* of each student's verbal performance. Such a record is of great value in assessing his/her linguistic ability. He/she can keep a portfolio[1] for each of his/her students in which he/she can record his/her day to day impression of the linguistic development of the child. Such an act will be an arduous task for the teacher but it will help him/her immensely in the overall assessment of students. The purpose of an exhaustive evaluation in the primary school is to find what each child has achieved and what kind of help he/she needs. A good evaluation programme centres around constructive guidance to students. It includes all aspects of learning, including the student's effort to learn and his/her attitude towards the second language. Recent research in the child language development has emphasized these factors very much.

Errors or Interlanguage[2]

In recent years the philosophy of language teaching has changed remarkably. For instance, what was traditionally viewed as errors or mistakes and had a stigma on language learners is now looked at positively as a sign of effort to learn the correct form. Errors are taken to be instances of "interlanguage", a version produced by the language learner in his/her effort to have the standard forms. A student who uses *many childs* for *many children* know that the adjective *many* must have a plural noun as its head but does not know that the word *child* has an irregular plural. That student is more advanced than the one who uses *many child,* because the latter does not know that *many* needs a plural noun. This way of treating errors is developmental and helps the teacher to adopt a suitable strategy for corrections.

Self-evaluation

Experience in self-evaluation helps the learner to have pride in achievement. It gives confidence that is more valuable than an achievement score. The child who sees himself/herself growing and finds satisfaction in that growth feels encouraged to attain a higher goal. If his/her peers admire his/her achievement and growth, it boosts up his/her morale. Genuine friendly interest in each other's growth among the peers provides incentive for further growth because children value the opinions of their peers.

The purpose of a good evaluation programme is in the quality of inspiration it gives to learners for their self-improvement. The teacher's job is

---

1. a large, thin flat case to keep records of a person's action and achievement.
2. language used by a second language learner in course of his language development. A different term for developmental errors.

to find out what each learner has achieved and what needs to be done to enable him/her to have further achievement. A good evaluation programme centres its attention upon constructive guidance and that is what a good teacher is supposed to give.

Comprehensive and Continuous Evaluation (CCE)

To evaluate is to form an opinion of the value of what is being or has been taught or 'to estimate'. According to Alan Davies (1990:85-88), it may be considered from three points of view: (i) what is being taught, (ii) what is learnt out of what is taught and (iii) whether what is being taught is really what we think it is. Alan assumes that testing is central to evaluation and proposes some kind of proficiency test, but such tests can be given periodically during the course and not continuously. If one wants to test his/her students continuously, i.e. without any interruption, such a test is not appropriate. In other words, continuous evaluation means assessment of student's progress throughout a course of study, as distinct from periodic examinations. Besides, it has got to be comprehensive, i.e. it should deal with all aspects of teaching/learning. For example, continuous oral evaluation will pay attention to all aspects of listening and speaking, i.e. whether the learner can hear the speech of the teacher and his/her peers clearly and respond to it appropriately. The same yardstick will apply to reading as well. From this point of view, writing involves not only attention to correct responses but also to accompanying attributes, i.e. whether the handwriting of the student is clear and contains no spelling mistake.

The idea of comprehensive and continuous evaluation is laudable, for it removes the anxiety that a student has at the time of a formal test. It pays attention to the overall growth of a student in the use of language. However, it is not an easy task for the language teacher to study the language growth of every child in a class. The written tests are standardized and easy to evaluate but a comprehensive and continuous evaluation implies that the teacher will keep an eye on all aspects of linguistic behaviour of all students in the class. Some children may be vocal and extrovert but other may be silent and withdrawn. The teacher has to provide equal opportunity to all his/her students. He/she will have to have a separate portfolio for each of them in which he/she will note down his/her overall impression on the linguistic behaviour of the child not only when he/she is responding to a question or participating in a classroom discussion, but also when he/she is interacting with other students. Such a keen observation is absolutely essential to form an impartial opinion on the development and learning problem of the child.

Comprehensive and continuous evaluation of a child in elementary classes is intended to find out what a child has achieved and what help he/she needs for his/her further development. Watching development rather than grading a child should be the goal of the teaching programme. If such a scheme of evaluation is provided from this point of view, and is sincerely executed, it gives impetus to the creative development of the child. We have already discussed the techniques which the teacher should adopt to make the language class a fun. We hope the system of evaluation will add further to the fun.

Remedial Measures

The teacher should draw conclusion from CCE and all types of tests he/she has administered during the course with a view to finding out what kind of remedial measures need to be taken. If some features of teaching have not had impact on all (or majority of) students, they should be revisited in the class. If only some students have failed to comprehend what was done in the class, they should be tutored separately. In either case, the lacuna must be removed. The teacher who administers a test from a positive point of view, will not fail to do so.

UNIT VI: PRACTICUM

16

Practicum

LESSON PLAN (FOR CLASS I OR II): LESSON 1

Recognition of Sounds

General objective: Listening and speaking English.
Main objective: Focus on listening some sounds of English.
Specific objective: To acquire the ability to differentiate between

(i) /s/and/ʃ/
(ii) /dʒ/,/z/and/ʒ/

Teaching Aids needed

- A piece of chalk, duster, blackboard
- Diagrams showing the articulation of
  (i) /s/and/ʃ/
  (ii) /dʒ/,/z/and/ʒ/
- Slides (or charts) showing the points and manner of articulation of these sounds.

Previous knowledge assumed

Familiarity with/s, ʃ, dʒ/among Hindi speakers and also of /z/among Urdu speakers and some Hindi speakers.

Introduction

The teacher tells students that Hindi- Urdu have sounds such as/s/,/ʃ/and/z/, though some speakers do not have/ʃ/or/z/in their dialects. None of them have the sound/ʒ/.

Presentation

The teacher produces these sounds and explains them with the help of diagrams and slides (Or charts) how they are produced.

- The teacher raises his/her soft palate. The tip and blade of his/her tongues make a slight contact with the upper alveolar ridge and the side rims of his/her tongue are in close contact with the upper side teeth. The air-stream escapes by means of a narrow grove in the centre of his/her tongue and causes friction between the tongue and the alveolar ridge. There is very little opening between his/her teeth so that friction is produced between the blade of the tongue and the alveolar ridge. /s/is pronounced when the friction is voiceless and/z/ when there is some vibration in the vocal cords.

For pronouncing/dʒ/and/z/, the soft palate is raised and the tip and blade of the tongue make a light contact with the alveolar ridge. At the same time the front of the tongue is raised in the direction of the hard palate and the side rims of the tongue are in direct contact with the upper side teeth. The air escapes in a diffused manner and the friction occurs in a more extensive area of the tongue and the roof the mouth. In the case of/dʒ/, the friction is voiceless whereas/z/has some vibration.

For producing/ʒ/the soft palate is raised. The airstream is obstructed by a closure between the tip, blade and rims of the tongue and upper alveolar ridge and side teeth. The front tongue is raised towards the hard palate for the release of the air with a friction. The closure is released slowly by letting the air escape in a diffuse manner over the central surface of the tongue. The friction occurs between the blade/front region of the tongue and the alveolar/front palatal section of the roof of the mouth. The vocal cords vibrate. The following chart captures the main points (Please see the relevant figures on Page 47):

Table 15.1: Some Consonants

sounds	voicing	duration	articulator	Point of articulation
s	voiceless	continuant	tip of the tongue	tooth ridge
ʃ	voiceless	continuant	front of the tongue	hard palate
z	voiced	continuant	tip of the tongue	tooth ridge
ʒ	voiced	continuant	front of the tongue	hard palate
dʒ	voiced	affricate	front of the tongue	hard palate

- After demonstrating how these sounds are pronounced in isolation, the teacher asks students to listen to the sound/s/in the following words:

sin/sɪn/, *sing*/sɪŋ/, *sink*/sɪŋk/, *some*/sʌm/, *pass*/pa:s/, *mass*/ma:s/, *boss*/bɒs/, *toss*/tɒs/.

- He/she pronounces the sound/ʃ/in the following words:
  She/ʃi:/, *sheep*/ʃi:p/, *shell*/ʃel/, *sheet*/ʃi:t/, *shall*/ʃæl/, *shame*/ʃeim/, *shampoo*/ʃæmpu:/, *show*/ʃəu/.
- He/she draws the attention of students to the contrast between/s/and /ʃ/.
  See/si:/and *she*/ʃi:/, *sell*/sel/and *shell*/ʃel/, *so*/səu/and *show*/ʃəu/, *same*/seim/and *shame*/ʃeim/, *suit*/su:t/and *shoot*/ʃu:t/.
- He/she asks them to listen to the following sentences:
  She showed the *same* thing without any *shame*.
  The man in the blue *suit* will not *shoot* the deer.
  She *saw* the *show*.
- Then he/she asks them to listen to the following sentence and tell which sound is /s/and which is /ʃ/.

She	sells	sea	shells	on the	sea	shore
1	2	3	4	5	6	7

Student1: first, fourth and seventh words begin with/ʃ/.
Student 2: the second, third and sixth words begin with/s/.
The teacher asks every student to speak the sentence in chorus.

ʃi: selz si: ʃelz ən ðə si: ʃɔə:

Teacher: I now produce words beginning with/z/, as in *zoom*/zu:m/, *zeal*/zi:l/, *zest*/zest/, *zoo*/zu:/, *zero*/zɪərəu/, *zip*/zɪp/.

The following words are pronounced with initial/dʒ/

gin/dʒɪn/, *jar*/dʒa:r/, *Jew*/dʒu:/, *Jewel*/dʒu:əl/, *Jam*/dʒæm/, *jungle*/dʒʌŋgl/, *Jute*/dʒu:t/.

- The following words have/dʒ/ sound
  Jazz/dʒæz/, *gems*/dʒemz/, *germs*/dʒə:mz/.
- Look at the contrast between/dʒ/and/z/sounds in the following words:
  Jest/dʒest/and *zest*/zest/, *Jealous*/dʒeləs/and *zealous*/zeləs/, *fudgy*/fʌdʒi/and *fuzzy*/fʌzi/.
- Now listen to the following:
  He made the *jest* with *zest*.
  He was *fuzzy* but *zealous*.
  She gave me something *fudgy* which made him entirely *jealous*.

In the first line which word begins with/dʒ/

Student 1: Jest.
Teacher: and/z/?
Student 2: zest.
Teacher: In the next two lines which word begins with/dʒ/?

Student 3: 'fudgy'
Teacher: and with/z/?
Student 4: *zest* and *zealous*.
Teacher: does *jealous* begin with/dʒ/or/z/?
Student:/dʒ/
Teacher: well done. Now practise the following sentences at home:

1. The judge of jazz music was judicious.
   /ðə dʒʌdʒ əʊ jæz mjuːzik wəs dʒuːdiʃəs/
2. To serve junk food was no joke for the zamindar.
   /tu səːʊ dʒʌŋk fuːd wəs nou dʒəuk fər ðə zəmindaː/
   By now you know how to differentiate between the sounds
   /s/from/ʃ/
   And/dʒ/from/z/.

The sound/ʒ/does not occur in many words.

- It does not occur in the beginning of a word in English.
- It occurs in the middle, as in *pleasure*/pleʒəː/, *leisure*/leʒəː/, *measure*/ məʒəː/.
- It occurs at the end of a word, as in *beige*/beiʒ/.
- Note the contrast between/dʒ/and/ʒ/:
  leisure/leʒə/and *ledger*/ledʒəː/,
  vision/viʒn/and *pigeon*/pidʒin/.

LESSON PLAN- 2 (FOR CLASS III)

Listening Comprehension

General objective: Listening and speaking English
Specific objective: Listening Comprehension
Task: Listen to the story and answer comprehension questions
Preparation: Vocabulary

Roam about- move about unsystematically
Desperate- showing little hope, hopelessness
Withdraw- retreat, leave a place
Hurried back- move back in haste
Look after- care

Teaching Aids- black board, pen, a piece of chalk, duster

Presentation

Teacher: Today, I will tell you the story of 'The Blue Jackal'. Listen carefully and be ready to answer questions that follow it.

"Once upon a time there was a jackal. He was very hungry. He roamed about the forest to get some food but failed. He became desperate and entered a city in search of food. He knew he was in danger of being attacked by men and dogs but he did not withdraw. Suddenly he was attacked by dogs. He ran fast and went into a house. It was the house of a dyer. It had a large tub full of blue dye. When dogs came close to him, he jumped into it. He hid himself there. The dogs could not find him and went away.

When the jackal came out of the tub, he was all blue. He hurried back to the forest. When other animals saw a blue creature, they were scared. They started running away. He shouted and asked them not to be afraid of him. He told them that he was their friend. God had sent him to protect them. The animals were assured. They took him as their protector and accepted him as their king. They declared their loyalty to him. They told him that they would supply him food regularly. They looked after him and he ruled over them. If they quarrelled, he judged their cases. He solved their day-to-day problems.

Once, when Jackal, the king, was holding his court, he heard a pack of jackals howling at a distance. He was pleased to hear their voice. He forgot that he was no longer a mere jackal but a king. He lifted his head up and howled. The animals knew now that he was merely a jackal. They rebelled against him and rushed at him. They wanted to kill him for he had cheated them. However, the jackal became alert and wanted to run away, but the tiger who was standing close to him killed him.

That is how the rule of the jackal ended."

Interaction: The teacher will give some time to students to recollect the gist of the story and then ask questions to find out whether they followed him.

Teacher : How did the jackal become blue?

Student 1 : Because he jumped into a tub full of blue coloured water.

Teacher : Why did he jump into the tub?

Student 2 : He wanted to save himself from the dogs who were attacking him.

Teacher : Why did the dogs attack him?

Student 3 : Because he had gone to the city in search of food. Dogs always attack a jackal when they see him.

Teacher : What happened next?

Student 4 : The dogs could not find him. When they were gone, he came out and ran towards the forest.

Teacher : What happened when he went to the forest?

Student 5 : When other animals saw a blue animal, they were afraid and started running away.

Teacher : What happened then?

Student 6 : The jackal asked them not to be afraid of him. He told them that God had sent him to protect other animals.

Teacher : Did the animals accept him among them?

Student 7 : Yes, Sir They accepted him as their king and decided to look after him well.
Student 8 : He became their protector and judge.
Teacher : What did he do as a judge?
Student 9 : He solved their disputes and gave them advice.
Teacher : What happened then?
Student 10 : One day he heard a pack of jackals howling at a distance. He was so pleased that he raised his head and howled.
Teacher : How did other animals react?
Student 11 : Other animals came to know that he was merely a jackal. They rebelled against him.
Teacher : Did the jackal die?
Student 12 : Sir, he was killed by a tiger.

Such a question and answer session will satisfy the teacher. It shows that the students had comprehended the story. If a student fails to answer, another student gets the chance to reply.

Recapitulation: The teacher will tell the students that the story had a moral. One can deceive others for sometime, but one day the truth is bound to come out.

A student: It shows how clever the jackal was. He took advantage of his new appearance and ruled over other animals for a while.

Teacher: That is true.

LESSON PLAN 3

READING

General objective: To develop the reading skill

Specific objective: To read and understand the text given to every student.

Manner of reading: It depends on the nature of the text. This has to be read for details.

Teaching aid: Pictures or drawings of butterflies; if possible, showing their evolution from eggs.

Pre-reading: The teacher gives some general information about butterflies. He/she tells students about the meta-morphosis of an insect egg into a butterfly. It goes through stages of development. The egg hatches into a caterpillar which becomes a pupa. It is in the resting stage before it breaks out of its case and becomes a fully grown insect.

Reading the Text

The text is made available to all students in the class. The teacher reads the text slowly and clearly so that it is audible to all. Then he asks students to read it silently.

THE BUTTERFLY

Butterflies are perhaps the most beautiful of the insect species. They are of several shapes, sizes and colours. They undergo several changes in life.

Butterflies are of several kinds. The Red Admiral Butterfly is very striking. There are Swallowtail Butterflies and grey butterflies ornamented with golden colour. Then there are blue butterflies and butterflies of brown colour with orange spots on the edges of its wings. The large blue butterflies are rarely seen.

1. Admiral 2. Swallowtail and Caterpillar 3. Adonis

Fig. 15.1: Butterflies

The female butterfly lays its eggs on leaves. She lays one egg per leaf. These eggs hatch in a week or two. The newly hatched eggs are known as caterpillars. They are very small. They can grow for days without being noticed. They shed their skins four or five times as they grow. After a caterpillar has molted a number of times, it wanders from feeding site and searches for a place to dangle from and pupate. After attaching its posterior end to an object, the caterpillar molts again. A different skin comes out which hardens with pupa. It reorganizes its body plan inside the pupa and finally emerges as an adult butterfly.

- The teacher allows the student to read the text silently and then asks them if they know all the words used in the text. He asks them to guess their meanings.
  He asks them: What does *hatch* means?
  No student answers. Then he explains.
  Teacher: To *hatch* means to come out of an egg.
  Again he asks: What does *shed* means?
  One student: to change.
  Teacher: Yes, it means 'to allow its skin to come off'.
  What does *wander* mean?
  Another student: 'to move'
  Teacher: Yes, it means 'to move in a leisurely way'
  Teacher: What does *dangle* mean?
  No students responds.
  Teacher: To *dangle* means 'to hang from', 'to swing'.
  To *pupate* means 'to develop into pupa'.
  Pupa is an immature form of an insect between larva and adult.
  Now, what does *reorganise* mean?
  A student: organises.
  Teacher: It means organizes again 'to change the way it is organised.
  What does *emerge* mean?
  Another student: It means 'to come out'.
  Teacher: Now that you know the meaning of every word, read the passage again.

Post-reading

After some time, the teacher asks the following questions:

1. What are the butterflies like?
2. Do they go through changes in their life?
3. What is the first change of a butterfly?
4. When does an egg become a caterpillar?
5. When does a caterpillar become a pupa?
6. When does a caterpillar become a butterfly?
7. Does a butterfly undergo any further change?

Some more questions may be asked.

8. When does the female butterfly lay its eggs?
9. Does it lay all its eggs at the same place?
10. How much time is needed for an egg to be hatched?
11. What is molting?

- The teacher can explain that molting is a process the caterpillar undergoes before it turns into a pupa.

12. What does a pupa look like?
13. Is it the same as the butterfly.

- The teacher will patiently wait for the answer.
- He/she will not interrupt a student while he/she is speaking.
- He/she will not make any grammatical correction.
- His/her aim is to encourage the student to speak fluently. The correction can be made after the student has stopped.

Recapitulation

After the question answer session, the teacher asks students to write about *butterflies.* It will be a home assignment.

LESSON PLAN 4 FOR CLASS IV

WRITING

General objective: To cultivate the habit of writing composition.

- How to choose the topic
- How to think of several ideas on the topic.
- How to put these ideas into sentences.
- How to organise and connect those sentences around this topic.
- How to conclude.

Specific objective: To write a passage on *Kite Flying*

Preparation-

Material: To have a picture involving a scene of children flying kites.

Language: words for various colour and shapes of kites.

Background brief by the teacher

Teacher: Kite flying is a very old hobby. Children love to fly kite. It needs a lot of preparation. One must have an attractive kite, good and strong thread, a good roller to which the thread is tied and the skill to control the movement of the kite while it flies. The kite should be made of good quality paper. Its frame should be light. Only then it will withstand the wind. It must not be very heavy. Otherwise it will not start flying. The kite flyer must be able to move quickly to keep the flying kite under his/her control.

There are kites of various types. Artisans in Delhi and other cities make kites of various designs, kites which look like birds, animals and other objects.

Children as well as grown up people fly kites. It is fashionable to do so in Delhi on Independence Day, Deepawali and other festivals. You must have an experience of flying kite. If you do not have it so far, try it, you will enjoy it.

The teacher shows a picture of a kite flying in the class (See Fig. 15.2) and asks students to tell him what they see. There are some questions the answer to which tell us about the scene.

Fig. 15.2: Kite Flying

1. What is the picture about?
2. What does it show?
3. Who are flying kites?
4. Where are they flying kites? Are they in a room or in an open space?
5. Where are the kites? Are they in the hands of the children?
6. How do the children keep control over their kites?
7. What do the kites look like? Are they white or coloured?
8. What colour do they have?
9. What shape do the kites have?
10. Do all kites have the same shape?
11. Are they all of the same colour?
12. When kites fly, what does the sky look like?
13. Are the kites flyers sitting or standing?
14. Some children do not have kites in the picture; what are they doing?
15. Are all kite flyers flying their kites separately or is it a team work?
16. How many teams are there in the picture?
17. Do you fly kites?
18. Do you play alone or in a group?
19. How do you like it?

- The teacher will put questions to students one by one and wait for their answers,

- He/she will ask them to write down the answers to these questions in two paragraphs. The first paragraph will describe what kite flying is and how it is played. The second paragraph will contain the experience of individual students when they flew kites.

PRACTICUM

WORD GAMES

(A) Chain Spelling (*Antakshari*)

Teacher: Let us play a game. I will give you a word. You spell it and give us another word which begins with the last letter of the word I gave you. The next student will spell the word you mention and will give us a new word that begins with the last letter of your word. This process will go on till all of you have participated in it. Anyone who misspells the given word or gives a new word beginning with the wrong letter will be out of the game. All right. Let me start the game. The word is "game".

Student A: g-a-m-e. 'egg'
B: e-g-g. 'good'
C: d… dog
D: g… get
E: t… time
F: e… easy
G: y… young
H: g… great
I: t… thing
J: g… go
K: o… orange
L: e… end
M: d… different
N: t… think
O: k… king
P: g… give
Q: e… eat
R: t… toy
S: y… you
T: u… us
U: s… such
V: h… house
W: e… ear
X: r… rat
Y: t… the
Z: e… east

(B) Anagrams: Rearrangement of sounds of words

Teacher: I give you a word. One of you will spell it and give me another word which has the same letters in a different order. The word you give must be meaningful. O.K. Let us begin.

'BUT'
A: *Tub*
B: Part
C: *Rapt* (i.e., completely absorbed)
D: Life
E: *File*
F: mean
G: *name*
H: god
I: *dog*
J: was
K: *saw*
L: and
M: *Dan* (a name)
N: take
O: *Kate* (a name)
P: what
Q: *thaw* (i.e. become liquid and soft)
R: raw
S: *war*
T: rat
U: *tar*
V: mug
W: *gum*
X: read
Y: *dear*
Z: not
A: *ton*

(C) Opposites (Antonyms)

Teacher: I give you a word. You give me another word which has its opposite meaning. You give another word to the person sitting next to you. He/she will give its opposite word and give another new word. That way the game continues till all of you finish your turn.

Teacher	old	
Student1	new	now
Student2	then	good
Student3	bad	right

Student4	wrong	large
Student5	small	young
Student6	old	high
Student7	low	full
Student8	empty	easy
Student9	difficult	public
Student10	private	similar
Student11	different	dry
Student12	wet	

(D) Words Defined

Teacher: I will define a word. You will tell us what the word is.

1. Teacher: something you put your books in and carry to school is a....
   Student: Bag
2. Teacher: A person who works without payment is a...
   Student: Volunteer
3. Teacher: A person who teaches in a school is a...
   Student: Teacher
4. Teacher: An instrument for writing with ink which has a metal nib or ball and is fitted in a metal or nylon holder is a ...
   Student: Pen
5. Teacher: An instrument for writing or drawing consisting of a thin stick of lead enclosed in a long thin wood or fixed in a cylindrical cane is a ...
   Student: Pencil
6. Teacher: A work that the teacher asks students to do at home is a...
   Student: Homework
7. Teacher: A book used as a standard work for the study of a particular subject is a ...
   Student: Textbook
8. Teacher: A person who participates in sports and other forms of physical exercise is...
   Student: An athlete
9. Teacher: An activity involving physical exertion and skill in which an individual or team competes against other individual or team is...
   Student: Sport
10. Teacher: A form of competitive activity or sport played according to rules is a ...
    Student: game
11. Teacher: A sequence of action regularly followed is...
    Student: routine

(E) Scrambling

Teacher: I will write some scrambled letters on the board. Please think quickly and tell me which word can be formed out of them.

The teacher writes: lalsm

Student: small **Another student:** malls

Teacher	**Student**
Knith	think
alsoci	social
feli	file - life
trpa	part - trap
naem	mean - name
giben	begin
pleh	help
gourp	group
arye	year
gerla	large
evig	give
embeco	become
brenem	number
temyss	system
lepoep	people
krow	work
drowl	world
sace	case

(F) Scrabble

Scrabble is a board game in which players try to make words by filling up the spaces with letters printed on small plastic blocks and connect them to words that are already on the board. For instance,

They ... ... s h ... ... out of the room. (rushed)

We ... ... *the whole night.* (talked)

This game helps the players in choosing an appropriate word in a given context. The clue is provided by the space left vacant for the blocks. There are other types of word games also.

Glossary

Acceptable usage: an expression that is normally and suitably used.

Acculturation: the way in which a second language learner adapts to the life with two languages.

Achievement test: A test based on the work done by the learner during a course; it aims to establish what he/she has learnt during the course.

Acquisition: Learning or development of a skill or knowledge.

Acquisition order: The order in which items (of learning) are acquired.

Adult language learner: A learner who begins to learn a language after he/she attains puberty.

Accent: A distinct emphasis given to a syllable in a word; e.g. ex´port (as a verb) vs ´export (as a noun).

Aptitude: Innate language learning ability.

Basic English: (British, American Scientific International Commercial) English; natural language modified by C.K. Ogdon and I.A. Richards.

Bilingual Acquisition: The simultaneous acquisition of two languages since childhood.

Bilingual medium of education: When two languages (e.g. Hindi and English) are used to impart education.

Child language acquisition: Language acquisition during one's childhood, i.e. before puberty.

Communication: An exchange of message between two or more persons.

Communicative competence: ability to communicate ideas or information in a language.

Communicative approach: A method of teaching a second/foreign language with emphasis on acquiring ability to communicate.

Contrastive analysis: The comparison of structures of two languages with a view to finding out differences between them. The grammatical features which are in L_2 but not in L_1 are supposed to be the areas of difficulty for L_2 learners.

Critical period hypothesis: The hypothesis is that there is a stage in human development, namely before puberty, during which natural language acquisition is easier than later on.

Curriculum: The subjects that are in a course of study.

Context of situation: The relationship between external world features (e.g. place of utterance, role of participants, etc.) and the actual language utterance.

Context of utterance: The expressions that come just before and after an utterance; a purely linguistic context.

Contextualization: The process of putting an utterance in a context.

Contrived: Planned in advance and not natural or realistic.

Conversational language: A colloquial language, not formal.

Contraction: the short form of an expression e.g. *I'm* for I *am*.

Declension: The way in which nouns, adjectives and pronouns change their forms or attach some endings (suffixes) to indicate case, number or gender.

Decoding: processing language to get the meaning.

Developmental error: The error that suggests the stage of development in the process of language acquisition; e.g. 'five childs' the speaker knows that five will have a plural noun but does not know that it has an exceptional plural.

Dialect: A regional or social variety of a language.

Discourse: A speech or writing larger than a sentence; the use of language in a speech or writing in order to communicate.

Dialogue: conversations, discussion.

Diagnostic test: A test administered to find out gaps in learner's acquisition.

Dictation: The act of speaking or reading so that somebody can write it down.

Drill: Repetitive oral practice for language learning.

Error: A mistake that causes problems, inaccurate use of language.

Error analysis: Listing and classification of errors contained in a speech or writing.

Extensive reading: reading fluently for enjoyment, reading some parts rapidly and others in detail.

Feedback: The (teacher's) specific response to specific aspects of learner's utterance.

Fluency: Producing spoken language without hesitation or unwanted pauses.

Fill-in the gap: An activity in which the language learner provides words missing from the text.

Filter: That part of the internal processing system which subconsciously screens incoming language.

Foreign language: A language not used by the residents of a country in which it is being learnt/taught, e.g. Russian in India.

Formal operation: When a thinker acquires a new concept from verbal, rather than concrete, experience. It is a term used by Piaget.

First language acquisition: The normal linguistic development of a child in his/her first language.

Functional linguistics: A linguistic theory that takes verbal interaction into account. It analyses how a language is used in communication.

Genre: A particular type or style of literature.

Gist: General idea of a text.

Grading: The usual order of organizing items in a syllabus from the simplest to more complex items.

Grammatical Model: A method of explaining a linguistic theory.

Global error: A mistake that hinders communication.

Idiomatic language: a language containing expressions that are natural to its native speakers.

Idealization of a language- the representation of a language that is considered to be perfect or better than a usual language.

Integrated skills: classroom activities which combine a variety of language skills.

Integrative test: An activity which tests many areas of language simultaneously (e.g. vocabulary, grammar, pronunciation, etc.)

Internalization: a process by which a child assimilates the external social use of language in internal mental use.

Immersion Programme: A form of bilingual education in which children are taught some content subjects through the medium of their second language (e.g. English speaking Canadian children through the medium of French)

Interlanguage: various stages of the learners' second language development. It is a term that is widely used for what was initially called developmental errors.

Inclusive reading: reading a text minutely for details.

Input: the language data one puts into work in order to make it illustrate a point.

Language specific grammar: It involves a set of grammatical rules that are applicable to a specific language (e.g. English or Hindi).

Lexis/lexicon: all the words and phrases of a particular language, vocabulary.

Lexical item: a word or phrase of the lexicon of a language.

Lingua Franca: a shared language of communication between people whose mothertongues are different, e.g. English between a Tamil speaker and a Hindi speaker in India.

Local error: mistake belonging to a particular area of sentence, it does not affect the overall meaning.

Macro-environment: the broad overall environment of a language.

Micro-environment: an environment covering a small area.

Monitor: that part of the learner's internal system that consciously inspects and sometimes alters the form of the learner's production (utterance).

Medium of instruction: the language used for teaching subjects other than the language itself.

Metalanguage: a language people use to talk about or describe a particular language (or languages).

Module: a unit as a part of a set of units, a unit that can form part of a course of study.

Morphology: the forms of words studied as a branch of linguistics.

Mothertongue: the language that one learns first as a child, the first language.

Multilingual: one who speaks or uses several different languages.

Native speaker: a person who speaks a language as his/her first language.

Narrative: a description of events, especially in a fiction.

Norm: a situation or pattern of behaviour that is usual or expected.

Notional: based on a theory but not existing in reality.

Objective: the main purpose, principle goal.

Overview: a general description or an outline.

Organizer: the part of the internal processing system that is responsible for the learner's gradual and subconscious organization of the new language system.

Parameters: A set of constraint that decides or limits the way a language works. Parameters vary from language to language.

Parsing: the process through which the mind processes the grammatical structures and meaning of a sentence.

Passive listening: listening without active response. (Opposite of active listening).

Pattern: A regular way in which words are arranged in a sentence.

Phoneme: Sounds of a language that are systematically distinguished from one another.

Phonetical alphabet: a way of transcribing the sounds of speech through a set of designed symbols, e.g. IPA symbols.

Phonetic transcript: the phonetic rendering of a written or spoken text.

Phonic method: the method of teaching reading by sounding out each letter. (Phonic= relating to sounds).

Portfolio: A large, thin flat case to keep records of a person's action and achievement.

Pragmatics: the study of language from the point of view of its uses, i.e. the choice they make.

Prescriptive grammar: a grammar that tells people how language should be used, rather than describing how it is used.

Presentation: Showing a piece of work or presenting a new idea to a group of people with the help of a series of computer slides or in stages that accompany the task.

Principles: refer to a set of abstract principles that explains how a language works.

Productive skills: the skills which involve language production, i.e. speaking and writing.

Proficiency: ability to use a language.

Proficiency test: a test which aims at establishing a candidate's readiness for a particular communicative role.

Prototype Theory: A theory that divides words into various groups based on the basis of their resemblance with the prototypical object. A prototypical object is one which has all the typical features of that basic category.

Register: A variety of language defined according to its social use.

Reliability: consistency of measurement of individuals by a test, e.g. reliability coefficient test.

Rating: Assessment of performance, recorded as scores on a rating scale.

Receptive skills: the skills which involve internal response to language, rather than language production, i.e. listening and reading.

Remedial work: work designed to help a learner overcome gaps and errors in language acquisition.

Role play: An activity in which the learner takes on different roles and acts out.

Scanning: reading a text quickly to find specific information.

Schema: an outline of a plan or a theory (Plural: Schemata).

Schematic: in the form of a diagram that shows the main features or relationships but not the details.

Self-assessment: the process of judging one's own progress or achievement.

Self- correction: correction without outside help.

Simulation: a situation in which a particular set of conditions is created artificially in order to study something that could exist in reality.

Skill: a particular ability or type of ability, e.g. language skills.

Skimming: Reading something quickly to get a general idea or gist.

Stress: An extra force used when pronouncing a particular word or syllable.

Second language acquisition: the process of learning another language after the basics of the first language have been acquired. A second language may be another language spoken in the country or a foreign language.

Silent period: The initial phase of language learning process during which the learner simply listens to the new language and does not produce it.

Saliency: the ease with which a structure is heard or seen.

Structural grammar: is concerned with the description of the phonological, morphological and syntactic structures of a language.

Substitution drill/practice: A teacher- controlled practice where the learner produces sentences of the same grammatical structure with some changed elements.

Substitution table: a table of grammatical pattern showing the elements that can be substituted on the basis of its successive columns.

Task: An activity which has a purpose and an outcome, e.g. dramatization to illustrate events narrated in a story, use of language to clarify a point.

Taxonomy: classification (of grammatical categories, errors, etc.)

Text: Written material, especially the one to be studied; a passage that is read out and discussed.

Text message: a written message that can be sent using a mobile, computers (e-mail) or phone.

Traditional grammar: is concerned with the traditional (or conventional) method of teaching grammar, rather than modern.

Transitional construction: the interim language that a language learner uses while learning a new language.

Transcript: the written copy of a spoken text.

Universal grammar: It involves a set of grammatical rules that is thought to be applicable to all languages. It is believed to exist in the human mind.

Vernacular: the language spoken in a particular area or by a particular group, especially one that is not an official language.

References

Aitchison, Jean.2003. *Words in the Mind.* Oxford: Blackwell.

Alatis, James E. and Kristie Twaddell (eds.) 1976. *English as a Second Language in Bilingual Education.* Washington: Teachers of English to Speakers of Other Language.

Allright, Richard L. 1975. Problems in the Study of Teachers' Treatment of Learners' Errors, in Burt and Dulay (eds.) 1975: 96-109.

Arena, Louis A. 1975. A Method for Improving the Writing Skills of Foreign Students, In Burt and Duley (eds) 1975: 281-291.

Asher, James. 1986. *Learning Another Language through Action: The Complete Teacher Guidebook.* Los Gatos, CA: Oak Productions.

Bansal, R.K. 1967. Spoken English in India; Suggestions for Improvement. *Bulletin of the C.I.L.* 6:95-116.

Bansal, R.K. 1967. A Study of the Intonation Patterns in Educated Indian English. *Bulletin of the C.I.E.* 6, 117-122.

Bansal, R.K. 1969. *The Intelligibility of Indian English.* Hyderabad: Central Institute of English.

Banich, Marie T. and Molly Mack (eds.) 2003. *Mind, Brain and Language.* Mahwah, N.J.: Lawrence Erlbaum.

R Beathie, 1983. *An Analysis of Speech and Non-Verbal Behaviour in Conversation.* Milton Keynes: Open University Press.

Bernstein, Basil. 1971. *Class, Codes and Control.* Vol. 1 *Theoretical Studies Towards a Sociology of Language.* London: Routledge & Kegan Paul.

Bernstein, Basil. 1973. *Class, Codes and Control.* Vol II. *Towards a Theory of Educational Transmission.* London: Routledge & Kegan Paul.

Birdsong, David (ed.) 1999. *Second Language Acquisition and the Critical Period Hypothesis.* Mahwah, N.J. Lawrence Erlbaum.

Brown, H. D., C. Yorio and R. Crynet (eds) On TESOL 77: *The Teaching and Learning of English as a Second Language. Trends in Research and Practice.* Washington: TESOL.

Brumfit, Christopher and K. Johnson 1979. *Communicative Approach to Language Teaching.* Oxford: Oxford University Press.

Bruner Jerome 1966. *Towards a Theory of Instruction.* Cambridge, Mass: Belkapp Press

Bruner Jerome 1966. *Studies in Cognitive Growth*. New York: John Wiley.

Burt, Marina and Heidi Dulay (eds.) 1975. *New Direction in Second Language Learning, Teaching and Bilingual Education.* Washington: TESOL.

Burt, Marina, Heidi Dulay and M. Finccehiaro (eds) *Viewpoints on English as a Second Language*. New York: Regents.

Candlin, C.N., J.M. Kirkwood and H.N. Moore. 1978. Study Skills in English, Theoretical Issues and Practical Problems. In Mackay and Mountford (eds.) 1978: 190-219.

Chomsky, Noam. 1967. A Review of B.F. Skinner's *Verbal Behaviour*. *Language* 35: 26-58

Chomsky, Noam. 1968. *Language and Mind*. New York: Harcourt, Brace & World.

Chomsky, Noam. 1986. *Knowledge of Language: Its Nature, Origin and Use*. New York: Prague.

Chomsky, Noam. 1988. *Language and Problem of Knowledge*. Cambridge, MA: MIT Press.

Chomsky, Noam. 2000. *New Horizons in the Study of Language and Mind*. New York: Cambridge University Press.

Chomsky, Noam. 2002. *On Nature and Language*. New York: Cambridge University Press.

Cook, Guy and Sarah North (eds.). 2010. *Applied Linguistics in Action: A Reader*. London: Routledge.

Cook, Vivian. 2008. *Second Language Learning and English Teaching*. London: Hodder (Hachette).

Carver, R. 1992. Reading Rate: Theory, Research and Practical Implications. *Journal of Reading* 36: 84-95.

Cazdan, Courtney B. 1965. Environmental Assistance to the Child's Acquisition of Grammar. Cambridge, Harvard University PhD Thesis.

Cranston Alan. 1974. Why the Bilingual Education Amendment Needs Support. *Phi Delta Kappan* September. 58-60.

Crystal, David. 2003. *English as a Global Language*. Cambridge: Cambridge University Press.

Corder, S. Pit. 1957. The Significance of Learner's Errors. *Internal Journal of Applied Linguistics,* 5: 161-170

Corder, S. Pit. 1983. *Error Analysis and Interlanguage*. Oxford: Oxford University Press.

Cummins, J. 1982. Bilingualism and Special Education: Issues in Assessment and Pedagogy. Clevedon: Multilingual Matters,

Davies, Alan. 1990. *Principles of Language Testing*. Oxford: Basil Blackwell.

Davies, N. 1976. Receptive Versus Productive Skills in Foreign Language Learning. *The Modern Language Journal.* 60:440-443

Dulay, Heidi, Marina Burt and Stephen Krashen.1982. *Language Two*. New York: Oxford University Press.

Ellis, R. 2003. *Task-based Language Learning and Teaching*. Oxford: Oxford University Press.

Ervin-Tripp, Susan. 1974. Is Second Language Learning Like First? *TESOL Quarterly* 8:111-127.

Fairclough, N. 1995. *Critical Discourse Analysis*. London: Longman.

Firth, J.R. 1968. *Selected Papers of J.R. Firth* (1952-1959) ed. By F.R. Palmer London/ Bloomington: Indiana University Press.

Flege, James 1999. Age of Learning and Second-Language Speech. In D. Birdsong (ed.). pp. 101-132.

Fries, C.C. 1963. *Linguistics and Reading*. New York: Holt, Rinehart and Winston.

Gardner, R.C. 1983. *Frame of Mind and the Theory of Multiple Intelligence*. New York: Basic Books.

Gattegno, Celeb, 1972. *Teaching Foreign Language in Schools. The Silent Way* Reading: Educational Explorers Ltd.

Graddol, David. 2000. *The Future of English*. London: British Council.

Greenbaum, Sydney (ed.) *The English Language Today*. Oxford: Pergamon.

Halliday, M.A.K. 1985. *An Introduction to Functional Grammar*. London: Edward Arnold.

Howatt, A.P.R. 1984. *A History of English Language Teaching*. Oxford: Oxford University Press.

Hunt, Kellogg W. 1970a. How little sentences grow into big ones, in Lester, Mark (ed.) 1970; 162-178.

Hunt, Kellogg W. 1970b. Recent Measures in Syntatic Development, in Lester, mark (ed). 1970; 179-192.

Hymes, Dell. 1974. *Foundations of Sociolinguistics*. Philadelphia: University of Pennsylvania Press.

Jokobovits, Leon. 1970. Implications of Recent Psycholinguistic Developments for the Teaching of a Second Languages in Lester, Mark (ed.) 1970; 245-283.

Jesso-Acquilar, Rebeca 2010. Sources, Methods and Triangulation in Needs Analysis. In Guy Cook and North (eds.) 2010: 60-99.

Johnson, J.S. and E.L. Newport. 1989. Critical Period Effects in Second Language Learning: the influence of maturational state on the acquisition of English as a second language. *Cognitive Psychology* 21: 60-99.

Johnson R.K. and M. Swain 1994. From Core to Content: Bridging the L2 proficiency gap in the late immersion. *Language and Education*, 8(4), 211-229.

Kachru, Braj B. 1985a. Institutionalised Second Language Varieties. In Greenbaum (ed.) 1985: 211-226.

Kachru, Braj B. 1985b. Standards, Codification and Sociolinguistic Realism: English Language in the Outer Circle. In Randolph Quirk and H.G. Widdowson (eds) 1985, pp. 11-30.

Kachru, Braj B. 2001. World Englishes and Cultural War. In Kiong, *et al.* (eds.) 2001: 392-414.

Katz, Jerrold and Jerry Fodor 1963. The Structure of a Semantic Theory. *Language* 39, 170-210.

Kiong, T.C., A. Fakir, B.K. Choon and R.B.H. Goh (eds) 2001 *Ariels: Departures and Returns: Essay for Edwin Thumbro*. Singapore: Oxford University Press.

Kim, R. 1995. The Effect of Age of L_2 Onset on the Ultimate L_2 Production. *English Education* 50:257-279.

Kothari, D.S. *Report of the Education Commission* (1964-66) New Delhi: Government of India.

Krashen, Stephen. 1977a. Some Issues Relating to the Monitor Model. In H.D. Brown, C. Yorio, and R Crymes (eds.), 1977, pp. 144-158.

Krashen, Stephen. 1977b. The Monitor Model for adult second language performance. In M. Burt, H. Dulay and M Finocchiaro (eds.), 1977, pp. 152-161.

Krashen, Stephen. 1983. *The Input Hypothesis: Issues and Implications*. London: Longman.

Krashen, Stephen and T. Terrell. 1983. *The Natural Approach: Language Acquisition in the Classroom*. Hayward, CA: Alemany Press.

Kroll, B. (ed). 2003. *Exploring the Dynamics of Second Language Writing*. New York: Cambridge University Press.

Labov, William. 1970. *The Study of Non-Standard English*. Champaign, All National Council for Teachers of English.

Labov, William. 1972. *Language in the Inner City: Studies in Black English Vernacular*. Philadelphia: University of Pennsylvania Press.

Lado, R. 1957. *Linguistics across Culture*. Ann Arbor: Michigan University Press.

Langendoen, D. Terence. 1968. *The London School of Linguistics*. Cambridge, MA: MIT Press.

Lenneberg, Eric. 1967. *The Biological Foundation of Language*. New York: John Willey.

Lester Mark. 1970. The Value of Transformational Grammer in Teaching Compositions in Lester Mak (ed.). 1970; 193-201.

Lester, Mark (ed.) 1970. Readings in Applied Transformational Grammar. New York: Holt, Rinehart and Winston.

Lippi-Green, R. 1997. *English with an Accent: Language, Ideology and Discrimination in the United States*. London: Routledge.

Lozanov, G. 1978. *Suggestology and Outlines of Suggestopedia*. New York: Gorden and Brench.

Malinowski, B. 1935. *Coral Island and Their Magic* Vol II, New York: American Book Co.

Marckwardt, Albert H. 1970. *Linguistics in School Programme*. Chicago: The National Society for the Study of Education.

McCarthy, M.J. 1991. *Discourse Analysis for Language Teachers*. Cambridge: Cambridge University Press.

McCarthy, Michael. 2000. *Issues in Applied Linguistics*. Cambridge: Cambridge University Press.

McClelland J. and D. Rumelhart (eds.) 1986. *Parallel Distribution Processing: Exploration in the Microstructure of Cognition* Vol. 2 Cambridge, MA: MIT Press.

McNeill, David 1970. *The Acquisition of Language*. New York: Harper and Row.

Mack, Molly 2003. The Phonetic System of Bilinguals. In Mary T. Banich and Molly Mack (eds.), pp. 309-349.

Macky, R. and A.J. Mountford. 1978. *English for Specific Purpose: A Case Study Approach*. London: Longman.

Miller, George A. 2003. The Cognitive Revolution: A Cognitive Perspective. *TRENDS in Cognitive Science*. Vol. 7, No. 3: 141-144.

Munby, John.1978. *Communicative Syllabus Designs*. Cambridge: Cambridge University Press.

Mitchell, W. Keith 1990. On Comparisons in a Notional Grammar. *Applied Linguistics*, 11(1): 52-72.

Nash, Ogden. 1945. *The Selected Verses of Ogden Nash*. New York: Modern Library.
Nation, Paul.2001. Learning Vocabulary in Lexical Sets. *TESOL Quarterly Journal*, 9: 6-10.
National Knowledge Commission, 2006. *Report to the Nation*. New Delhi: Government of India.
NCERT.1999. *National Curriculum Framework for School Education: A Discussion Document*. New Delhi: NCERT.
Nemser, William. 1971. Approximative Systems of Foreign Language Learners. *International Journal of Applied Linguistics*, 92: 115-123.
Ohmann, Richard. 1970a. Generative Grammar and the Concept of Literary Style, in Lester, Mark (ed.) 1970; 109-128.
Ohmann, Richard. 1970b. Literature as sentences, in Lester, Mark (ed.) 1970; 129-140.
Oller, J.K. 1973. Cloze Tests of Second Language Proficiency and What They Measure. *Language Learning*, 23:105-118.
Oyama, S. 1995. A Sensitive Period for the Acquisition of Non-Native Phonological System. *Journal of Psycholinguistic Research*, 5(3): 261-283.
Palalas, Agnieszka. 2011. Mobile Assisted Language Learning: designing for your students. In S. Thouësny & L. Bradley (Eds.), pp. 71-94.
Pattanayak, D.P. 1997. *Language Curriculum for Teacher Education*. New Delhi: National Council for Teacher Education.
Piaget, Jean. 1974. *The Language and Thought of the Child*. New York: The New American Library.
Pinker, Steven. 1997. *How the Mind Works*. New York: W.W. Norton.
Quirk, Randolph and H.G. Widdowson (eds.) *English in the World: Teaching and Learning the Language and Literature*. Cambridge: Cambridge University Press.
Ravem, R. 1968. Language Acquisition in a Second Language Environment. *International Journal of Applied Linguistics* 6: 175-185.
Ravem, R. 1972. The Development of Wh-questions in First and Second Language Learning. In Richards, J (ed.) 1972: 134-155.
Richards, Jack C. (ed.) 1972. *Error Analysis*. London: Longman.
Rosch, Eleanor 1978. Principle of Categorization. In E. Rosch & B.B. Lloyd (Eds.), pp. 27-48.
Rosch Eleanor and Barbara Lloyd (eds.) *Cognition and Categorization*. Hillsdale, NJ Lawrence Erlbaum.
Rumelhart, P.E. and J.L. McClelland 1986. On Learning the Past Tense of English Verbs, in McClelland and Rumelheart (eds) 1986: 216-217.
Selinker, L. 1992. *Rediscovering Interlanguage*. London: Longman.
Selinker, L., M. Swain and G. Dumas. 1975. Interlanguage Hypothesis Extended to Children. *Language Learning*, 25:139-155.
Sinha, Anjani, K. 2016. *The Teaching of English in Indian Context*. New Delhi: Shipra Publication.
Skinner, B.F. 1957. *Verbal Behaviour*. New York: Appleton-Century-Crofts.
Skinner, B.F. 1974. *About Behaviourism*. New York: Vintage Books, Random House.
Strickland, Ruth G. 1969. *The Language Arts in Elementary Schools*. Lexington, MA D. C. Heath and Co.
Slobin, Dan 1971. *Psycholinguistics*. Glenview; IL: Scott Foresman.

Swain, M. and S. Lapkin. 1982. *Evaluating Bilingual Education: A Canadian Case Study*. Clevedon, England: Multilingual Matter.

Swain, M. and S. Lapkin. 2000. Task-based Second Language Learning: the use of the first language. *Language Teaching Research* 4: 251-274.

Taylor, William 1952. Cloze Procedure

Thomas, Owen and Engene R. Kintgen. 1974. Transformational Grammar and the Teacher of English. New York: Holt, Rinehart and Winston.

Thouësny, Sylvia and Linda Bradley. 2011. *Second Language Teaching and Learning with Technology: Views of Emergent Researchers*. Dublin: Research Publications.

Vygotsky, Lev S.1962. *Thought and Language*. Cambridge MA: MIT Press.

Vygotsky, Lev S. 1978. *Mind in Society: The Development of Higher Psychological Processes.* Cambridge, MA: Harvard University Press.

Watson, John. 1924. *Behaviourism.* Chicago: Chicago University Press.

Widdowson, H.G. 1979. *Exploration of Applied Linguistics*. London: Oxford University Press.

Wilkins, D.A. 1976. *Notional Syllabuses*. London: Oxford University Press.

Williams, M. 1994. Motivation in Foreign and Second Language Learning: An Interactive Perspective. *Educational and Child Psychology*, 11: 77-84.